Corporation 2020

To the lucky winner!
Enjoy the book — & hope
we are all lucky enough
to see serious changes
by 2020!

Pavan Sukhdev

CORPORATION 2020

Transforming Business for Tomorrow's World

Pavan Sukhdev

Washington | Covelo | London

Library of Congress Cataloging-in-Publication Data
Sukhdev, Pavan.
   Corporation 2020 : transforming business for tomorrow's world /
Pavan Sukhdev.
      p. cm.
   Includes bibliographical references and index.
   ISBN 978-1-61091-238-9 (cloth : alk. paper) -- ISBN 1-61091-238-1
(cloth : alk. paper) -- ISBN 978-1-61091-239-6 (pbk. : alk. paper) -- ISBN
1-61091-239-X (pbk. : alk. paper) 1. Social responsibility of business.
2. Corporations--Environmental aspects. 3. Industries--Environmental
aspects. I. Title.
   HD60.S8844 2012
   658.4'08--dc23

                                                          2012020609

ISBN-13: 978-1-61091-238-9 (cloth)
ISBN-13: 978-1-61091-360-7 (e-book)

Printed on recycled, acid-free paper ✴
Manufactured in the United States of America
10 9 8 7 6 5 4 3 2 1

Keywords: Island Press, economics, sustainability, business, corporate
responsibility, corporate externalities, environmental commons,
sustainable economy

To today's students, tomorrow's corporate leaders
This is your book, make it happen

Contents

Foreword

Our oceans are severely depleted, deforestation continues apace, biodiversity is dwindling and concentrations of greenhouse gases continue to rise rapidly. The lives and livelihoods of the world's people are under increasing risk as a result of the damage our activities are doing to the ecosystems and environment of the planet. The risks of profoundly damaging irreversibilities and tipping points are increasing. As a result, inaction is dangerous: indeed the dangers are intensified by the ratchet effects of accumulation processes such as greenhouse gas concentrations and the lock-in of long-lived polluting capital. It is the poorest who are and will be hit earliest and hardest. But all of us will be profoundly affected by continuing neglect and delay, including by major movements of population and the tension and conflict these are likely to bring.

Many or most of our problems lie in combinations of market failure and irresponsible and short-term behaviour. We have it in our hands to overcome these problems through sound policy, collaborative behaviour, a more far-sighted approach to the consequences of our action, and the processes of discovery about technology, organisation and policy. All of these reinforce each other. And they can bring advances in material living standards, particularly for poor people, greater social and economic inclusion and equity, and a more attractive and hospitable environment for us all. In other words greater economic, social and environmental sustainability. Indeed, unless we act to put all three together, each of them is likely to be undermined.

This book sets out these arguments strongly and clearly. And it shows the key details of actions and policy that are necessary. The policies are designed to go to the heart of the problem and particularly the market failures involved. It shows how the entrepreneurship and creativity of firms, individuals and communities can be re-oriented away from the damage caused by distorted markets and irresponsible behaviour towards actions and discoveries that are economically and socially profitable for firms, individuals and communities and the world as a whole. To fail to correct gross market distortions is to grossly distort markets. If we pursue these policies we will create a much sounder, stronger and more attractive way to produce and consume: more secure, cleaner, quieter, more bio-diverse and more equitable.

Specifically the book argues that UNEP's Green Economy Initiative showed that building a new economy—one which promotes economic development and social equity while reducing environmental risks and ecological scarcities, is not only possible, it is necessary for sustainability. But for too long we have been talking about making directional changes at the "macro" level without recognising that economy-wide changes can happen only if we build them up from the "micro" level. That means sound micro-policy which gets to grips with market failure.

This leads us to think about the economy's largest agents: corporations. What will change how corporations operate? Like any species, their "environment" has to change for them to evolve, and that comprises institutions, policies and prices. But it also requires greater discussion and social engagement about what works, what is sustainable and what is responsible in relation to all the relevant stakeholders.

Corporation 2020 proposes four primary changes in what could be called the "enabling conditions" for the development of a more responsible kind of corporation:

- Disclosing externalities: to provide both investors and consumers with more information to make decisions based on criteria broader than just shelf price or return on investment.
- Resource taxation: taxing "bads" rather than "goods."
- Accountable advertising: to provide real information to consumers, rather than just sales pitches.
- Limiting leverage: especially companies considered "too-big-to-fail," whose leverage is essentially a negative externality on taxpayers.

Action now is critical. We cannot wait until 2050 or 2100 to make changes in environmental performance. The science tells us that dramatic changes must be made to "business-as-usual" within the *next decade* if we are to maintain hope of building a sustainable economy.

As we build action we must recognise that:

- International negotiations tend to speak in generalities and at the "macro"/country level, but we must also look at the "micro"/company level for real change to take place.

- Competition often produces efficiency if resources are properly valued, but our current system undervalues non-financial forms of capital as well as public capital generally.

- We should not be worrying about whether Corporation 2020-type policies "hurt growth." Indeed, that is often to misunderstand growth and development. The policies described are essential if living standards are to be sustained and the aspirations to overcome poverty are to be realised. Of course measures of progress must go beyond narrow GDP, as most of those who think seriously about development and living standards have long realised.

- The private sector, civil society, and governments must work *together* to make significant changes in "business-as-usual"—no single institution nor any "silver bullet" can solve the complex problems we face in today's world.

We have it in our power to create a much better, fairer and more productive world. We can see the destructiveness of our current path and its causes. This book sets out clearly what we must do and particularly the role of markets and corporations. There is no excuse for inaction.

Nicholas Stern

July 2012

The "Green Economy" work of the United Nations Environment Programme (UNEP) shows that a new, inclusive green economy is the only path forward for a truly sustainable world. But a green economy cannot be realized without first thinking deeply about the roles and responsibilities of the actors involved in building it. Macro-level changes can only be constructed through the cumulative efforts of many micro-level entities. As such, the private sector must become the primary agent of innovation and problem-solving on which governments and other stakeholders depend if we are going to make real strides towards a green economy.

Corporations may have created the situation we are in today, but they are also the very institutions that are best placed to bring the quantum changes which are required for solutions on a global scale. As businesses, we have a responsibility to move from doing business with collateral damage to doing business with collateral benefits. This movement is critical because nothing can be gained from the current race to the financial top if it is coupled with a race to the environmental and social bottom.

Until now, nature's complexity and the "free services" it provides have been disregarded and degraded because they escape pricing and do not trade in markets. Valuing natural capital and reflecting the true cost of conducting business on nature is essential in the overall "sustainable economy" equation. Measuring externalities and placing an economic value on a business's environmental impacts is not just a question of taking full responsibility for nature—and hence our quality of life and livelihood—but also of risk aversion and the search for innovation and new opportunities for the benefit of long-term sustainability. This approach must be applied to all businesses—to be aware of and to measure their costs to nature, to draw clear conclusions, and to find appropriate solutions—in order to move toward a more equitable and sustainable future.

Such an approach is a key focus of this book, and it makes a clear case for this new business model. Corporations stepping up, being accountable and leading the way is a belief and vision I share with Pavan Sukhdev and I hope that it will be a given for the next generation of business leaders to not even question that business must be a "win-win" for all stakeholders, including nature and society. Undoubtedly, there will still be competition in the world of Corporation 2020 but companies will compete more on the basis of innovation, resource conservation, and serving consumers' needs, rather than by pursuing tax avoidance, lobbying, and externalizing costs.

I for one know that the world of Corporation 2020 is one in which I am looking forward to contributing to business.

Jochen Zeitz
July 2012

Editor's note: Jochen Zeitz conceived and developed the first-ever Environmental Profit and Loss Account statement which places an economic value on a business's environmental impacts across the entire supply chain during his tenure as CEO and Chairman of PUMA.

Acknowledgements

After three and a half years of frenzied writing (and managing others' writing) to deliver "TEEB" and "Towards a Green Economy" for the United Nations, it might seem odd that I would once again throw myself into writing. I am not a writer by training, and neither do I enjoy it. However, I could see that 'Green Economy' would remain just an aspiration unless the biggest "agency problem" of our times were not disclosed and solved: that the main agent of today's economy, the corporation, was neither persuaded nor incentivized to deliver a green economy. And failing this, I could also see that TEEB, a toolkit to value the unaccounted public benefits of nature, would merely adorn bookshelves, unused.

But even this logic would have failed to move me to write had it not been for two friends who convinced me otherwise.

Meenakshi Menon, CEO of Spatial Access, made me see that I was far too committed to TEEB and Green Economy as changes that 'must happen' to *not* take that additional step of writing about 'Corporation 2020.' A media and advertising expert, she volunteered to organize the campaign and the web platform that would be needed alongside the book. She also offered to prepare a key chapter for the book: on accountability in advertising, a crucial plank of change that can drive the transition towards "Corporation 2020." Meenakshi, I cannot thank you enough.

Sanjeev Sanyal, Deutsche Bank economist, my partner in the green accounting project of 'GIST,' and author of a recent best-seller *(The Indian Renaissance: India's Rise after a Thousand Years of Decline)* encouraged me to take the plunge. His early advice on the "how and why" of writing was invaluable. Sanjeev also framed and supervised a chapter on the world of Corporation 2020. Many thanks, Sanjeev, for being with me all the way from 'GIST' to 'Corporation 2020.'

Purpose had thus been found, but the means were missing. M. K. Gandhi had said, "Find purpose, the means shall follow," and as if on cue, Yale University stepped forward. A meeting in September 2010 with

Sir Peter Crane (Dean of the Yale School of Forestry and Environmental Studies) on how Yale might create educational value from the forthcoming "TEEB" reports, turned into a recruitment discussion. Before long, I had accepted an offer from Yale University as their McCluskey Fellow for 2011. Their offer included graduate research support for a book called "Corporation 2020." Thank you, Peter, for visioning this partnership and making it happen.

To my research team at Yale, who researched and drafted many of the chapters of this book, my deep appreciation. This group of excellent graduates gives me hope for the future. Bryant Cannon researched and wrote an "e-book" (just published) on the corporation's legal history, which Michael Parker summarized for Chapter 1. John D'Agostino researched post-war economic history for Chapter 2. Namrata Kala researched and drafted both Chapters 4 and 5, and richly deserves her team epithet "Miss Externalities." Brian Marrs lived and breathed "Resource Taxation" for many months while drafting that chapter. Joseph Edgar researched corporate lobbying, a strand which runs through several chapters. Rafael Torres drafted the "leverage" chapter, covering in depth a crucial plank of change. Michael Parker researched the final chapter, on the "World of Corporation 2020." Alisa May gave us excellent visuals for our covers and e-books. And Star Childs carefully designed all our diagrams, a painstaking task very well delivered. To this Yale team, a very big "thank you."

The onerous task of organizing the extensive effort and network that the project "Corporation 2020" had become, and doing so to very demanding timelines, fell on Kevin Kromash, another graduate at Yale. As my Research Supervisor for this project, Kevin not only organized (and patiently chased) everyone, including me, to do what we had to do on time, but edited and proof-read all chapters and researched and wrote on several topics that had fallen between stools. If 'Corporation 2020' were a business, he was its "Chief Operating Officer." Well done, Kevin, and many thanks.

I thank Brad Gentry, Stuart DeCew and Amy Badner of CBEY for hosting "Corporation 2020," advice and assistance in coordinating our activities at Yale. I also thank George Joseph, Eugenie Gentry, Jeanette Gorgas, Marian Chertow, Susan Welles, Victoria Manders, and Jessica Foote of Yale University for their help at various stages of the project.

For their thorough and thoughtful reviews of various "Corporation 2020" chapters, I am indebted to several reviewers. I thank Ed Barbier for his review of both the 'externalities' chapters. Thanks to Allen White for his review and detailed comments on the Introduction and the chapters describing 'Corporation 1920' and 'Corporation 2020' respectively. I thank Camilla Toulmin for her review of 'The Great Alignment' chapter on post-War economic history, and Gautam Patel and Connie Bagley for their reviews of the 'Legal History' chapter. My thanks to Tom Lovejoy for reviewing "Why 2020?," the scientific rationale for early action, which eventually became an introductory "e-book" to introduce the topic. Thanks also to Rajiv Sinha and Sanjeev Sanyal for reviewing several chapters.

For taking the time out of their busy schedules to be interviewed for our website www.corp2020.com, I thank Romesh Sobti, Paul Abraham, Alessandro Carlucci, Mohandas Pai, Jochen Zeitz, Michael Izza, Julie Katzman, Jon Anda, Partha Bhattacharyya, Daniel Esty, Jochen Flasbarth, Stuart Hart, Andrew Kassoy, Tom Lovejoy, Juliet Schor, Peter Seligmann, Erik Solheim, Gus Speth, Rob Walton, Adam Werbach and Allen White. I thank Michael Parker from Yale for arranging these video recordings, often in remote locations. My thanks to Rick Leone, Doug Forbush, Phil Kearney, and Lucas Swineford of Yale Broadcast and Media Center for their excellent recording of many of these interviews.

For their encouragement and support with launch events for this book and our ongoing "Corporation 2020" campaign, I thank Camilla Toulmin, Steve Bass, Tom Bigg and their colleagues at the IIED; Peter Seligman and Conservation International teams in the US and in Brazil; Richard Spencer and his colleagues at ICAEW; Laurene Powell Jobs and her team at the Emerson Collective; Julia Marton-Lefèvre, John Kidd, and their IUCN colleagues at Cheju; Miriam Lyons and team at CPD in Sydney, and our collaborators from the Cambridge Program for Sustainability Leadership.

For research support, thanks are due to my friends and ex-colleagues Anirban Lahiri, Saurabh Sen, Rajesh Tolani, Sunil Rangaiah, Abheet Dwivedi, Mohit Agarwal and others at Deutsche Bank's CIB Centre in Mumbai (erstwhile "GMC Mumbai"), as well as to Amod Shah and the team at GIST Advisory.

Island Press has been a wonderfully supportive publisher at every level and at every stage of this book. Chuck Savitt backed my proposal to run a campaign around the ideas in this book, indeed to launch it ahead of the book despite the risk of unveiling its ideas too early. David Miller gave constructive and critical editorial feedback of very high quality. I also thank Sharis Simonian and Mike Fleming for production and copyediting, and Maureen Gately, Denise Schlener, Meredith Harkel, Jaime Jennings, and Rebecca Bright for their assistance throughout.

For managing my impossible schedule during the writing of this book, I thank my assistant Gloria d'Souza at GIST Advisory, as well as William Walker and Ashley Maignan at Yale, and Cynthia D'Souza at Spatial Access.

Anita Horam, Ruchir Joshi, Nayantara Kotian and others at *Via Earth Productions* did an excellent job of designing our website and editing our CEO interviews.

The work of Johan Rockström and colleagues at Stockholm Resilience Centre inspired urgency, and that of Tomorrow's Company (Tony Manwaring) and Tellus Institute (Marjorie Kelley and Allen White) emphasized the importance of transforming the corporation. Authors quoted by us are too many to thank individually, but their work has been referenced.

Many others helped and hosted me during the writing of this book, including Keshav Varma whose garden balcony at home near Washington helped end my "writers block" and write the Introduction. My family and friends have seen even less of me than usual during the writing of this book, and I thank them for their understanding.

Introduction

Failure is simply the opportunity to begin again, this time more intelligently.

— Henry Ford

If you search the Internet for the words "I'd like my life back," you will find a video of Tony Hayward, the former CEO of BP.[1] His remarks—not a great example of corporate diplomacy—made headlines everywhere on May 30, 2010, just a month after the BP oil spill in the Gulf of Mexico. Hayward, apparently, was trying to pacify the inhabitants of Venice, Louisiana, who had been affected by the spill.

What is noteworthy is not Hayward's lack of success in placating his audience, but rather, the context from which his remarks arose. Just a year before, Hayward had said that "a duty of care" was the key driver in his professional life.[2] While readily admitting to BP's history of safety disasters in Texas, Alaska's Prudoe Bay, and elsewhere, he declared that he had tried ever since his appointment as CEO in 2006 to refocus BP on improving safety, while emphasizing that their primary purpose was to meet shareholder expectations, not to save the world. Scarcely a year later, he was responding to a safety failure of tragic proportions—the largest accidental oil spill in history.[3] As a result, BP's share price had collapsed, wiping out $70 billion of shareholder wealth in less than a month and a half.[4]

After the *Deepwater Horizon* disaster, Hayward had another agenda: damage control. He took issue with findings by at least three separate and independent scientific teams that vast plumes of oil measuring up to 22 miles long were lurking below the surface of the sea. BP's own studies, he claimed, had found no evidence of such a phenomenon.[5] He also had to answer questions being raised about decisions at the *Deepwater Horizon* site just days before the blowout, suggesting that BP managers had not selected the safest option.[6]

Was Hayward at fault as a CEO because his company failed to deliver on the first of his stated priorities, operational safety, and because he had thus presided over the worst-ever drop in its shareholders' wealth? BP had broken no laws, nor had they led the way in asking for regulatory relaxations for drilling in the Gulf of Mexico, as some US companies had done.[7] And yet, BP's "footprint" on the Gulf of Mexico was immense— biodiversity lost, beaches destroyed, oyster and sea fisheries damaged, and nature-based leisure and tourism and local livelihoods disrupted—an overall environmental cost calculated by one group of researchers to be as high as $34–670 billion.[8] The incident led to BP establishing a $20 billion claims fund.[9] These are all giant problems, but beyond them, BP's future as a company was at risk in the wake of public anger about the oil spill. So on May 30, Hayward was doing what any CEO does when his company causes a social problem: trying to contain damage to the company's reputation and retain its social licence to operate. Even on this count, however, BP's performance got in the way.

BP's environmental impact assessment (EIA), a prerequisite for obtaining rights to drill in the Gulf of Mexico, appeared to be a shoddy example of "cut-and-paste" from an earlier EIA. It listed the conservation of the walrus, a mammal only found in the Arctic, as one of BP's objectives. It also suggested Professor Peter Lutz, an expert on the impact of oil spills on sea turtles, as a "go-to" person in case of an emergency, although the venerable scientist had died in 2005.

In "The Walrus and the Carpenter," Lewis Carroll's famous rhyme from *Through the Looking-Glass*, the two fictitious beings in the title lead a troupe of oysters on an aimless expedition around a beach before devouring them. BP's sloppy EIA brought forth, in addition to its own two fictitious beings, destroyed beaches and oyster fisheries along the Gulf of Mexico, and a corporate culture that did not respond to its own CEO's publicly avowed first priority. It also set the stage for operational decisions that had just cost society billions of dollars and its shareholders around $70 billion, not to mention a CEO who made matters worse with numerous public relations gaffes. All this from a company that had spent an estimated $200 million on a global advertising campaign about BP being "Beyond Petroleum."[10]

On what kind of imaginary expedition was BP leading an outraged world? Is this what today's multinational megacorporations are all about?

A Year Later . . .

A year later, at the end of May 2011, more than twenty Nobel laureates were gathered together in Stockholm to apply their exceptional minds to the world's greatest challenges and to prepare a communiqué for Rio+20, a major environmental conference which was just a year away.[11]

To launch their discussions, they held a mock trial of Humanity, in which the plaintiff was Planet Earth, and the charge was serious damage inflicted to it by the defendant. Over the next couple of hours, Humanity was put through the grinder. Counsel for the defense tried valiantly to defend his client, but with little success. The Nobel laureates who had been nominated as "judges" finally ended the trial and declared Humanity guilty on most counts. They proposed several remedies, including a 1,000-year period of community service! Enjoyable though this mock trial was as a humorous start to serious proceedings, it left some worrying undertones hanging heavy in the air. Was Humanity actually capable of changing its ways, let alone willing to change them? If not, then why not? Was there something *pathological* about humanity's suicidal intransigence? And was it already too late even to *bother* about discussing the issue?

I attended this event as an expert witness on the "green economy" and the invisible economics of nature. My only formal observation on these proceedings was that they were infructuous, because counsel for the plaintiff had failed to call to the box Humanity's invisible codefendant, the Corporation, which had been the main economic agent for Humanity during its sixty-odd years of alleged misdemeanors toward Planet Earth. Just a year after BP's staggering oil spill in the Gulf of Mexico, perhaps the single largest and most talked-about misdemeanor to Planet Earth in the recent past, why was the *Corporation* entirely missing from this mock trial conducted by twenty Nobel laureates?

The Invisible Foot and Its Visible Footprint

In 1759, the moral philosopher Adam Smith described the market as having an "invisible hand" that steered the economy and achieved well-being—some combination of the market forces of self-interest, competition, supply, and demand.[12] One of the main criticisms of his "invisible hand" hypothesis explaining why selfish market behavior apparently delivered social benefits is that it ignores the very significant social costs that businesses pass on to the wider world: their so-called "negative externalities."[13] Indeed, if market forces are the market's "invisible hand," then the corporation—the economy's main agent and the market's main player—might perhaps be called an "invisible foot." For what would be the impact of Smith's four market forces, in the absence of the corporation?

Without today's corporations, most supply would either not be produced or it would be produced inefficiently. Much demand, spurred today by corporate advertising, would just be missing. Market competition without its most aggressive agents would be stunted at best, and of course, self-interest would be diluted by social purpose—this fourth outcome being perhaps not such a disastrous problem! But the reality is that the corporation, in all its profit-seeking, externality-churning glory, is very much the cornerstone of today's economy. Indeed, it is the sheer size of its externalities that is making this "invisible foot" recognizable through its very large and visible "footprint."

The costs to society of corporations doing "business as usual"—that is, the so-called negative externalities—are well known. These include damage to health and natural environments from pollution and toxic-waste discharge as well as the economic costs and poverty implications of climate-changing greenhouse-gas emissions. They also include many non-environmental impacts, such as the loss of livelihoods as local businesses are gradually replaced by worldwide corporate supply chains and distribution networks, or the public-health costs of cigarette smoking.[14] Indeed, among the most transformative impacts of the corporation are two huge and pervasive categories of negative externalities. The first is damage to our environmental and ecological commons through unconstrained greenhouse-gas emissions, excessive waste generation, and excessive use of energy, land, and freshwater. The second is damage to human health through polluting residues, and mismanaged waste, as well as manufacturing harmful products and promoting their use. A recent study estimated the environmental and ecological externalities of the top 3,000 stock-exchange-listed companies as close to $2.15 *trillion* and estimated that economic activity overall has undisclosed costs to society of $6.6 trillion—in other words, "business as usual" is already costing human society an estimated 11 percent of global GDP every year.[15]

My contention in this book is that all material externalities deserve measurement, disclosure, and management—be they negative or positive. They are the increasingly visible "footprint" of today's corporation. The multi-billion-dollar footprint that BP left on the ecosystems, communities, and economy of the Gulf of Mexico is just one example, albeit a powerful and visible one, of the billions of dollars' worth of negative externalities that many corporations rack up every year. But some corporations, on the other hand, also create at least two huge *positive externalities*. Corporations offer skills training that builds earnings potential or "human capital" for employees. This enables the creation of new relationships and new communities that build "social capital" among employees, suppliers, and customers. One company, Infosys, creates valuable job skills for hundreds of thousands of young Indians. Another, Natura, builds greater economic security and improved family and social status for the million housewives who are its sales agents in Latin America.[16]

With such a large, visible contribution to economic development and growth, and with four such significant and large invisible impacts, today's corporation is perhaps the most important institution in modern society. There are good questions about it and its role in the world, however, that deserve answers. What defines today's corporation? When and how was it born? What drives its singular success and pervasiveness? What problems are associated with it, and how can society solve them?

"Corporation 1920"

Today's corporation is something of an anachronism, the result of a long history of development which began in ancient India and Rome, continued in medieval Europe, and culminated in nineteenth-century America and England. However, most of the development of today's corporation happened during an eventful century beginning in the early 1820s and lasting until early in the twentieth century. These hundred years achieved limitations on shareholder liability, established corporate personhood, and unshackled the corporation's operations from restrictions on time, place, and purpose, enabling the corporation to engage in any business, anywhere, for as long as its shareholders desired. These hundred years also freed the corporation from social purpose, and established the primacy of profits as the corporation's *raison d'etre*. A landmark judgment in the United States (*Dodge v. Ford*, 1919) affirmed that the purpose of the corporation was indeed its own self-interest. By 1920, therefore, the corporate form had crystallized as the corporation we recognize today, and for the purposes of this book, I shall refer to today's corporate entity as "Corporation 1920."

The key drivers of Corporation 1920's success are demand creation and expansion, product innovation, and low-cost production. It is characterised by its multinational presence, as well as its success at employing large-scale and international "price arbitrage" in every aspect of its operations. It arbitrages raw-material costs by sourcing cheaply from resource-rich, ill-governed developing countries in Africa and Asia, or from Australia. It arbitrages labor costs by hiring labor cheaply from populous developing countries in Asia to expand its manufacturing capacities. It arbitrages foreign direct-investment benefits from source countries, and investment subsidies from development-hungry destination countries keen to grow their manufacturing and services sectors.[17] Last, but not least, it arbitrages demand from rich consumer markets (particularly Western demand for branded consumer goods) by branding and selling goods at hefty premiums that translate to substantial profit margins.

As technology is forever evolving, the successful corporation needs to grow turnover at a rate *fast enough* to cover the costs of product obsolescence (through technological innovation and rapidly changing products—as we see with cars, cell phones, and laptops). Indeed, the most successful corporate models (such as Apple) actually *build* obsolescence into their product and marketing strategies. The successful corporation also needs to grow volume to counter competitive losses of margins (such as air travel in real terms, microchips, etc.). Corporation 1920's basic mantra is "more is better." It needs and feeds that other central mantra of today's dominant economic model, "GDP growth."

Corporation 1920 has four defining characteristics. First, determined pursuit of *size and scale* in order to achieve market dominance. Second, aggressive *lobbying* for regulatory and competitive advantages. Third, the extensive use of *advertising*, largely unhindered by ethical considerations, in order to influence consumer demand and, often, to create entirely new demand by playing on human insecurities and "turning wants into needs" which can only be satisfied by new products.[18] And finally, aggressive use of borrowed funds to "leverage" the investment that shareholders have made in their corporation.

Leverage, advertising, and lobbying often combine to drive size, thus creating positive feedback loops. Size, in turn, creates cost efficiencies and economies of scale which can deliver more competitive pricing that, in turn, leads to more sales. In the corporate quest for growth, even without the excess, misuse, or abuse that so often attends lobbying, advertising, and leverage, the collateral damage inflicted by corporations on society is not small. This damage typically leads to three exclusions: the exclusion of small- and medium-sized companies through lack of access to leverage; the exclusion of poor consumers from public alternatives to manufactured and marketed private goods; and the exclusion of competing new products (especially clean-tech or green alternatives) by means of a corporate stranglehold on media and distribution networks.

In his book *The Corporation*, Joel Bakan presents today's corporation as a psychopath—devoid of moral compass, relentless in the pursuit of power and profits, an "externalizing machine."[19] Not all commentators are as damning of today's corporation, but several have taken issue with the corporation's focus on shareholder interests to the exclusion of other stakeholders,[20] with its enormous and growing environmental and social cost externalities, and with its tendency toward unethical conduct (including bribery, inducement, lobbying by connected parties, irresponsible advertising, and public misrepresentation, among a long list of scandals).[21] All this is justified to achieve business advantage and higher short-term returns.

It is a moot point whether or not the average corporation shows *more* than the average human tendency for unethical behavior. There is no study that argues that corporations transact to *higher* ethical standards than individuals. On the contrary, there are mountains of evidence of the distancing or subjugation of *individuals'* normal moral compass when they act on behalf of their soulless corporate *employers*. Whistle-blowers in many industries have been effective precisely because they are the exception and not the norm. They are mostly people who at some stage in their working lives have become unable to bear the disjointedness of their personal response from their professional response to situations that require an ethical stance.

Elinor Ostrom, winner of the 2009 Nobel Prize in Economics for her work on the significance of community-based management of common-pool resources (CPRs),[22] in conversation described the Corporation as a CPR owned by a community of shareholders.[23] But it does not appear to be managed even to their advantage, given the long-term and reputational costs of most corporate misconduct. Hence, perhaps Corporation 1920 might be best described as a *dysfunctional* CPR.

This is particularly worrisome when one considers that the archetype of today's corporation operates across dozens of national boundaries, through thousands of employees and hundreds of suppliers, and serving perhaps millions of people as their customers. Should there be *any room for dysfunctionality at all* in the design of the corporation?

Tilting the Field

Corporate proponents of a green economy, low-carbon growth, and other economic recipes that target the goals of sustainable development are often frustrated by market-entry barriers and hostile economic policies, unhelpful laws and taxes, and perverse subsidies. Public policies, public investment, taxes, subsidies, and laws are sometimes collectively referred to as "enabling conditions" that could, if properly calibrated, provide fertile ground for "green" business strategies to take root.[24] Instead, they usually face market barriers put up by large incumbents, they are confronted with consumer resistance to greener products, and they experience the frustrating power of enormous subsidies supporting the opposite economic model—the incumbent "business-as-usual" model, or so-called brown economy. For example, fossil-fuel subsidies add up to an estimated US$650 billion per year globally, or about 1 percent of global GDP.[25] Subsidies for fisheries—mainly ocean fisheries—represent almost a third of the total value of fish caught in the oceans. Agricultural subsidies worldwide are over a tenth of total agricultural output.[26] It is hardly surprising, therefore, that renewable energy, sustainable fishery, and ecologically friendly agriculture have a hard time competing with their brown economy alternatives. Country after country provides examples of tax exemptions, import duties, export incentives, and a plethora of subsidies that favor a status-quo brown economy. The question begs to be asked: How did the playing field in so many sectors of the economy get so tilted, and how did corporations manage to achieve such outcomes?

A globally tilted playing field with around $1 trillion per annum in subsidies favoring a business-as-usual model over greener alternatives is, by definition, anything but a free market. Ironically however, an almost religious fervor for free markets has become the cornerstone of the public narrative told by corporations and amplified through advertising campaigns, PR firms, lobbyists, and even shareholders. For example, US corporations activate shareholders across multiple voting districts to flood the offices of Congressional representatives with phone calls decrying "legislation against the free market."

But the free market they seek to preserve is most often the status-quo market, and their large spending to lobby politicians is fundamentally a reflection of the value that the status quo represents to their bottom lines. Indeed, managing the regulatory landscape is among the most cost-efficient ways by which a corporation can sustain its dominance. Corporate lobbying is a pervasive and potent tool to interact with the regulatory process in a way that tilts the playing field further in their favor, or alternatively, prevents change in the status quo. Often, such change might have helped to foster a healthier balance among private risks, private gains, public risks, and public interests.

Although lobbying is part of the operational toolkit for almost all large companies, it is particularly important for those operating in realms of public trust, including oil, gas, coal, and other extractive industries. And as it happens, these corporations are also among the world's corporate behemoths: of the world's ten most profitable companies, four sell energy products and three base their global operations in the United States.[27]

It is not difficult to see why lobbying is such an attractive proposition for corporations seeking market dominance and profits, whether through new competitive advantage or by preserving the status quo. But why does lobbying deliver its punch with such apparent ease into the political world? No doubt party political funding matters, and (in some countries more than others) corruption in politics and government adds to the success of lobbyists. But that is not the case in every nation. Checks and balances are quite strong in most democracies, and the risks of exposure are real and politically costly—and yet, in every capital city from Washington to Wellington, corporate lobbying and influence is visible and successful.

The most pervasive reason for the ease with which corporate lobbying reaches into political decision making is that the corporation today is the most important and pervasive institution in political economy. The private sector delivers nearly 60 percent of GDP worldwide,[28] employs 70 percent of workers,[29] and corporate taxes comprise a significant slice of government revenues.[30] In other words, the report card for today's politicians and their "grades" on the subjects of GDP growth, employment, and deficit management are largely written by corporations. Small wonder, therefore, that politicians today are so beholden to the corporation, or that they are constantly looking over their shoulders to check if this or that policy change might harm the profitability of some business sector. The last thing they want is that voters see a "failing" grade on their report card, which would prevent them from getting another term. Small wonder, too, that "crony capitalism," the cozy relationship of mutual favors between businessmen and government officials, is so ubiquitous,[31] no matter whether we look at Latin America in the pre-crisis 1970s, or at Asia pre-crisis in 1997, or the United States pre-crisis in 2007.[32] The revolving door between the US Treasury and Wall Street was just the crowning refinement of this crony capitalism and it has had a deep impact on the financial and economic history of our times, especially the financial crisis of 2008 and the economic recession that followed.[33]

Corporation 2020

Tellus Institute's "Corporation 20/20" is an international, multi-stakeholder initiative that seeks to develop and disseminate a vision and pathway for the twenty-first-century corporation in which social purpose moves from the periphery to the heart of the organization.[34] In a 2007 position paper "Corporate Design: The Missing Business and Public Policy Issue of Our Time," the authors remark that "business leaders operate today inside a corporate design largely inherited from the nineteenth century, with ownership and governing structures put in place during the horse and buggy era."[35] The report sees the challenge of creating a new kind of corporation as "*the* design challenge of the twenty-first century."

This book reflects many of the concerns raised by the Corporation 20/20 project, and it proposes a composite solution to the problem of corporate design. *Corporation 2020* argues that endogenous changes will not suffice, notwithstanding exceptional leadership from some corporations, and that exogenous changes with the collaboration of governments, businesses, media, and civil society will be required to make a new design arise from the old. It contends that a safe timeline for these changes (taxation reforms, leverage limits, externalities disclosure, and advertising standards) to be introduced into policy frameworks and business practices is probably the next ten years, rather than the next fifty or a hundred years.[36] A new DNA of the corporation must begin to make its presence felt in the global economy by 2020, by which time we shall be dangerously close to many planetary limits or will have actually exceeded them. The 2050 or 2100 scenarios that are still reflected in UN climate negotiations and economic literature on the subject are too far off to be of any relevance. This is why the new corporation is termed "Corporation 2020" in this book. And there is an increasing convergence of opinion that vision, action, and timelines must converge; "20/20" and "2020" are therefore two sides of the same coin.

The New DNA That Business Needs

This book makes the case that Corporation 1920 has had its day. What attributes does today's corporation need to evolve in order to secure not only the corporate form but also the future of mankind on our only home, Planet Earth? What kind of corporate agent, in other words, do society and the economy need today if they are to forge an "economy of permanence,"[37] also known as a green economy[38] or a sustaining economy,[39] one which increases human well-being, increases social equity, decreases environmental risks, and decreases ecological scarcities?

A new DNA for the corporation needs to have numerous strands, but our focus will be the four key strands that are likely to make the most difference: corporate goal alignment with society, the corporation as community, the corporation as institute, and the corporation as a capital factory. As early as the early 1900s, Henry Ford was *aligning his company's goals with society*: he wanted every American farmer and his wife to have mobility and he wanted the farmer to grow his own fuel—ethanol from corn, fruit, or almost any biomass. Natura in Brazil prides itself on a *community* which is anchored in the company's relationship with over a million housewives who sell the Natura "story" and through that sell their cosmetics and personal products. Infosys in India has built the largest corporate university ever, and trains over thirty thousand young software professionals every year—in fact, Infosys is as much a *training institute* as it is a corporation. Creating social capital (like Natura) and human capital (like Infosys) are activities that are very valuable to society at large—not just to the company. In Japan, more than fifty large corporations maintain natural forests as their contribution to the society where they do business. It is the thesis of this book that such activities will make the corporation of the future a veritable "capital factory"—not just creating one line or category of capital (financial profit) but a whole array of capitals (physical, social, human, and natural), and not just for itself, but also (in the form of positive externalities) for society at large. This behavior at the "micro" level will make way for a very different world at the "macro" level, the world of Corporation 2020.

We are not compelled to live with the risks and costs of Corporation 1920 as the main agent of our economy and the most significant institution of our times. We can instead collaborate to create an environment for the success of a new species of corporation. Corporations, like biological species in a dynamic environment, respond to external stimuli which, in their case, include policies and prices. They adapt and evolve, with the strongest and fittest surviving over time. Changing external conditions such that the input costs of natural and social resources converge with their true value to society would enable a Darwinian process by which corporations most able to adapt in this efficient environment would survive and facilitate the creation of more such businesses. In the long run, therefore, the social benefits and social costs of corporations' activities would be reflected in their accounts as much as possible, thus realigning the corporations' profits with society's gains.

The World of Corporation 2020

Today's enabling conditions favor the DNA of Corporation 1920 and engender a brown economy. For our survival and success in Earth's biosphere, tomorrow's enabling conditions will have to be at least neutral if not explicitly supportive of Corporation 2020, which will become the dominant agent in a global green economy. So what would this "brave new world" look like, both for these corporations and the economies they would dominate?

The operating environment for corporations would have changed. Perverse subsidies would have been reduced, taxes reformed, new incentives added, public procurement "greened" and public investments focused on public wealth—especially ecological infrastructure. Private ownership and free markets would no longer be considered the panacea for all ills. Public ownership of the commons and community ownership of common-pool resources would be understood as economic *reality*, and not disparaged as "market failure." And the private sector would actually benefit from this improved understanding. Just as trusted corporations today are contracted to deliver public services such as waste management or road maintenance, so they would also win contracts to manage common-pool resources and public reserves such as forests, wetlands, or coral reefs on behalf of and according to the dictates of their host societies and communities.

Financial leverage would be limited by regulations which align corporate interests better with societal goals such as economic stability. At present, this task is left largely to investors, with fund managers becoming the unlikely conscience-keepers of society. Capital adequacy requirements would be introduced for corporations above a certain size—at present, they apply only to banks and financial institutions. The idea that car companies, utilities, insurers, and mortgage originators can also be "too big to fail" would be accompanied by its logical corollary, that public capital is either invested in or is being put at risk by these corporations, so they must also conform to prudential capital management standards just as banks are required to do.

"Selling good, not good selling" would become the norm rather than the exception. The legal status of an advertisement would no longer be a place to hide. Today, an advertisement is a non-actionable inducement (or an "invitation to treat" in Common Law), and not an actual offer, so in law there is no automatic recourse to misleading advertising, and specific product laws or sectoral laws or rules have to be introduced on a case-by-case basis, such as with advertising for cigarette smoking. Lessons learned in the context of the tobacco industry would be used to map wider solutions. Advertising would become accountable, and ethics in advertising would no longer be optional.

A new capitalism would prevail in the world of Corporation 2020, one recognizing and rewarding the creation of natural, social, and human capital as well as traditional physical and financial capital. Growth in complexity—rather than just size—would be an underpinning principle of the emerging green economy. Innovation would be an increasingly important driver for growth and employment. We can only manage what we measure; thus national capital stock (not just value-added turnover) would become central to measuring national economic performance. International projects such as Beyond GDP[40] and WAVES[41] would have provided the launching pad for a system of national accounting that recognizes and accounts for natural capital—its invisible benefit flows as well as its unaccounted loss or degradation. Fiscal gap management would not be affected by a switch to resource taxation for extractive industries, but it would motivate much greater resource efficiency. Likewise, for non-extractive but greenhouse-gas-emitting industries, taxing these "bads" would gradually replace corporate taxes. Near-term green economy forecasts for labor losses would take place, but well-managed transitions would lead to many more (and more-satisfying) green jobs within a decade.[42] Economics and politics would finally be aligned. On all counts—innovation, decent jobs, wealth, systemic risks, and income distribution—Corporation 2020 would gradually build up a successful and green macroeconomy.

The time to begin is now.

CHAPTER ONE

The Legal History of the Corporation

*If you would understand anything, observe its beginning and
its development.*

— *Aristotle*

To tell the story of the corporation is to tell the story of a grand bargain
gone awry.

Through history, governments have granted corporations special
privileges such as corporate personhood and limited liability, with the
expectation that corporations would serve the interests of the state and
the broader public. And yet legislative history and the ascendancy of free-
market capitalism have ensured that most modern corporations seek only
to advance their own self-interest. Billions of dollars are spent every year
on corporate and trade association lobbying to tilt the field of commercial
opportunity toward maximizing private financial capital. Responsibilities
of maintaining *public* capital are ignored, in particular those of natural
capital and social capital, even though these are respectively the ecological bedrock and institutional masonry of any successful human economy.
Dire results follow for both the public good and trust in the corporate
institution.

Civilizations have repeatedly recognized the value of corporations.
Henry Ford never visited the great Swedish Stora Kopparberg mine (chartered in 1347, the oldest corporation in continuous operation), but he
would have recognized its genius. Ancient Rome's *societates publicanorum*
and the Mauryan Empire's *sreni* in India arrived at astonishingly similar
approaches to pooling capital and reducing risk. History suggests that the

corporation is one of mankind's most useful inventions, as essential for continuity and achievement in commerce as the advent of the written word was for ideas.

At the same time, corporations have always come with risks, and they are centrally implicated in many of today's most serious problems. While the history of corporations reaffirms their value, it is also replete with examples of governments struggling to constrain corporate power and negative externalities. This chapter narrates the history of the legal innovations that have given us today's corporation.

Early History

The earliest attempts to share risk and pool capital occurred in ancient Mesopotamia. However, not until the Mauryan Empire in India and the rise of the Roman Republic did the concepts of limited liability and corporate personhood emerge. It should be said in this context that the early official accreditation of the corporation into civilized society occurred unfettered by societal controls designed to protect those outside the corporation. The notion of "undue corporate influence" would not emerge until nearly the eighteenth century. The early corporation completely lacked introspection.

From 800 BC to AD 1000 India experimented with a powerful tool: the *sreni*. Like later corporations, *sreni* had dispersed ownership structures, with shares that could be sold. Unlike modern corporations, *sreni* operated under a pro rata system, in which shareholders were liable for the *sreni*'s debts in proportion to their investment.[1] When engaging in expensive and risky endeavors, such as international trade, merchants could create an entity holding assets separately from its owners.[2]

The *sreni* were the engines of ancient India's economic growth. Because of their power, they were also highly regulated.[3] While the security provided by the Mauryan dynasty fostered the development of the *sreni*, it was the fall of the Mauryan Empire in the second century BC and the emergence of smaller and less centralized states that allowed India's *sreni* substantially to expand their influence, control, and wealth over the next 1,200 years.

Although India's *sreni* prove that it is untrue that the invention of companies "belongs entirely to the Romans,"[4] Rome did play a crucial role in advancing the idea that a corporation can have an identity separate from its human components.[5] Rome's *societates publicanorum*, or "societies of government leaseholders," were constituted to meet state goals such as providing public works, manufacturing weapons of war, and collecting taxes.[6] Beginning in the third century BC, groups of investors (the *publicani*) would bid on state contracts for activities deemed vital for the advancement of the republic. Although for business done in the private sector Rome provided essentially no protection from liability, in the public sector, government-granted limitations on liability allowed investors to purchase shares without absorbing personal responsibility. Within two centuries of the formation of this business structure, the largest *societates publicanorum* resembled modern companies, with hundreds of limited partners trading their shares on a stock exchange.[7] These vibrant exchanges were promoted by the limited liability of investors, with the tradability of shares in turn encouraging increased capital formation and corporate growth.[8]

In ancient Rome, corporations only provided services to the state and not to private parties. Thus, the state would maintain a strong interest in ensuring that the firm was managed efficiently and honestly, and it could readily take action against corporate misdeeds. For business in the private sector, however, there was essentially no ability to shield the entity from liability, although the Romans did indeed build some corporate structures that could be used for general purposes. They developed and made extensive use of a corporate form that looked remarkably similar to that of a modern public corporation, which could easily have been utilized for general business endeavors. The reason that this did not happen might be due to the high transaction costs for ensuring governance structures sufficient for protecting investors and the public. After Rome's transition from a republic to an empire in the first century BC, the emperors grew wary of the influence of the *publicani*, so the state began to take over public works projects.[9] The role of the *publicani* was limited to collecting taxes, but they were barred from even this activity by the end of the second century as Rome entered its slow decline.[10] By the fall of Rome in AD 476, the *societates publicanorum* had dissolved into the fabric of history.

The Era of the Social Corporation

It would take almost a millennium for governments and commercial enterprises to once again develop a robust corporate form within Europe. The Middle Ages saw the incorporation of Europe's nonprofit social institutions, such as churches and universities.[11] In the case of for-profit corporations, the important limitation of the times was that incorporation occurred only via royal charter.[12] Frequent reference is made nowadays to a corporation's "social license to operate," or its implicit acceptability to society at large, but royal charter was in essence an early, explicit, and legal form of a "license to operate," a contract between society and the corporation.

The oldest commercial corporation in continuous operation—Stora Kopparberg—obtained a charter from King Magnus Eriksson in 1347, and still maintains a strong presence (as Stora Enso) in Northern Europe.[13] The evolution of royal charters reached a watershed in 1600 in England with the creation of the East India Company, which became the first truly multinational corporation.[14] Shortly thereafter, in 1602, the chartering of the Dutch East India Company followed this multinational model, eventually becoming perhaps the most powerful corporation ever formed.[15] Both of these corporate giants' charters, as a result of the risks associated with global commerce, granted shareholders limited liability on ventures related to their respective investments. More significantly, they also represented two of the earliest examples of the role of corporate influence in shaping policy. As attested in the annals of both the British and Dutch governments, these companies shaped the foreign policies of their respective countries for nearly two centuries.[16]

By the early eighteenth century, corporations were increasingly common and were moving away from a system based on royal charter. In England, however, the Bubble Act of 1720 banned all corporations not authorized by royal charter, putting a halt to British corporate evolution. Ostensibly a response to a series of speculative frenzies, the Bubble Act was in fact originated by the South Sea Company, which sought to protect its monopoly. What began as a cynical attempt to manipulate investment patterns turned into a condemnation of "[a]ll undertakings . . . presuming to act as a corporate body."[17] Its official name gives a hint of the vitriol heaped on the corporate form: it was entitled *"An Act to Restrain the Extravagant and Unwarranted Practice of Raising Money by Voluntary Subscriptions for Carrying On Projects Dangerous to the Trade and Subjects of this Kingdom."*[18] The Bubble Act meant that England's Industrial Revolution, perhaps the most significant turning point in recorded history, took place outside the corporate form.[19]

Because of this, the next great shift in the corporate model would occur in the United States. There, every state could issue corporate charters; in 1832 authors Joseph Kinnicut and Samuel Ames Angell complained of "an infinite number of corporations aggregate, which have no concern whatever with affairs of a municipal nature."[20] The proliferation of corporations rekindled debate about the relationship between shareholders and the state, which Justice John Marshall reflected on in the 1819 case, *Trustees of Dartmouth College v. Woodward*. In this case, the state of New Hampshire had attempted to alter the charter of Dartmouth College.[21] In his final opinion, Marshall asked whether the act of incorporation by the state made it possible for the state to take over the corporation. In oft-quoted language, Marshall held that "[a] corporation is an artificial being, invisible, intangible, and existing only in contemplation of law."[22] Having created the corporation, the state could not simply treat it as an extension of itself.[23]

Marshall's decision established the legal principle that private corporations can exist in isolation from the state. Though still typically "imbued with public purpose," corporations were evolving into more independent entities—a trend that would accelerate dramatically in the coming decades.

Private Enterprise and the Corporation

Traders, merchants, craftsmen, and their guilds were the mainstay of commerce in medieval times. However, the nineteenth century saw private enterprise discover and rapidly embrace the benefits of corporate personhood and limited liability that came with incorporation. In 1800, there were just 355 corporate charters in the United States. By 1890, the number was almost 500,000.[24] Two legal developments lay behind this explosion: the advent of general incorporation statutes and the adoption of limited liability.

Starting in the 1830s, state-level incorporation statutes in the United States began to allow individuals to form corporations without special charters from legislatures.[25] In 1844 the Supreme Court stated that a corporation "seems to us to be a person, though an artificial one . . . and therefore entitled, for the purpose of suing and being sued, to be deemed a citizen. . . ."[26]

The rise in general incorporation statutes and their increasing popularity with business entrepreneurs and their investors mirrored a rise in limited-liability acts. Protected from risk, shareholders increasingly bought stocks as investment vehicles.[27] The resulting growth of corporations led to a change in the impacts corporations had on stakeholders. As opposed to shareholders, stakeholders are those who lack an ownership role in a corporation, but are still affected by its actions. Historically, corporate stakeholders were mostly limited to customers, but in the nineteenth century the growth of corporations expanded the stakeholder sphere. In particular, the negative externalities of railroads affected larger and larger numbers of people.[28] Because of limited liability, defrauded stakeholders became unwilling creditors for corporations, with no way to seek compensation.[29] This unintended consequence of limited liability remains one of the central negative realities of the corporate form today.

At the same time, Britain was also engaging in a debate over limited liability, though preoccupations with class provided a twist that would not have been familiar to an American.[30] With lords and ladies disdaining industry, commerce was seen as the province of the lower and middle classes. Partly because of this it was not until 1850 that the House of Commons appointed a committee to "inquire into the subject of investments of the middle and working classes."[31] In 1855, the English Parliament passed the Limited Liability Act, which conferred limited liability on most joint-stock companies.[32] While this event would eventually have profound effects on the way that corporations were structured, it is interesting to note that *banks* were at first hesitant to take up this form, as their owners' unlimited liability was regarded as a "badge of prudence."[33] The banks weighed the benefits that the two systems provided; the new law of limited liability afforded the value of investor protection, while the previous system of unlimited shareholder liability could drive business by giving confidence to depositors that their funds were secure. It was not until the failure of the City of Glasgow bank in 1878 over two decades later, causing 80 percent of the bank's shareholders to go broke, that banks realized the value of limited liability and quickly adopted this form. By 1889, there remained only two British banks with unlimited liability.[34] A recent extension of the concept of limited liability is the emergence of "limited liability partnerships" in the United Kingdom.[35] This shows that liability limitation has crept into even the partnership form which, thus far, had not provided safety from losses beyond invested capital to its owner-partners.

Following the rapid evolution of corporate law in the United States came competition to attract corporations to particular states. Beginning in the 1870s, this competition led to major legal innovations. The first important development, albeit with limited effect, was an attempt by Congress in 1876 to control the influence of corporate lobbying by requiring the registration of lobbyists with the Clerk of the House of Representatives.[36] The second was the rise of the business judgment rule, which holds that boards of directors possess powers not delegated by shareholders. By 1905, the principle was so well established that a court could write that "it is [the board's] judgment, and not that of its stockholders outside of the board of directors . . . that is to shape [a corporation's] policies. . . . This principle is not disputed, and the citation of authorities in its support is unnecessary."[37]

Equally important was the decline of the ultra vires doctrine, which held that a corporation could not act contrary to the powers conferred on it by the state. The doctrine was a response to the potential for abuse that came with limited liability.[38] Yet competition for commerce now offered states an incentive to loosen corporate regulations. In 1896, New Jersey eliminated its prohibition against corporations owning stock in other corporations.[39] The spread of corporate laws permitting incorporation for "any lawful activity" sealed the decline of the ultra vires doctrine.[40]

Absent the ultra vires doctrine, corporations were not compelled to meet society's needs. From 1865 to the early 1890s, large corporate enterprises became the norm for American business activities.[41] Following a wave of consolidation, corporations grew even larger, and Americans got their first taste of the Robber Barons. Names like John D. Rockefeller and J. P. Morgan became symbols of both the promise and perils of corporate growth. Indeed, the reign of these influential barons' corporations occurred with virtually no government efforts to control how their influence was wielded. Despite President Theodore Roosevelt's use of the Sherman Anti-Trust Act (which actually existed for nearly 15 years before its first use),[42] it would not be until 1936 that the government took a consistent stance on limiting corporate influence on the political process.[43]

The Nail in the Coffin

The final blow to the social corporation came with a 1919 Michigan Supreme Court case, *Dodge v. Ford*. Prior to this case, the centrality of the profit motive of the corporation was like an old wives' tale—frequently repeated, but never tested. After *Dodge v. Ford*, the corporation could exist only to promote financial gains for its shareholders.

The defendant in the case, Henry Ford, wanted to "employ still more men; to spread the benefits of this industrial system to the greatest possible number."[44] Ford's reasoning was that it is better to sell many cars at a small profit than few cars at a large profit, because "it enables a larger number of people to buy and enjoy the use of a car and because it gives a larger number of men employment at good wages."[45] The plaintiffs in the case, the Dodge brothers, were major early investors in Ford, and wanted a larger dividend. When Ford planned to reinvest cash assets for a plant expansion, the Dodge brothers sought an injunction.

The decision of the Michigan Court did not alter the law of the nation, but it did profoundly shape legal and popular perceptions about what it meant to be a business in modern America. The Court wrote,

> There should be no confusion . . . of the duties which Mr. Ford conceives that he and the stockholders owe to the general public. . . . A business corporation is organized and carried on primarily for the profit of the stockholders. The powers of the directors are to be employed for that end.[46]

Ford's appeal for social welfare would not again be voiced so insistently for several decades. Ford emphasized that his company was "an instrument of service rather than a machine for making money"—but the twentieth century would indeed be defined by the corporation as money-making machine.

As the Dodge brothers and Henry Ford contested the future of corporate control, a parallel shift in corporate law was under way. Corporations had always presented a paradox. In legal terms, they had some human attributes. Yet many of the defining qualities of corporations, such as limited liability, were also distinctly nonhuman. As the twentieth century progressed, courts increasingly answered the corporate legal paradox by granting corporations more of the kinds of rights historically reserved for people.

The originating case for corporate personhood was *Santa Clara County v. Southern Pacific Railroad Co.* (1886),[47] which went to the U.S. Supreme Court, and resulted in a statement indicating that the right to set off mortgages from the taxable value of properties belonged as much to corporations as to people.[48] A rush of cases followed, steadily expanding corporate personhood.[49] Looking back in 1949, Justice William O. Douglas wrote that "the Santa Clara case becomes one of the most momentous of all our decisions. . . . Corporations were now armed with constitutional prerogatives."[50]

The Birth of "Corporation 1920"

It is evident from the above that the hundred years from 1820 to 1920 were a veritable crucible in the legal history of the corporation. Heating this crucible were the entrepreneurial fire of America's early decades of freedom, the economic fuel of a vast and still expanding British colonial empire, and the creative yet disruptive churning of inventions and innovations—giant new mills and factories, expanding railway networks, ocean liners, automobiles, the telegraph, etc. During this period, the corporation became the preferred market agent for rapid growth in manufacturing and trade. It was gradually unshackled from its state-granted "charter" history and from its community moorings. It became unconstrained in time, space, and lines of activity. Its independent identity was legally established as "corporate personhood" and became an accepted feature of everyday business. Its purpose was defined and formally accepted as profit for its shareholders, and social purpose was no longer a driving force. This corporation became the main agent of modern, market-centric economies in the twentieth century, a poster child and champion of free-market capitalism.

The corporation that emerged from this "crucible period" embodied a paradoxical mix of human and nonhuman qualities, which has made it difficult to address its externalities. Punishments such as fines and penalties, effective in controlling human behavior, were extended to corporations. However the limitations of this approach can be seen from Baron Thurlow's famous comment that corporations have "no soul to damn" and "no body to kick." Most modern corporations, nearly human in the eyes of the law but inhuman in their practices, treat penalties and fines as simply the "cost of doing business."[51]

This new corporation grew from strength to strength in the twentieth century. It was aided and abetted by governments keen to use the energy of entrepreneurship and the scale and efficiency of the corporation to reset their economies on a path to growth and prosperity from which they had been derailed—first by the buffeting of the Great Depression (1929–1930s) and then by the disruptions of the Second World War (1939–45).

It was no small leap of faith for governments to forgo control in this manner, as the purpose of the corporation had been firmly established as self-interest (*Dodge v. Ford*, 1919) and not social improvement. Through this landmark case, by 1920 the stage had been set for the corporation we see today: Corporation 1920 had been born.

CHAPTER TWO

The Great Alignment: 1945–2000

The Convergence of Deregulation and Innovations in World Trade and Capital Markets, and Its Impacts on the Corporation

One of the most significant human commitments of the last half of the twentieth century has been to economic growth and trade expansion, and we have been spectacularly successful in accomplishing both.

— *David Korten*

The period 1820–1919 was in many ways the crucible of today's corporation: it gave the corporation identity independent of its shareholders, empowering it with rights and capacities which were equal to those of living individuals and it limited the liability of shareholders to their invested capital. After World War II, the power of all these privileges was force-multiplied by simultaneous waves of deregulation and innovation, both in world trade and in capital markets. This great alignment of forces provided the fertile economic soil on which the corporation grew into its most successful avatar, the multi-billion-dollar, multinational, corporate behemoth which dominates economies and permeates societies today.

Postwar economic history is largely the history of the rise of free-market capitalism and its aiding-and-abetting democracies. This economic model gradually replaced other forms of economic management everywhere: the command and control of communism in the Soviet bloc; India's Fabian-socialist, public-sector "commanding heights"; China's communism-and-manufacturing revolution and its subsequent "state capitalism"; and the many resource-cursed economies of Africa's electoral and military dictatorships. Several national success stories, some real and some contrived, are rolled out as icons of success for this expanding economic paradigm.[1] In most nations with different political models, a democratization of the political fabric accompanied and helped accelerate free-market capitalism—mainly through legislative relaxations that opened up these economies to increasingly global and deregulated trade and capital markets, while also, unavoidably, increasing the power that corporate interests exert in the global marketplace.

The increasing dominance of free-market capitalism had several drivers—from trenchant international political and institutional changes (such as the introduction of GATT and WTO, and the dismantling of Bretton Woods, among others) to innovations in world trade (including two revolutions in logistics and several innovations in capital markets). The invisible engine that drove this economic transformation and benefited most from these avenues of deregulation and innovation, however, was today's corporation. The free-market-capitalist, "brown economy," cost-externalizing DNA of Corporation 1920 responded to the benign enabling conditions in the postwar years and flourished as never before, becoming increasingly pervasive and powerful.

The Prize of Size

Peter Drucker observed that a century-old "trend toward an employee society of big organizations gathered rapid momentum . . . especially, after World War II."[2] This trend can be evidenced in many ways, but perhaps the simplest is to observe the number of corporations whose revenues exceed one-tenth of a percent of global Gross Domestic Product as it rises from under 20 in 1970 to over 120 in 2010 (see Figure 2.1). This is in relative terms, of course, but if we look at absolute size, the trend is even more startling: the number of corporations with sales turnover exceeding $25 billion (inflation-adjusted 2010 dollars) increased from fewer than 20 in 1970 to a staggering 320 in 2010 (Figure 2.2).

It is also worth stating that this trend toward the "bulking up" of corporations was not a result of the private sector as a whole increasing in size compared to the global economy, as that ratio tends to remain more or less steady at between 55 and 60 percent (Figure 2.3).

The deregulation in trade and in capital controls that punctuated most

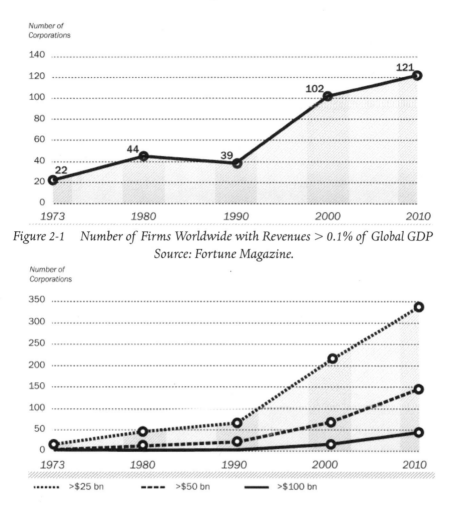

Figure 2-1   *Number of Firms Worldwide with Revenues > 0.1% of Global GDP*
Source: Fortune Magazine.

Figure 2-2   *Number of Firms above Threshold Revenue (2010 US$)*
Source: Fortune Magazine.

postwar economic history was closely aligned to the goals of the corporation: the pursuit of private profits in the most advantageous manner
possible. Trade and capital market deregulation provided today's corporation with the opportunity to grow. It became a "price arbitrageur" *par*
excellence in terms of its increasingly unfettered access to cheap natural-
resource inputs, cheap labor markets, subsidized manufacturing capacity,
and perhaps most important of all, rich consumer markets in Europe,
North America, and Japan.

This new era of access prompted the corporation to promote its

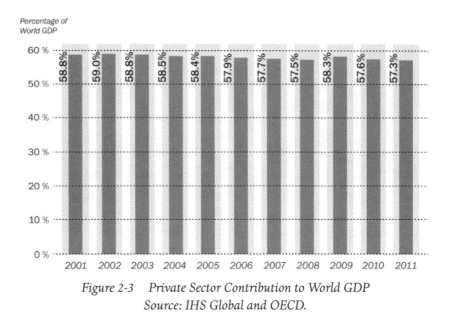

Figure 2-3   Private Sector Contribution to World GDP
Source: IHS Global and OECD.

interests aggressively within the political fabric of these booming consumer markets in order to ensure continued growth. The creation of
the General Agreement on Tariffs and Trade (GATT) and its subsequent
implementation by the World Trade Organization (WTO) have, in theory, minimized the impact of corporate influence on trade liberalization
while still lowering worldwide trade tariffs.[3] In practice, however, this has
not been the case. One of the sharpest criticisms of the WTO is its lack
of transparency during its negotiation rounds, where member nations directly discuss trade issues affecting the corporate interests of their respective countries.

It is difficult to quantify the number of corporate lobbyists swarm-
ing around the WTO's headquarters in Geneva, Switzerland (it does
not require lobbyists to register, unlike Capitol Hill in the United States)
but the number is large. Given the informal nature of day-to-day operations, many industry groups maintain permanent lobbying offices in Geneva, and often travel to WTO ministerial meetings around the globe.[4]
Although there was a sharp decline in corporate lobbying during the
WTO's recent Doha Development Round of negations,[5] this is widely attributed to the substance of the negotiations and may not continue.[6] The
stalling of this multilateral process and a corresponding rise in bilateral

trade negotiations suggests that trade lobbyists have not disappeared, but have merely refocused their efforts elsewhere.

Trade Deregulation and the Multinational Corporation

In the period 1913–1950, during which world GDP had approximately doubled in spite of two world wars, the volume of world exports tripled from US$19.5 billion to $60.9 billion. However, this growth in trade was actually minor compared to what would develop in the coming years. Only a decade later, world exports had again doubled, to US$127.3 billion. By 2010, this value would rise more than *300-fold* from its 1950 value to US$18.8 *trillion*.[7]

The origins of today's global, multinational, trade-intensive corporate economy can be found in a 1945 State Department report, *Proposals for the Expansion of Trade and Employment*. This report sought to catalog and characterize the poor decision making by political leaders that had led to the withering of international commerce since its height in the early 1880s. In doing so, *Proposals* was designed as a blueprint for unraveling the preponderance of global protectionism that had emerged in the wake of the Fordney-McCumber and Smoot-Hawley Acts in the United States, and also establishing the United States as the uncontested leader in the global economy.

Utilizing *Proposals* as a guiding framework, in 1947 trade officials from 22 major nations convened in Geneva to construct a policy framework that would become known as GATT, ratified on November 18, 1947. Three days later, officials from 56 nations entered negotiations in Havana, Cuba, for the formation of the International Trade Organization (ITO), an institution whose purpose was to act as coordinator and manager of ensuing GATT rounds. Although the ITO as an entity eventually dissolved shortly following its inception, by the third round of GATT negotiations in 1951, prewar tariffs and restrictions on the trade of industrial products had been overwhelmingly dissolved.

From 1945 to 1998, the loosening of international trade law under GATT yielded annual increases in the real value of world trade of 6.4 percent, almost doubling every decade for five decades in a row. This period also saw an increase in the volume of world trade relative to production, from <5 percent to >15 percent of world GDP (see Figures 2.5 and 2.6).[8]

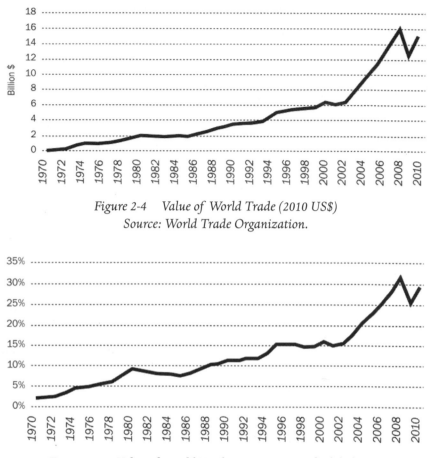

Figure 2-4   Value of World Trade (2010 US$)
Source: World Trade Organization.

Figure 2-5   Value of World Trade as Percentage of Global GDP
Source: World Trade Organization, World Bank.

Two Revolutions in Logistics

World trade grew not only on the back of deregulation, but also on the back of two major logistics innovations, in shipping and telecommunications technology. Shipping saw an unprecedented boom with the invention of the cargo container and the reconfiguration of ports to handle the rapid transport of cargo containers from ship to barge to rail and truck. A second era of innovation, even more powerful, came with the telecommunications revolution and the advent of bar-coding, the Internet, and e-commerce, making it not only practical but even cost-effective to operate through global supply chains that were tracked and managed electronically as part of multinational corporations' increasingly harmonized, global operations machinery.

The Rise of Containerization

Since the 1800s, merchants had sought an intermodal shipping device that could be seamlessly loaded and unloaded among train, truck, and ship. Although a number of innovations had been pursued over the course of the nineteenth and early twentieth centuries, none had been able to escape purview and rejection by the federal Interstate Commerce Commission (ICC) in the United States.[9]

This rejection of containerization technology, and the inertia behind Congressional expansion of ICC policy, was in part due to the Commission falling prey to regulatory capture by vested corporate interests that sought to block a technological advancement that allowed both cheaper and faster logistics.[10]

The rapid development of logistics, however, did not occur purely under widespread corporate influence, but was achieved more organically.

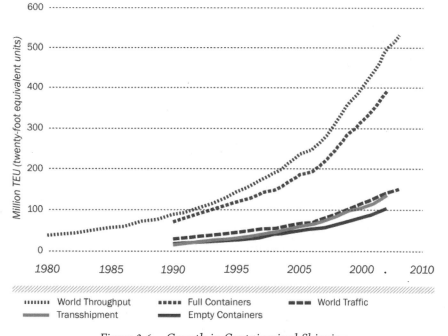

Figure 2-6   Growth in Containerized Shipping
Source: *Jean-Paul Rodrigue, Claude Comtois, and Brian Slack,* The Geography of Transport Systems, *2nd ed. (London, New York: Routledge, 2009).*

In 1940 and 1942, the ICC's jurisdiction expanded to cover interstate water carriers and then freight forwarders, in effect charging the ICC with coordination for all modes of transportation. In 1956, however, a federal court ruling removed intermodal containers from the purview of the ICC. Although specialized intermodal shipping containers had been used by some railroad companies as early as 1926, it was the insistence of the US Army from the end of World War II to the Korean War that underlined the need for a standardized reusable container to optimize the efficiency and integrity of long-distance shipping.

By the 1970s, the era of containerized traffic had begun. Volume grew by leaps and bounds. The number of freight containers handled annually by the world's ports increased from 6.3 to 163.7 million from 1972 to 1997.[11]

At the same time, transportation providers turned themselves into "logistics firms" capable of handling the movement of both products and information. Mainly as a result of this transformation, the cost of transport as a percentage of the total cost of goods dropped between 1961 and 1999 from approximately 10–12 percent to 1 percent.[12] (See Figure 2.6)

Telecommunications as a Force Multiplier

Telecommunications innovations in the postwar years significantly enhanced the capacity to track business globally. The invention of bar codes, electronic scanners, databases, tracking software, high speed communications networks, and portable wireless devices paved the way for the multinational corporation to become the natural unit of business. Connectivity, uniformity, and digitization radically increased the ease with which goods could be delivered from the factory floor to the consumer with unprecedented ease and efficiency across countries and continents, and the multinational corporation was the natural beneficiary of this newfound ability to size and scale.

The technological developments that have contributed most significantly to the emergence of multinational corporations in the twentieth century have come from the telecommunications industry. At the macro scale, in the century following the laying of the first transatlantic telegraph cable a series of transatlantic telephones began to lay the foundation for modern international telecommunications. Where the earliest transatlantic cables were galvanic, beginning in 1988 these cables were replaced with more-advanced fiber-optic material, enhancing both the speed and clarity of communications. At the micro scale, the evolution of cellular telecom systems in the postwar period has contributed tremendously toward building efficient communities within multinational corporate networks. In the United States, the first generation of analog cellular networks came to fruition over the extended period from 1947, when AT&T first requested spectrum for cellular service from the Federal Communications Commission, until 1982 when service authorization was finally granted.[13] After these initial delays, cellular telecommunications grew by leaps and bounds. In the early 1990s, new high-tech telecommunication companies began to usurp the market capital of older industry stalwarts. The transition to a second generation of digital transmission yielded significant improvement in cellular communication cost, speed, and power efficiency.

The ability to track supply chains changed dramatically with the invention of bar codes and bar code scanners in the mid-twentieth century. In 1970, four years after its first commercial application, the Universal Grocery Products Identification Code established the first industry standard bar code. It would in short order evolve to become the Universal Product Code (UPC) and give rise to commercial bar code scanners which could be used to rapidly track, evaluate, and communicate product sales and supply chain locations that once demanded physical inspection. The growing ranks of multinational corporations recognized that it was a means of better monitoring and greater control of product inventory, and before long, UPC barcodes were found everywhere, from factory shipping depots to retail outlets, from metropolitan megastores to remote village shops, from the developed world to the developing world. This innocuous signature of modern producers and distributors of consumer goods was soon in use almost everywhere anything was bought or sold.

The effects of trade deregulation and innovation on the business of multinational corporations in the postwar period were palpable. In 1938, on the eve of World War II, the value of production by firms coordinating their operations on a global basis (i.e., early multinational corporations) was only one-third that of total international trade. Liberalization of trade markets fueled strong growth right through the postwar period to the point at which, by 1976, the value of multinational global production actually exceeded that of global trade.[14] This was a sign of the meteoric growth of the multinational corporation in domestic markets as well as export markets, especially considering how fast trade had expanded during the same period.

During the so-called Bretton Woods era of fixed exchange rates in the 1950s and 1960s, trade innovation and deregulation were the dominant forces driving the emergence of the multinational corporation as the model of corporate success. An instance of the "great alignment" of forces during this era, they were supported by exchange-rate stability and predictability—a nurturing backdrop for the success of multinational corporations' productivity- and efficiency-driven export strategies. Toward the end of that period, however, the global financial arrangements set in place after World War II began to crumble. The forces of deregulation and innovation found a new playing field: the world's capital markets.

Capital Market Deregulation

In the period from 1914 to 1945, the global economy was ravaged by a succession of two world wars, a Great Depression, and a rise in nationalism and noncooperative economic policymaking. By World War I, the gold standard was largely abandoned as monetary policy become a mere agent of domestic political goals, first as means to finance wartime deficits, and later as a tool to engineer beggar-thy-neighbor devaluations under floating exchange rates.[15] As a result, in the period leading up to the war, capital controls proliferated in an effort to guard against currency crises, and as a result international investment became less pronounced.

Even before the end of World War II, in July 1944 at Bretton Woods delegates from Allied nations forged what became known as the Bretton Woods monetary system, which sought to establish a framework for commercial and financial relations among the world's major industrial states. This meeting established both the International Bank for Reconstruction and Development (IBRD) and the International Monetary Fund (IMF). The Bretton Woods arrangement established a system based on fixed but periodically adjustable exchange parities. The prime responsibility of the newly formed International Monetary Fund (IMF) was to act as a source of hard-currency loans to governments, which were likely to lapse into recession, in order to maintain a standard fixed exchange rate.

The IMF initially sanctioned capital controls as a mechanism to prevent currency crises and runs, lending autonomy to governments by providing more power to activist monetary policy. However, by the 1960s capital flows could no longer be restrained. In 1971, President Nixon de-linked the US dollar from the price of gold, creating a fluctuating US currency that necessitated a floating-exchange-rate regime, and the Bretton Woods system was dismantled. IMF control on currency exchanges and capital flows had given way to private-sector trade and capital flows, with exchange rates determined by market forces driven by these same trade and capital flows. The combination of floating-rate currencies and reforms to foreign investment rules yielded an international economic system with greater ability to reduce transaction costs, accommodate market developments, and stimulate net capital investment. In the process, the multinational corporation became the main agent in the growing success of free-market capitalism.

The advent of capital-account convertibility in the 1970s, the creation of offshore or "Euromarkets" from the 1960s, and the invention and increasing use of an entire family of financial derivatives from the late 1980s and early 1990s made financial capital readily available, and also made leverage increasingly easy to obtain and increasingly difficult to control. All these capital-market trends converged to favor the success of the modern corporation as a large, international, unconstrained seeker and arbitrageur of access to resources, capital, labor, and consumers.

Post–Bretton Woods, it was found that floating rates could generally accommodate market developments, and this encouraged capital flow internationally. In many developing countries, economic reforms reduced transaction costs and foreign investment risks, leading to an explosion in foreign direct investment. This trend was in fact a hallmark of the successful emerging multinational corporation and a reflection of its expanding access to financial leverage.

The Power of Foreign Direct Investment

As deregulation grew, corporations once constrained to their domestic markets were now able to establish international footprints. Opportunities for foreign direct investment (FDI) consisted broadly of two types: greenfield investment, and mergers and acquisitions. Greenfield investment, which results in a wholly new operation in a foreign country, was subject to the demands for knowledge of the host nation's business and political culture and a working familiarity with its investment environment. Although mergers and acquisitions required a similar body of knowledge on the front end, it held the greater advantage of allowing foreign firms a means by which to gain experience operating within international business cultures through a foreign intermediary. As an investment strategy, mergers and acquisitions were easier, more expedient, and less risky to execute than building greenfield investments from the ground up. They also provided an operating mechanism to import firm capital, technology, and management skills as strategic assets in increasing the efficiency of foreign companies.

Foreign direct investment was driven by a number of factors, among them business's aversion to threats of protectionism in important export markets in the developing world, the shift toward democratic political institutions and free market economies, and, with the gradual emergence of a global marketplace, the importance to firms of having a significant global presence. Another driver of FDI was the accelerating global demand for energy and minerals, which not only fed off and bred bad governance, but in some cases also led to "de-industrialization" in natural-resource-dominated economies in Africa and in Latin America. As trade liberalization grew under GATT, increased FDI was encouraged through the establishment of government-backed insurance programs to cover major types of foreign investment risk, the elimination of double taxation of foreign income, and the relaxation of restrictions on inbound investment by host nations.

In the 1950s, FDI was confined largely to primary sectors and manufacturing, as firms were motivated by access to large national or regional markets and the opportunity of arbitraging low-cost foreign production and natural resources. FDI has seen its greatest growth from the mid-1980s on, most notably since the World Trade Organization established a set of rules to promote FDI liberalization. With the rise of modern telecommunications, FDI has become increasingly service-oriented as the economies of developed nations evolve. In fact, while FDI stock has increased in almost all sectors over the past decades, it has notably grown even in sectors not traditionally associated with FDI. Between 1990 and

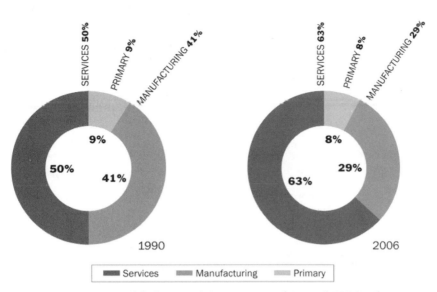

Figure 2-7   Global Sectoral Composition of Inward FDI Stock
Source: Zbigniew Zimny, "Foreign Direct Investment in the World and in Africa:
Long-term Trends and Current Patterns," in UNCTAD Virtual Institute
Training Package on Economic and Legal Aspects of International
Investment Agreements (IIAs).

2006, inward FDI increased more than two and a half times in the "agriculture, hunting, forestry, and fishing" category, but eight times in the service sector as a whole globally—compared to roughly fivefold increases
for inward FDI in manufacturing and extractive industries.[16]

Throughout the postwar period, the origination of FDI also shifted
significantly. While FDI origination was dominated by the contingent of
the United States, the United Kingdom, the Netherlands, and France for
the two decades following World War II, the rise of developed economies
in Korea, Taiwan, Singapore, Hong Kong, and China has significantly re-
distributed cross-border capital flows in recent years.

The free-market capitalist view would be that international production should be distributed among countries according to the theory of
competitive advantage, and having the capacity to exploit such competitive advantages increases the efficiency of the global economy. In theory,
FDI stimulates home-country economic growth by freeing resources employed less gainfully and making them available for activities where they
can be used to maintain or build competitive advantage.

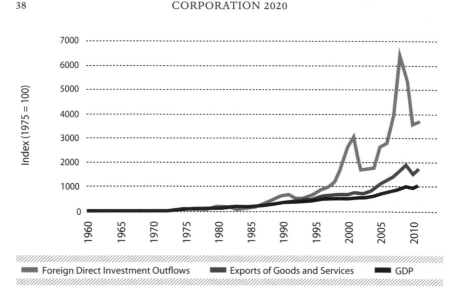

*Figure 2-8   Indices of World FDI Outflows, GDP, and Exports
(Base year 1975: 100) Source: World Bank World Development Indicators.*

In developing countries, however, the long-term sustainability of FDI-induced efforts to exploit competitive advantage is not without issue. In these growing markets, a relative lack of safeguards against illicit lobbying (in the form of bribery) and government corruption creates intense obligations on the corporation to use FDI responsibly.[17] While corporations have created investment mechanisms such as Private Public Partnerships and Power Purchase Agreements to safeguard their FDI investments abroad, they have little to show in terms of institutional innovation (other than basic self-accountability) to safeguard host nations and their citizens from the negative effects of FDI.[18] After two decades of FDI buildup which has seen global FDI rise more than fivefold, civil-society activism and (in a few countries) public-interest litigation are often the only host-nation responses that could be described as "checks and balances." This is by no means an outcome that satisfies even the basic principles of equity or social responsibility, and yet, such a lack of governance is commonplace among multinational corporations in host countries across the developing world.

One further facet of FDI is worth noting, and that is its connection with the growth of firms' leverage and their persistent drive to obtain capital more cheaply and in larger quantities than the traditional banking system permitted.[19] Empirical studies have indicated that the acquisition of foreign subsidiaries tends to result in an increase in the amount of leverage taken on by multinational corporations.[20]

That point brings us to look at capital markets, and how the forces of innovation and deregulation in postwar years provided the essential fuel for the corporation to evolve into the multinational, expanding, leveraged arbitrageur of resources, labor, capital, and consumer markets that defines its success today.

Financial Innovation: The "Brave New World" of Euromarkets, Tax Havens, and Financial Derivatives

Technological innovation has dramatically changed the way firms develop, produce, and deliver most goods and services in the economy over any time period one would care to examine. In a similar vein, entrepreneurs in the financial industry—driven by the prospect of increased profits—have continually experimented with and sought out new financial structures that reallocate risk or amplify returns. These institutions have developed new financial products to satisfy demand for growth just as older, established types of transactions were reaching unprofitable commoditization or saturation in the marketplace. With each new generation of financial products, the complexity of the financial system grew and attempts to regulate these instruments were fought back in order to preserve profits above all. Three of the most prominent examples of financial innovations that came with negative side effects are the evolution of offshore money markets, tax havens, and financial derivatives. All three are interrelated and each has played an enabling role for today's cost-externalizing corporation.

Eurodollar Markets

The first of these financial innovations was the birth and growth of the offshore money markets, also referred to as Eurocurrency or Eurodollar markets. Eurocurrency markets were initially developed by British banks in the late 1950s to avoid central bank restrictions on the use of the pound sterling for external loans by conducting transactions in US dollars.[21] Under these arrangements, banks could offer higher interest rates to attract deposits and make loans denominated in dollars. During the 1960s several factors contributed to growth in the Eurodollar markets, including significant demand for offshore dollars by Russia, credit restrictions and capital controls attempted in the United States and other financial centers, and differential regulation between offshore and onshore banking operations. Of these three drivers, the latter—differential regulation—has been the continuing force behind the growth in Eurodollar markets, as banks used the vehicle to engage in regulatory arbitrage, taking advantage of increasingly interlinked financial centers across the world to exploit favorable credit spreads. The Eurocurrency deposit market went from virtually nonexistent in 1960 to over $4.5 trillion on a gross basis ($2.2 trillion on a net basis) as of March 1988, with a compound annual growth rate of roughly 20 percent; those amounts compare with a U.S. money stock (M2) of $2.9 trillion in March 1988.[22]

National authorities initially attempted to regulate this market but eventually gave in, and instead structured accommodating rules in order to court this mobile bank capital. With Eurocurrency unbound by much regulation, financial institutions were free to use these funds to experiment with the creation of new products and trading schemes not tied to domestic financial measures and regulations. Eventually, this market's evolution contributed to the dissolution of the Bretton Woods fixed-exchange-rate system, and it has increasingly become a source of short-term bank liquidity, contributing to the development of floating-rate instruments (including those linked to the London InterBank Offered Rate, or LIBOR). Special-purpose vehicles were created to warehouse many of these transactions hidden from the prying eyes of regulators and other interested stakeholders. More innovation ensued, as floating-rate instruments gave rise to the world's first interest-rate swap, between IBM and the World Bank in 1981, setting the stage for a swap market that would reach a total notional value of $866 billion in 1987 and then grow to $250 trillion by mid-2006, representing a turnover roughly five times the GDP of the world.[23] Other forms of derivative contracts sprouted throughout the financial system, with instruments like the Three-month Eurodollar Future of the Chicago Mercantile Exchange (CME) becoming the bellwether exchange-traded contract, further linking Eurocurrency and derivatives markets.

Tax Havens

The second of the innovations, tax havens, gained prominence as a natural extension of the same activities and incentives that gave rise to the Euro-currency markets: regulatory arbitrage, this time not relating so much to banking regulation as to tax regimes. Tax avoidance is a practice as old as taxation itself, and the idea behind tax havens—of governments establishing low hurdles to incorporation and low taxes in order to attract foreign capital—though not all that new in the 1960s and 1970s, did reemerge with newfound vigor. The history of tax havens appears to be one of evolutionary financial innovation across geographies, as model after model of tax favor was tried and subsequently "improved upon" elsewhere. Easy incorporation regimes in New Jersey and Delaware in the 1880s were precursors to more-modern tax havens.[24] Then, in the early twentieth century, British courts legitimized the concept of "virtual" residencies, allowing corporations with few physical operations to incorporate in Britain without having to pay taxes.[25] Further innovations followed in the late 1920s, as the Swiss strengthened their banking secrecy and protection laws, and Luxembourg developed income-tax-exempt holding companies. The next wave of tax-haven innovation arrived with the birth of the Eurocurrency market, which resulted in an accumulation of enough critical mass of mobile capital to set off tax-regime competition paralleling the race to the bottom in banking standards. Tax havens spread within Europe and out to dozens of states in the Caribbean and Asia as well. Using reported data from the Bank for International Settlements, the IMF calculated that cross-border assets in overseas financial centers (tax havens) totaled $4.6 trillion at June 1999, or about 50 percent of total cross-border assets, and this didn't include nonreported information.[26]

Financial innovation thus resulted in the spread of preferential tax regimes meant to court corporations whose only demonstrated interest is to maximize profits by avoiding their fair share of taxes (even as they exploit workers and deplete nations' natural capital). In some cases, these tax havens have been used to launder money obtained from illegal activities like drug trafficking. Recognizing the dangers of allowing such rampant abuse of tax arbitrage, the Organization for Economic Cooperation and Development (OECD), in parallel with other international governance institutions, studied the problem and in 2000 issued a report

titled "Towards Global Cooperation: Progress in Identifying and Eliminating Harmful Tax Practices."[27] In it, the OECD tried to infuse stopgaps
on tax-haven member countries by recommending that economic sanctions be used as a deterrent. But because concrete sanction designs were
never released by OECD, and because the imposition of such sanctions
would likely have run afoul of the WTO, the OECD's efforts never gained
traction. Importantly, though, the OECD explicitly recognized the power
of corporate interests as, throughout its push to limit the detrimental
impact of tax havens in the developed world, it effectively excluded corporate interests from its internal decision making.[28]

Financial Derivatives

The third of the significant financial innovations of interest to us is the
financial derivative, a type of financial instrument which can be used by
institutions at once for hedging, investing, and speculating. Derivatives are
securities whose price or cash flows are dependent on or derived from one
or more underlying assets or indices. Thus, the derivative's value is determined from fluctuations in the specified "underlying," as it is often called,
which can include stocks, bonds, commodities, currencies, interest rates,
market indices, or even the weather. Most notably, derivative instruments
are often characterized by little or no initial net investment in the transaction, which enables contracting parties to essentially make highly levered
bets such that gains or losses can be many times the value of the initial
cash exchange (infinitely so, if it involved no initial investment at all).[29]

Derivative instruments did not come into being recently. In fact, one
can trace early uses of derivatives to the seventeenth century, when commodity futures markets emerged for rice in Japan and for tulip bulbs in
the Netherlands during the tulip mania of the 1630s. Futures for many
other commodities sprouted throughout the eighteenth and nineteenth
centuries, although the *financial* species of derivatives (that is, those not
based on physical goods) had their genesis when the Chicago Mercantile Exchange allowed trading in currency futures. The ensuing wave
of financial innovation produced offspring instruments such as interest-
rate futures, Treasury Bill futures, swaps of assorted types, options on
almost any instrument, "swaptions" (options on swaps), and eventually
the now well-known credit default swap (CDS), a prominent feature of
the 2008 financial crisis. In parallel to the traded-derivatives exchanges,

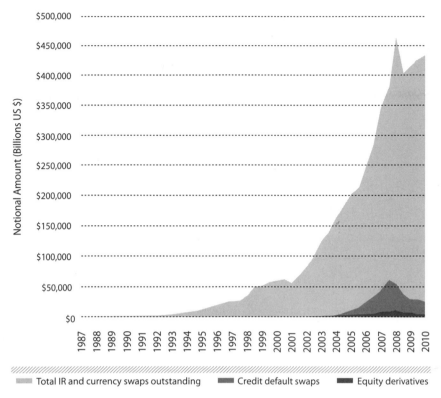

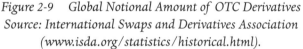

Total IR and currency swaps outstanding   Credit default swaps   Equity derivatives

Figure 2-9   *Global Notional Amount of OTC Derivatives*
Source: International Swaps and Derivatives Association
(www.isda.org/statistics/historical.html).

over-the-counter (OTC) derivative transactions grew, wherein institutions contracted with each other for tailored transactions. Figure 2.9 highlights the explosive growth in OTC derivatives.

Regulators struggled to keep pace with these financial innovations, and they were often successfully fended off by other institutions or persuaded that intervention was unnecessary. Often, fragmented regulatory structures left gaps which financial innovators could exploit. The US Commodity Future Trading Commission (CFTC), created in 1974 to regulate derivatives transactions affecting commodities, issued its famous CFTC swaps exemption in 1992, confirming the legality of OTC swaps in the United States—that is, not treating them as illegal bets—and declaring them outside its regulatory control. Other regulators in Europe and the United States also refused to impose regulations on assorted types of derivatives transactions, believing the markets to be best equipped to manage their risks. In 1998, Brooksley Born, chair of the CFTC, issued a proposal to regulate derivative instruments, citing their inherent dangers, but she was stopped in her tracks by Deputy Secretary of the US Treasury Larry Summers, Federal Reserve chair Allan Greenspan, and SEC chair Arthur Levitt, all of whom issued a joint statement that same year condemning derivatives regulation. Derivatives remained a largely unconstrained market.

The 1990s saw a large number of spectacular losses, corporate collapses, and bankruptcies closely related to derivatives. Metalgesellschaft AG, a large and respectable German corporation, lost between $1.3 billion and $2.1 billion in 1993 from trading in oil futures.[30] Barings PLC, Britain's oldest investment bank, collapsed in 1995 due to uncontrolled Nikkei options-derivatives trades gone awry. Long-Term Capital Management (LTCM), was driven to near insolvency and eventual buyout by $4.6 billion in losses in 1998, some of which were from trading emerging-markets currency and interest-rate derivatives.[31] Bankers Trust, a Wall Street giant, saw its share value drop from $120.63 to $49.19 between July 14 and October 7, 1998, due to rumors of losses (it did end up losing $488 million in the quarter).[32] CSFB's losses in Russia alone were estimated at over $1 billion in the wake of LTCM's collapse.[33] Scarcely five years after this avalanche of misfortunes from LTCM's collapse and the Asian debt crises, Credit Default Swaps (through a series of operations and control lapses) caused mayhem for many hedge funds and their bank counterparts in the mid-2000s. They were also instrumental in the near failure of insurance giant AIG in the 2008 financial crisis—AIG survived solely as a result of a $182-billion bailout from the US federal government, earning AIG the title of the first "too big to fail" insurance company. Corporations' exploitation of financial derivatives to magnify their returns shows, time and again, how financial innovation can be used to circumvent risk-management safety measures and can lead to excessive leveraging and its expected consequences.

Outcomes of the "Great Alignment"

The advent of deregulation and technological innovation—both logistical and financial—greatly increased the ability of firms to achieve relative autonomy and, in the process, to assert control over their value chain as a whole without having to resort to formal integration (also known as "action at a distance"). Firms found themselves dissolving old hierarchical forms and engaging in business-process innovation in earnest—as a business priority, and not as a luxury for managers with time on their hands. Global businesses grew to make their money through arbitrage between prices at the point of production and prices at the point of consumption. For arbitrage to be possible, and for its exploitation to create business advantage, the flow between these two places has to be impeded—by government regulation and borders, by coordination and communication problems, by transportation costs, and so forth. The strategy of the multinational corporation became to arbitrage this "space of flows."[34] Cheaply transportable goods could be sourced from accessible lowest-wage areas; heavier goods would come from points geographically closer to market. Capital, of course, flows more easily than either goods or labor, and a combination of deregulation and financial innovation made this even easier.

Today, in lieu of moving cash to counter unfavorable shifts in exchange rates (the original meaning and context of "arbitrage"), entire supply chains can be reconfigured to move production itself to other regions of the world. Firms look to balance variables such as labor, inventory costs, transportation, quality, concentrations of valuable knowledge, and proximity to customers. Firms in different business sectors have very different "winning combinations" of these diverse factors. It should be noted that relocation is constrained by the capabilities of the workforce—design, R&D, and marketing have still largely remained in traditional havens, while manufacturing has relocated. More recently, however, firms have been offshoring business-process divisions. Financial services in general and investment banking in particular have demonstrated the profitability of this trend, but it remains to be seen how sustainable it is. Rising costs and declining skills availability in major offshoring destinations such as India may change the picture. The key point to note is that the increasing modularity of design and production—and the increasing globalization of markets, production, ownership, and products—creates an ever-evolving field. The constant, however, has been the delivery mechanism, and that is today's dominant multinational corporate model, or what in this book is referred to as "Corporation 1920."

It all appears to be a globally winning proposition! Reduced trade frictions and transaction costs fed by innovation and deregulation reduce logistics costs, lower product prices, and increase demand for goods and services produced by increasingly complex but increasingly efficient global supply chains. Unfettered access to global capital provides leverage at the best available prices to the corporation willing to invest in its own future success. Increasing consolidation and FDI can free capacity in-country and can add to more competitive sectors within, and the resulting outsourced production will increase growth of both wages and demand in destination countries. More-buoyant economies will arise on either side, both sides nourishing the ever-expanding, evermore international, increasingly efficient engine that enabled it all: Corporation 1920.

But is it really all that simple? First, as we've seen, these factors were enabled by a remarkable congruence, a "Great Alignment" of exogenous forces in the postwar years, 1945–2000. This consisted of an entire suite of epoch-marking trade and capital-market deregulations, innovations in trade facilitation and supply-chain management, and innovations in capital-market disintermediation. How much of this Great Alignment was inevitable or natural, and how much was attributable to political choices and private-sector lobbying, due to corporations and banks seeking self-interest through unfettered growth? How much of this growth and success is repeatable, and for how long? Was the desire for this growth not also the genesis of increasing leverage, which sowed the seeds of our largest crises and recessions since the 1980s?

And what were the main outcomes of this Great Alignment, and of the new model of business success that it created, the large multinational Corporation 1920?

To what extent was this model of corporate success also a model of resource preemption that institutionalized corruption in developing countries, of labor arbitrage that carried deep social costs, of FDI investment subsidies that cost taxpayers in both source and destination countries, and of an ever-spreading global epidemic of consumerism that converted wants into needs with no thought of resource limits and no heed of environmental consequences? Did the growth in size of this twentieth-century baby, like the fattened cuckoo in a warbler's nest, happen at the cost of fledglings that were unceremoniously bumped out of their home markets, never again to be seen? What losses in market access, economic diversity, financial inclusion, alternative products, and economic stability does the success story of this cuckoo chick hide in its billowing wake?

The answer to those questions is the story of Corporation 1920—the subject of the next chapter.

CHAPTER THREE

Corporation 1920

*For years I thought what was good for the country was good
for General Motors and vice versa.*
— *Charles Erwin Wilson, former US Secretary
of Defense and former CEO of GM*

"Who is in charge of *bread* in London?" asked an impressed but puzzled Soviet bureaucrat visiting London in the late 1960s.[1] He saw that supermarkets and even small shops had shelves full of bread and that there were hardly any queues: quite unlike the situation back home in Moscow. Who managed this? How astonishing that his English friend's answer was "nobody"! Of course, that was not strictly correct. Several corporations invisible to the consumer managed this—*they* were in charge of production and distribution, working collaboratively in a sophisticated supply chain from farm to mill to bakery to transporter to supermarket.

Almost everything you use or consume, including this book, has such a supply chain built behind it, and every aspect of production and distribution along this supply chain is most probably managed by a corporation and transacted at market-determined prices at every point along the way. So much that is taken for granted is the result of the success of a market system that produces and delivers our needs through the work of today's corporations—especially large multinational corporations.

The fact that multinational corporations today deliver a vast array of products and services along complex global supply chains, across countries and continents, to societies at various stages of development is proof

enough of their success in making these goods available at affordable prices. The fact that names such as Unilever, Ikea, Sony, IBM, and Nokia are
household names throughout the world demonstrates the power, reach,
and value of such organizations.

As we have already seen, Corporation 1920 is typified by its ability
and success at employing large-scale "price arbitrage" in every aspect of
its operations. All this is not without costs, however. A paper by Kelly
and White, cofounders of the Corporation 20/20 Initiative, describes four
major problems with today's corporations:[2]

- *Short-termism*, reflected in an "endless quest for short-term earnings, heedless of long-term social costs" . . . which is "virtually
  on autopilot." The constant scrutiny of stock analysts, employee stock options, and speculative interest from hedge funds all
  result in enormous pressures on executives to produce and profit quickly
- *Company transience*, manifested in the search for the cheapest
  locations for production and the rapid pace of mergers and acquisitions, has led to the corporation being detached from local
  communities and lacking in loyalty to any nation.
- *Wealth disparities*, exemplified by the enormous gap between
  CEO packages and the lowest-paid employee, by multiples as
  high as 500 or 1,000
- *Lack of accountability*, due to diversified ownership and the ubiquitous "business judgment rule" (established since the late nineteenth century, which grants decision-making power on corporate policy to corporate boards and management, not to shareholders), as a result of which, shareholders have little power to
  influence company decisions

Three of these four problems are part the very nature of Corporation 1920 and the free-market-capitalist, "brown economy" model that it
needs and feeds. Short-termism, company transience, and compensation
disparities are each the result of the free-market, profit-seeking model
of the modern corporation, and are in that sense integral to the legal
history of the corporation, which has established its purpose as being
self-interest. The fourth problem is a problem of agency, of true owners

being distanced from what they own. This too is bound up in the corporation's legal history and the introduction of limited liability, as it encouraged widely-held corporations with small, working-class shareholders (the term "ha'penny stocks" derives from an apocryphal coal miner's investment of just half a penny in industrializing England). All of these problems reflect the fact that as an outcome of its legal history and the ascendancy of free-market capitalism, today's corporation has consciously and legally ceased to have either a de facto or de jure "social purpose," replacing it with a narrower focus on optimizing shareholder value.

If the main problems inherent in today's corporate model have their genesis in its legal history, what makes these historically rooted design flaws deliver such massive social costs today? What are the defining characteristics of the successful Corporation 1920 that contribute most to converting legal design into social costs? The answer would be *size, leverage, advertising,* and *lobbying.* These four create a powerful toolkit for what has been aptly described as "a relentless pursuit of profit" by constructing or influencing demand, increasing product distribution, reducing product costs, creating product opportunity and competitive advantage, financing business growth and creating positive feedback loops among all these drivers of traditional corporate performance.[3]

Big Is Beautiful

Traditionally, the drift toward greater size has been justified to reap economies of scale in production, but there are other drivers. Size is both an aspiration and a measure of success for the multinational corporation.

Size and success are not always positively correlated; indeed, the economist Ronald Coase presents a nuanced view of size as a form of market failure. His argument, in simple terms, is that production is possible without any organizing institution, so in theory, if markets are efficient (a big if), those best at providing a good or service most cheaply are already doing so and it should always be cheaper to contract out than to hire.[4] Corporations (or "firms," in his landmark paper "Nature of the Firm") only emerge when an entrepreneur begins to hire a large number of people, leading Coase to ask why and under what conditions we should expect firms to emerge. Coase explains that there are transaction costs to using the "efficient" market (i.e., the cost of obtaining a good or service via the market is actually more than just the price of the good). Other costs include search and information costs, bargaining costs, the costs of keeping trade secrets, and policing and enforcement costs, all of which add to the cost of procuring something from the market. These costs suggest that large firms will arise when they can arrange to produce what they need internally and find commercial advantage in avoiding these transaction costs.[5]

In essence, Coase saw the corporation as a way to circumvent market inefficiencies and transaction costs, arguing that very large corporations are the result of market failure rather than market success.[6] Two interesting implications for the potential size of both Corporation 1920 and Corporation 2020 follow. First, an improved legal system and the ability to enforce contracts lead to a large number of smaller companies that contract with each other rather than do things themselves. Second, improved communications can allow large organizations to extend management over huge geographies even while they can encourage outsourcing. Apple Inc. is a prime example where a design and brand specialist has become a global giant without owning the heavy infrastructure of a global giant. However, the more common model of the pursuit of size is perhaps best illustrated with an example from almost a century ago, the Ford Motor Company.

Ford's "1920" Footprint

Although the Ford Motor Company in its early days was far ahead of its time in many aspects, its early history was a very much a pursuit of size and scale, a characteristic of Corporation 1920. It also demonstrates the monstrous appetite for raw materials of large corporations even a century ago. A close look at one resource—wood—helps to tell this story.[7] The original Model T used a surprising amount of wood (mostly maple, elm, and ash) in its construction: about 250 board feet, or a whole tree, for each car. This added up to a need for 25,000 acres of forest per year. Ford was conscious of both the cost savings and the brand image it could reap by minimizing its impacts on these forest resources. The company used innovative and frugal techniques for minimizing waste of wood in order "to use every part of the tree except the shade." Ford also bragged about its selective harvesting techniques, in which it did not cut down any trees smaller than ten inches in diameter; however, the true extent to which it used this practice seems to be limited. Thus, we see that, like most corporations today, Ford in the early 1900s addressed the social impacts of its operations on the environment in part through true process changes and in part merely through public relations campaigns.[8]

This gigantic footprint was inevitable because of Ford's large-scale production model, driving economies of scale through mass production, which defrayed the fixed costs of factories and machinery, and broke down the production process into its smallest tasks so that labor inputs were simple and replaceable. Ford mechanized car making as far as possible to reduce labor inputs. At the same time, Ford led the market in high factory wages, encouraging employees to buy the Model T. This system of both mass production and mass consumption came to be known as "Fordism," and was best exemplified in the period of the 1940s through the 1960s, during which many in the United States benefited from sustained economic growth.[9]

The Unlimited Liabilities of the Limited Liability Corporation

Leverage is essential for corporations that need to finance their growth and supplement shareholder capital with credit, in order to ensure that the availability of shareholder capital not become a limitation on growth. Limited liability alone may not have sufficed to power the last century and a half of economic progress, were it not for the power of leverage, which was provided competitively to corporations by a financial sector of increasing depth and sophistication.

On the other hand, financial leverage also fueled all of the last four major economic crises in the world, including the Latin American debt crisis, the savings and loan crisis in the United States, the Asian debt crisis, and the recent housing-sector-led global financial crisis. It has also served to force-multiply the "brown economy" and increase the vulnerability of economies to asset bubbles.[10] Used appropriately, leverage can balance financing risks and support the steady growth of enterprises and economies. Used in ill-advised ways, a central feature of the near–global financial meltdown of 2008–9, leverage overexposes organizations to downside risks and creates or magnifies negative returns for corporate stakeholders and society at large.

One question that holds the key to the way forward is this: Should freedom from limits on leverage (a global norm for the private sector) also apply to the public sector and to nonfinancial companies considered "too big to fail" (TBTF), despite the systemic risk they represent to the larger economy and their de-facto recourse to the public purse?

High leverage enables institutions to grow to a size that can be considered "too big to fail." A TBTF institution *usually* refers to a bank or other financial institution that federal regulators determine is too important to be allowed to fail in a disorderly manner without protecting at least some creditors. Some of the factors that contribute to TBTF status include size, interconnectedness, and the degree of public visibility.[11] In practice, however, institutions from any industry can grow to become TBTF: mortgage originators (e.g., Fannie Mae), insurance companies (e.g., AIG), car companies (e.g., General Motors), banks (e.g., Citigroup), investment banks (e.g., Goldman Sachs), airlines (e.g., the airline industry in 2001), and even hedge funds (e.g., Long-Term Capital Management in 1998). Beyond presenting an increase in systemic risk for the economy, the implicit TBTF status of very large institutions also creates a problem of moral hazard. The managers of those institutions have increased incentives to take on leverage-related risk when they know their worst-case-scenario losses will be socialized.

In addition, the expectation of government bailouts can effectively lower the firm's cost of borrowing, further encouraging risk-taking behavior. Leverage by banks is part and parcel of their business—they exist to create credit, after all—and it is by and large well controlled by bank regulators. However, there is an untenable assumption behind society's current model of leverage that controlling this "source" of leverage creation is sufficient to control the misuse of leverage down the chain—by corporations and by consumers. Recession after recession has proved that assumption false. And the extent to which uncontrolled leverage can feed corporate misbehavior is best illustrated with the iconic example of Enron, an energy company.

Enron's Abuse of Leverage

Enron pursued risky investments under highly leveraged structures, seeking short-term profits without regard to the long-term viability of these deals. Enron's executives booked many such deals into special-purpose vehicles whose accounts were not disclosed, in order to avoid the glare of public scrutiny.[12] As the company levered up it grew to be the seventh largest company in the Fortune 500,[13] and its total revenues jumped from $31 billion in 1998 to $101 billion in 2000.[14]

During 2001 Enron's leveraged con game unraveled spectacularly. Beginning in the spring of that year, analysts became increasingly skeptical of the company's lack of transparency. Enron's CEO resigned abruptly in August 2001, the company announced a significant quarterly loss soon after, an SEC investigation was launched, and by the end of the year Enron filed for bankruptcy[15]

Turning Wants into Needs

A third defining characteristic of Corporation 1920 is advertising—which as an industry is a very small global business, although it commands an inordinate share of the world's attention. For 2012, global advertising turnover is estimated at about US$500 billion, smaller than the combined turnover of just two retail giants, Walmart and Carrefour![16] The United States (which accounts for 25 percent of global consumption) contributes a significant chunk of $180 billion to global advertising turnover—37 percent of the global total. Hence much of the following discussion of advertising is about American advertising.

The power of market research and advertising as a growth driver for business is second to none. It converts wants into needs, sometimes creating new needs that are nothing more than brand desires, with no functionality.[17] The essentials that you actually do *need* may include a handbag, and you may *want* a branded bag, but marketing and advertising will convince you that what you *need* is a Prada bag. What you *need* is just daily transportation to the office, but clever marketing convinces you that what you really need is a Toyota Lexus, because such a car tells your colleagues something positive about you. Thus advertising has created a need for Prada bags and Lexus cars, a market demand for branded goods.

An advertisement's legal form is not an offer, but an "invitation to treat"—a subtle, even quaint, but descriptive phrase. Someone acting on an advertisement is not accepting an offer, and is therefore legally not concluding a contract. Without contractual liability, the advertiser can be right or wrong, misleading or informative, but it is generally not liable for what is in effect just an opinion. Unless there is a regulation or law against misleading advertising, an advertisement can say practically anything and still not be actionable by a misled or an aggrieved party. For example, carbonated drinks are habitually advertised as "thirst-quenching," though this is not an objective claim. It is interesting, if academic, to ponder how Coke or Pepsi might respond to a proposed regulation to expunge the concept of "thirst-quenching" from their advertisements. At the time of writing, the EU Commission was in the process of introducing "claims regulation" for advertising such that food companies can only make advertising claims supported by science. The impacts of such regulation could be far-reaching.

Corporations lobby extensively to avoid regulations or constraints on advertising, and the emergence of a few forceful regulators in developed economies (in particular, from the US Federal Trade Commission [FTC]) is in part a reaction to that trend. The FTC has had a mixed record in attempting to regulate advertising, but let us begin by looking at one of their successes.

In 2003, the FTC established a National "Do Not Call" Registry to constrain unwelcome telemarketing calls, which numbered more than 16 billion such calls a year and had clearly become a too-frequent annoyance and disturbance to daily life.[18] The National "Do Not Call" (DNC) Registry gave US consumers a simple means to significantly reduce the number of such calls. By doing so it *shifted power from companies to consumers*, with immediate and profound impact.[19] Within three days of the DNC Registry's launch, over 10 million numbers were registered, and within a year, DNC registrations had grown to 62 million.[20]

Corporate lobbying contributed to some of the FTC's starker failures. In 1978, the FTC proposed a ban on TV advertising of highly sugared food (which exposes children to serious risk of tooth decay) at times when the TV audience is mostly "older" children (defined as between ages eight and twelve).[21] They also proposed a ban on all television advertising when the audience was mostly children "too young to understand the selling purpose of advertising" (i.e., children under eight). The failure to internalize the potential health damage from sugared food was in fact a classical example of "market failure"; however, corporations lobbied against these FTC proposals on grounds that they were "anti-market," and this utterly illogical point was amplified by media detractors.

Corporate lobbyists nevertheless succeeded in preventing such legislation on various grounds: that it prevented free access to information to adults as well, that identifying time slots was impracticable, that viewership is mixed at any time, that parental guidance must be respected, etc. While voluntary standards were attempted, they did not succeed, and so the FTC gave up on this battle.[22] However, a much longer and more serious war had recently been won: the ban on cigarette advertising on television and radio.

Or had it?

Tobacco's Misuse of Advertising

The liberating social climate of the 1920s and '30s gave tobacco companies an opportunity to exploit the ideas of emancipation and power in order to recruit an untapped female market. Earlier considered a social liability, cigarettes were turned into a desirable product for women to openly indulge in as an expression of freedom and gender equality. The American Tobacco Company in the1920s saw the additional potential in selling cigarettes as an appetite suppressant, since slimness was part of the allure of the emerging model of the modern woman. Their brand Lucky Strike's campaign—"Reach for a Lucky Instead of a Sweet"—was successful in getting women to see smoking as a means of weight control, a positioning that led to a tripling of sales for this brand in the first year of this advertising campaign. A "want" had been turned into a "need" by playing on a fundamental human insecurity, and advertising had successfully influenced the minds of a vast new consumer segment: women.

Cigarette advertising had in fact been on the radar of the FTC since the 1930s, when it tried to prevent companies from making health claims about smoking, but constraining legislation would not come for another 40 years. In 1964 the FTC announced that any cigarette advertisements that did not disclose health risks are "unfair and deceptive." This landmark conclusion eventually led to the ban on cigarette advertising on TV and radio in 1971. And while this societal reaction was in motion, in 1968 the Philip Morris Company took the women's market segment to new heights with the help of Leo Burnett, a Chicago ad agency. They launched Virginia Slims, the first cigarette designed specifically for women. The company had spent nearly a year, and millions of dollars, to develop the new brand "for the independent woman of today." The company further exploited women's desire for independence with the tag line "You've come a long way, baby."

Smoking-related cancer, its tragedy and its public health costs, now occupies the public mind, but the health risks of smoking were known even in those early days. Were Philip Morris and their agency, Leo Burnett, *ethical* in launching Virginia Slims? What kind of cigarette advertising, launched in the midst of a national move to legislate against cigarette advertising, would have constituted accountable advertising?

Tilting the Field

The fourth key characteristic of Corporation 1920 associated with its social costs is the nature and use of corporate lobbying. The word "lobbying" needs definition in the context of this book. Here it refers to the use of persuasion with government or industry regulators or lawmakers to create advantage through laws, regulations, taxes, and public investment, in order to promote private profit. The fact that lobbying is meant to create private advantage implies that it is by nature inequitable. The challenge for regulators is to create checks and balances on it.

Lobbying is as ubiquitous in business as the pursuit of profit itself. It presents an outstanding return on the investment of senior executive time. Managing the regulatory landscape is among the most cost-efficient ways by which a corporation can seek preferential treatment, or maintain exclusions that stymie competition and thus sustain its dominance. Corporate lobbying is a pervasive and potent tool for interacting with the regulatory process in a way that tilts the field further in their favor, or alternatively, prevents any change in the status quo. Often, a proposed change might have helped foster a healthier balance between private risks, private gains, public risks, and public interests.

Although lobbying is part of the operational tool kit for almost all large companies, it is of particular importance for those operating in realms of public trust, including the oil, gas, coal, and other extractive industries. These corporations are also among the global behemoths: of the world's ten most profitable companies, four sell energy products and three base global operations in the United States.[23] US electric utilities, for example, hold over $600 billion in assets and generate annual sales of around $260–300 billion.[24]

Clean Coal's Unclean Lobbying

It should come as no surprise that this economic power translates into influence. Legislative processes for the Waxman-Markey Bill featured 770 business groups lobbying Capitol Hill.[25] While the United States debated this bill in 2008, energy-intensive industries spent over $100 million on public relations and hired 2,340 registered lobbyists to shield their interests against climate legislation in the US.[26] Moreover, the American Coalition for Clean Coal Electricity (ACCCE) spent $38 million on public advertising to convince the US public that coal was a reliable, safe energy source too important to let climate legislation impact the industry.[27] The ACCCE also hired a small public relations firm which forged letters from community organizations to members of the US Congress who represented key votes on the Waxman-Markey Bill. Despite being made aware of the deception well before the vote, neither the ACCCE nor the management of the errant firm called the members of Congress to whom these forged letters were sent until after the vote.[28] As it happens, this particular scandal was investigated by NGOs and exposed by the popular media, but similar tactics are common around the world. Not every nation has civil society organizations energetic enough or a press that is fearless enough to research or report these stories. However, in the aftermath of the 2010 Supreme Court case *Citizens United v. Federal Election Commission*, efforts to limit political influence in the United States will be significantly more difficult in the years to come. The Court ruled in this case that the First Amendment to the Constitution allows corporations and unions to raise unlimited funds for political campaigns, as long as they maintain their "independence" by not *directly* contributing to candidates.

Australia's Super Profits

By its very nature, lobbying raises questions of ethics. The ethics are particularly poignant when lobbying on behalf of extractive industries, because they are in business to mine resources that were "public wealth" before they were leased or licensed or encumbered by governments in favor of these lobbying corporations. So what is a "fair price" for such an encumbrance? Should the public risks and costs typical of mining industries be ignored when setting these prices? And should the price be a fixed, long-term royalty oblivious of the paths of inflation, supply scarcities, and market prices, or should it be a variable royalty based on these drivers of mining profitability? Can "free markets" really determine "fair prices" that satisfy the principles of ethics and public equity? Finally, does aggressive corporate lobbying by extractive industries increase or decrease the chances of ethics and equity being applied in such executive decisions?

Any influence that distorts price in favor of private interests at the cost of public interest deserves to be a focus of *more* rather than less public scrutiny and regulatory control, and yet rarely is this the case. When a government actually tries to reverse a historic inequity, observe the corporate calisthenics!

In mid-2010, Kevin Rudd's new Australian Labor Party government proposed an additional tax on mining profits, in the face of a sharp escalation in commodity prices, especially coal. Their rationale was straightforward and very clearly stated: to return super-normal profits on extracting the public wealth of Australia to the people of Australia, and to do so by taxing these extractive industries' windfall profits and lowering the corporate tax rate generally by a few percentage points.[29] Wasn't this perfectly reasonable?

Not so, said the mining companies. They launched a lobbying and advertising blitz, appealing to public sentiment. They said Rudd's government was "killing the goose that laid Australia's golden egg!"[30] (Did Australia's coal and gold companies actually *lay down* the subsoil assets of Australia, or did they just get licensed to *exploit* them?) They claimed the government was destroying jobs (even though employment in mining was drawing Australia's labor force away from acquiring higher skills—a drag on growth according to Australia's Department of the Treasury). They argued that "Australia's exports would be decimated!" (Should Australia *not* aspire to export anything *except minerals*, a fate which even the most resource-cursed, least-developed nations would consider beneath their dignity and destiny?)

The most remarkable thing about such blatantly false rhetoric was that most Australians actually believed it. Kevin Rudd became politically vulnerable and paid the price. He had to resign and his deputy took over his party and his premiership. Perhaps this happened because Australians had inherited a belief in the principle of "finders keepers," a legacy of the days of their gold riots in the nineteenth century when gold miners refused to pay tax on profits because they saw the gold they mined as "theirs." Or perhaps it had to do with the clever messaging through some very effective advertisements by the mining companies. Or perhaps it was a combination of these factors. The fact remains that an appropriate tax reform was stymied by a combination of lobbying and advertising by vested interests, especially Australia's coal mining giants.

One can see why lobbying would be such an attractive proposition for corporations seeking dominance and profits. But why has lobbying been able to rise to such heights in the political world? Political-party fund-raising surely has a significant role, and in some countries corruption magnifies lobbyists' success. But checks and balances are quite strong in most democracies, and the risks of exposure are certainly politically costly—and yet corporate lobbying and influence likely exist in every capital city around the world. Why is this so?

Put simply, the main reason that corporate lobbying has such clout in political decision making is that the corporation is *the* most important institution in political economy. The private sector delivers nearly 60 percent of GDP worldwide[31] and employs 70 percent of workers;[32] further, corporate taxes provide a significant share of government revenue.[33] There should be little wonder that they have such power over the politicians and bureaucrats whose decisions impact their behavior and performance.

The Consequences of Corporation 1920

This chapter identifies and outlines the four defining characteristics of the successful Corporation 1920 (*size, leverage, advertising,* and *lobbying*), which contribute most to converting its legal history and design into social costs. The examples given above show that these social costs are of various kinds: environmental damage (e.g., Ford's forest footprint in the 1920s, ACCCE promoting fossil fuels in the 2000s), health damage (e.g., cigarette advertising, sugared foods advertising to children), and private profits at the expense of public losses (exceptional profits of Australian mining companies vs. suboptimal royalties for Australia's public funding.)

In addition to such forms of social costs, note these additional four general types of "exclusions" that result from the characteristics of size, leverage, advertising, and lobbying:

1. The exclusion of poor consumers from "natural public-good" alternatives to marketed products
2. The exclusion of small and medium enterprises (SMEs) through lack of access to leverage
3. The exclusion of competing products by a stranglehold on marketing and distribution networks as well as public infrastructure
4. The exclusion of competing products by vested-interest lobbying

An example of the first kind, the exclusion of those who do not have the wealth to buy market goods and services from their access to natural public goods alternatives is an effect seen most painfully in small-scale farming. Subsistence farming, in traditional contexts, benefits from the nutrient and freshwater flows from natural areas such as forests and wetlands. Furthermore, it has been shown by a research study of 286 ecologically-friendly farming projects covering several million farms in over 50 developing countries that yields in these farms increased 79 percent as a result of using simple ecologically-friendly farming techniques.[34] Most such farming, however, is under the threat of conversion to a conventional model of heavy use of fertilizers and pesticides, which is often government-subsidized. Corporations in the businesses of selling seeds, fertilizers, and pesticides benefit from the sale of their products to poor and subsistence farmers, but the jury is out as to whether the farmers themselves benefit. Indeed, they may well improve their traditional farming models even more simply with the help of better information and training and relying on what comes free from nature: freshwater cycling, soil enhancement, pollination, pest control, and other "ecosystem services" of the ecosystems where they live and farm. Indeed, if ecologically friendly farming were rewarded or intensive farming penalized for respective economic gains and losses of valuable ecosystems caused by their farming models, then the invisible but compelling economics of small farming might be better appreciated.

The exclusion of small and medium enterprises (SMEs) from equitable access to financing has become a serious concern across the world. This occurs not just in developing countries, such as India, where development banks have divisions dedicated to promoting such financing and where *all* scheduled commercial banks are given mandatory portfolio targets for "Small Scale Industry" (SSI) lending. It also applies in the *developed* world; for example, the British government is considering a new state-owned bank specifically to finance SMEs, because they are habitually excluded from being given sufficient leverage by "mainstream" banks. Institutions such as the US Small Business Administration partially mitigate the bias of large financial institutions toward large companies, but in times of recession it is the small companies that suffer most dramatically from credit freezes and rising costs of capital, owing to their perceived higher risk.

The third exclusion—from media, distribution, and other infrastructures—has many examples. Incumbent products and technologies usually get priority—all the way from product placement on shelves in supermarkets to public infrastructure. In the case of organic foods, there has been a constant debate for years about whether these should be placed in a separate corner of a supermarket, specifically for consumers who are disparagingly referred to as "greenies," or placed together with comparable (but perhaps more cheaply priced) food alternatives. The sale of electric cars suffers everywhere from a lack of investment in infrastructure to charge or exchange their batteries on city routes, whereas at the same time, governments continue to invest billions in building roads and highways, which are in fact today's largest invisible subsidy for private fossil-fuelled transportation.

Perhaps the most powerful examples of exclusions relate to the fourth category, those caused by lobbying, and this is because *creating exclusions* is in essence the central goal of corporate lobbying.[35] The case of tetra-ethyl lead (TEL)—whose use in gasoline was discovered by General Motors (GM)—illustrates this vividly (exemplifying both exclusions 3 and 4 above). No matter how much one objects to GM's ethics, one has to admire the consummate deftness with which the company handled the TEL issue through its use of information, misinformation, and disinformation to ensure that the solution of engine "knock" was the one most profitable for its patent holder, GM, even though it was not the cheapest for human health (not by any stretch of the imagination), nor was it the cheapest or

the only technological solution available at the time. Corporation 1920
behavior was in fact already well established by the mid-1920s.

The Story of Leaded Gasoline: Fooling
All the People, All the Time[36]

The youth of today may not be aware that gasoline ever had lead in it,
because after 20 years of political struggle, the sale of leaded gasoline officially ended in the United States in 1995.[37] It seems obvious that removing the lead from gasoline was the smart choice, as lead can ravage the
nervous system (especially in young children), and as today's vehicles do
not need the octane boost that lead provided. But even those who well
remember the fight to remove lead from gasoline in the 1970s and 1980s
may not be aware that the political saga in fact began six decades prior.

In 1921, researchers at General Motors discovered that the chemical
known as "tetraethyl lead" (TEL) could be added to gasoline to increase
the octane rating, which would help to prevent engine "knocking"—the
result of gasoline burning wrong, through detonation rather than defla-
gration.[38] TEL was brought to market in 1923, but it wasn't widely known
that it was being added to gasoline until 1924, when a number of workers
at a Standard Oil refinery in New Jersey "went violently insane and then
died."[39]

In a move that will be all too familiar to those who concern themselves
with the modern version of the corporate denial of wrongdoing, both
GM and Standard Oil insisted that TEL was not dangerous to the public,
that the only risk was in handling the material in high concentrations.
And likewise, though the federal government was well aware of the issue,
they were unable or unwilling to do anything about it. As it happened, the
true damages of lead to human health were confirmed over time.

An interesting corollary to the TEL story is that in fact another "anti-
knock" additive has been around since before TEL was even invented.
Ethyl alcohol, or ethanol, is the same type of alcohol that is found in
beverages, and it can be produced from a variety of crops, including corn,
sugarcane, and potatoes—in fact, any sugar-bearing plant product that
ferments. When blended with gasoline, ethyl alcohol can be used as a
fuel for automobiles, and it has the beneficial effect of reducing engine
knocking. It is not widely known that Henry Ford's Model T vehicles

were originally produced to run on both gasoline and ethanol. Ford believed that not only would ethanol allow the majority of the US populace to fuel their own cars, but it would also solve the farm crisis of the 1920s by increasing demand for farm products.

Though there were certainly disadvantages to ethanol as well, it is clear that powerful corporations were the true reason that TEL stuck around for so long in our fuel, polluting the environment and damaging the health of generations of people around the world. Thus, the TEL story perfectly illustrates the ability of powerful corporations to exclude considerations of broader social welfare from their cost-benefit analyses. It should be evident that the defining characteristics of these powerful corporations were all too well defined even a century ago. Today's corporation is truly Corporation 1920.

CHAPTER FOUR

Through the Looking Glass
of Corporate Externalities

True Measures of the Corporation

"The time has come," the Walrus said,
"To talk of many things . . ."
— *From "The Walrus and the Carpenter," in*
Lewis Carroll's Through the Looking-Glass

The *Deepwater Horizon* oil spill in the Gulf of Mexico in 2010 damaged fisheries and tourism, destroyed miles of beaches, and hurt thousands of livelihoods. It is an example of the so-called negative externalities of corporations. *Externality* refers to the impact of a transaction or activity on any person or institution that did not explicitly agree to this transaction or activity. Such third-party impacts can be either benefits (*positive externalities*) or costs (*negative externalities*). While *externality* is a general term, and its agent can be a person, company, or government, in common use it usually refers to the impact of corporate activities.

The litmus test of whether such an impact is an externality or not is whether its perpetrator accounted for it when deciding to undertake that activity. If it did not, then the third-party impact of the activity is an externality. Thus, if the impact on marine biodiversity and ocean fisheries caused by a company releasing pollutants into the ocean did not figure in the benefit-cost calculations of that company, that impact is an externality. However, if law required a company to pay the full price of these damages, then those impacts would be accounted for in its benefit-cost calculations while considering the decision. In such case, the externality would have been "internalized" and would no longer be an externality.

The key point to note about corporate externalities is that, although they represent costs to society, they are difficult to control because they are not *illegalities*, at least not at the time they were caused.

This chapter discusses how the generation of externalities obscures the true value and sustainability of corporations. The next chapter illustrates specific solutions to enable corporations to measure and disseminate this true value, which is a better reflection of their performance than current financial statements. The sections below describe the rationale behind corporations' large and increasing negative externalities as well as their long-term risks.

"Because That's Where the Money Is"

According to urban legend, Willie Sutton, the immaculately dressed bank robber who robbed more than a hundred banks over a forty-year career, was once asked why he robbed banks and succinctly replied, "Because that's where the money is."[1] Fittingly, then, activity-based costing in management accounting is known today as the "Willie Sutton rule": it should only be applied "where the money is," that is, in the largest expenses of an organization.[2] This rule illuminates the logic that underlies corporations' continual efforts to profit from avenues such as carbon emissions and freshwater use where costs are either unregulated or unrecognized, because "that's where the money is."

Corporate Externalities and the Natural Environment

Chapter 1 established the *raison d'être* of corporations as self-interest: to profit and to survive. Calvin Coolidge observed that profit and civilization go hand in hand,[3] a sentiment echoed by Samuel Gompers, the English-born American labor leader and first president of the American Federation of Labor (AFL), who said that "the worst crime against working people is a company which fails to operate at a profit."[4] From the perspective of a corporation's production process, the natural environment is viewed no differently than inputs such as labor, with the exception that it is available for free or at least much more cheaply than its economic value, if a free market existed for that natural resource. Thus, the corporation has the incentive to overuse cheaply available natural resources instead of pursuing another business route which might be the most cost-efficient strategy for society as a whole. At its most fundamental, this is the heart of the environment's externality problem—our inability to price natural resources at an amount that reflects their true value to society. The causes of this inability are complex: uncertainty associated with the benefits of ecosystem services which makes them difficult to evaluate, the "public goods" nature of many ecosystem services such that they escape valuation and defy pricing, and the lack of legal or institutional imperatives to measure and manage externalities, among other reasons.

It is important to mention here that the true value to society of *some* resources could well be infinite or impossible to price, such as the value of human life. A poignant example comes from the Dongria Kondh tribe in India, consisting of about 8,000 people living in the Niyamgiri Hills in Odisha. They have been battling a mining permit that gave a subsidiary of the British company Vedanta Resources plc authorization for an open-pit bauxite mine on Niyam Dongar, the hill that the tribe revere as the seat of their deity, Niyam Raja. These hills contain the forests that this community depends on for its livelihood (*Dongria* means "dweller of *donga*" or "hill" in the Oriya language), and is integral to their sacred beliefs.[5] Valuing these hills based on the forest resources that would be lost if mining were to proceed clearly does not, and cannot, fully account for its loss, because this is a matter of human rights. Since the property rights to the land are with the tribe, their valuation ought to have prevailed. The "price" of these hills, to this community, could well be infinity, rather than the effective $2 billion value that the mining company put on its use if one accepts at face value its statement about how much investment it had to deny India as a result of losing its license.[6]

Externalities Can be Positive

Any discussion of externalities needs to be balanced. Corporations are at least in part responsible for some externalities that are both enormous and unquestionably *positive*. For centuries, traders and entrepreneurs, and their modern avatar, the corporation, have been the harbingers of technology, information, and ideas. In the twentieth century this effect was explosive: innovations ranging from pharmaceuticals to the Internet, ideas ranging from Fordism in the West to the Kaizen system that Toyota cites as its philosophy.

One of the oldest and most benign externalities exerted by corporations has been the spillover from technological research and development (R&D). R&D and other investment by a corporation can generate benefits to other firms in the same industry as well as other industries, particularly in sectors where technology is developing rapidly. For instance, in 2002 Sung-Bae Mun and M. Ishaq Nadiri analyzed information technology (IT) externalities of 42 US private industries for about 50 years beginning in 1948.[7] They found that IT externalities help explain a considerable part of the growth in productivity for several other industries, particularly the services industry. Other research finds that foreign direct investment (FDI) can generate positive spillovers through technology transfer in manufacturing industries in developing countries such as China,[8] and that domestic sectors are the main beneficiaries of these spillovers. Furthermore, recent research from economists at Stanford and LSE estimates that gross social returns to R&D are at least twice as high as the private returns.[9] R&D is thus a classical "public good" in which investment is likely to be less than socially optimal, since the (private) entity who invests in it does not reap all the benefits. Government intervention in the form of R&D subsidies can help ensure that corporations have the incentives to invest in research that has powerful ripple effects in the growth of the wider economy.

Corporations have also indirectly contributed to ideas that have changed the world powerfully for the better, such as microfinance— which stemmed from a business model that sought to provide a service while ensuring efficiency and financial sustainability. The entire premise of social entrepreneurship is founded on sound business principles that seek low-cost, innovative, and sustainable solutions that provide goods such as decentralized energy and health, and that facilitate a billion people at the bottom of the economic pyramid to participate in and benefit from the global economy.

Two immense positive externalities of corporations are the human-capital creation they can facilitate through training their employees and the social capital they can create by fostering new communities—among employees, or suppliers, or customers.

Modern corporations spend billions of dollars on staff training, and while the rationale of increasing employees' human capital is for them to direct their enhanced skills toward creating value for the corporation itself, employees often take their newfound skills to new jobs with compensation premiums that are a direct result of this training. The American Society of Training and Development (ASTD) estimates that US organizations spent over $134 billion on employee learning and development in 2007 alone.[10] Even estimated at very low staff turnover rates of 1–3 percent per annum, that is on average a positive externality of $1.3–4 billion, the amount spent on training that firms did not directly benefit from.

Infosys: Positive Externalities in Human Capital

A leader in creating human capital has been Infosys, an iconic example of a corporation with leaders who thought "forward and fast," creating a corporation that is impressively close to the vision of Corporation 2020. Infosys started with an initial investment of about US$200 in 1981; by May 2010 Infosys had a market capitalization of about US$33 billion.[11] It was listed on the Bombay Stock Exchange in 1993, and its sales and earnings have grown at a compounded rate of 70 percent a year on average.[12] Winner of innumerable Best Employer titles, it extended offers to about 3 percent of the staggering 1.3 million job-seekers who applied to work at Infosys in 2007.[13]

Its primary training campus in Mysore is the largest corporate university in the world.[14] As of 2007, Infosys's Global Education Center had the capacity to house about 4,500 trainees at any given time, and over 15,200 employees are trained here annually.[15] With the recently added second Global Education Center in 2009, the Infosys now has the capacity to train 14,000 employees at a time.[16]

The campus is a remarkable testament to the vision that built and navigated Infosys through the many changes in the Indian economic scenario. It spans over 330 acres, including about 140 acres of green cover providing habitat to 63 bird species and over 45,000 trees. The residences have solar water heaters, there is a biogas plant in its pilot phase, and the elegant, eclectic architecture makes it easy to forget that thousands of people live and work here. Just walking around is inspiration enough to extend one's imagination and abilities and to reach for something truly extraordinary.

Simply due to the sheer scale of its training initiatives, Infosys is

Table 4-1   Total Value of Human-Capital Externality (HCE) Generated by Infosys Cohorts

	2012	2011	Annual Change
Number of Employees	149,994	130,820	14.66%
Value of Human Capital Externality (in million USD)	1,408	1,151	22.36%

Source: GIST Advisory, 2012.

probably one of the largest generators of human-capital externalities in the world, even though its attrition rates are well below industry average. They thus enhance the earning potential of thousands of people, and not all of them contribute to Infosys's value because some leave to work in organizations elsewhere. Thus, to the extent that employees trained by Infosys gain human capital through training and then leave to work for other organizations, the company generates a positive externality for society by enhancing human capital for which it receives no economic gain.

The human capital externality generated by Infosys was worth over $1.4 billion in 2012 (Table 4.1). Infosys's spectacular human-capital generation has been its value added to the economy, although there are no requirements to report this. Infosys does disclose such measures in its annual financial statements, a practise that ought to be emulated.

The leadership that molded Infosys into this kind of corporation emphasizes the importance of "earning the respect of all stakeholders," and as founder-CEO Narayan Murthy emphasized in his retirement address, Infosys has "demonstrated that businesses can be run legally and ethically; that it is possible for an Indian company to benchmark with the global best; and that any set of youngsters with values, hard work, team work, and a little bit of smartness can indeed be successful entrepreneurs."[17] This ethos and respect for their community is reflected in the many dimensions of the excellence that often follows such drive, ranging from a 98 percent buyback rate from their customers, and exponential growth, as well as innumerable awards for technical excellence, employee satisfaction, and partnerships, and even a special mention by Bill Clinton in 2000 when he praised India's achievements in the technology sector.

Natura: Positive Externalities in Social Capital

Natura, Inc., is a Brazilian cosmetics company that generates large positive externalities through its unique distribution model, which they have turned into a core business strength. Natura operates using a direct-sales business model with housewives as its sales agents, and it has harnessed and strengthened community ties into an economically rewarding institution. Analogous to the investment in community infrastructure by Toyota, Natura has generated positive externalities in local Brazilian communities by contributing to the enhancement of social networks and providing economic security to the women it employs, most of whom have no other employment. This strengthening of the social fabric is Natura's first positive externality.

Natura employs about 1.2 million sales agents, almost all women. It empowers women economically and trains them to become skilled salespeople, many of whom go on to represent other companies, including Natura's competitors. Future-oriented corporations like Natura frequently train large numbers of employees and enhance their earning potential. If Natura trains an employee who goes on to work and earn elsewhere, the newly created skill of the employee is a second positive externality.

Third, by operating in a manner that enables these women to work part-time, Natura is in a sense mitigating a labor-market bottleneck. Jobs usually come in the form of a certain number of hours paying a certain wage, depending on factors such as skill and experience. Many women, particularly in developing countries, choose not to participate in the labor market since jobs that match their preferences and skill set and that have flexible hours are difficult to come by. According to a recent International Labour Organization study, "Among married couples with children, men's paid working hours tend to increase while women's paid working hours decrease." It points out that in Malaysia, an estimated 23 percent of women stop doing paid work entirely due to the demands of childcare.[18] By enabling women to participate in the labor market in a flexible manner, Natura is filling a gap in the market. Furthermore, to the extent that they are spurring other firms to consider providing this kind of part-time employment opportunity, they are creating positive externalities for the people who participate in these jobs as well as for these other firms.

Finally, by empowering women economically, Natura may have initiated powerful ripple effects on children's and household welfare more generally. Intra-household economics studies how the income that each member brings into the household changes the type and amount of goods that the household as a whole buys. The premise is that each member of the household may have different preferences for goods, and since the income contributed by each member is a factor that affects their bargaining power, women's earnings affect the household's final choice of goods and services. Beyond income, institutional factors can be determinants of bargaining power. Studies have shown that the effects of giving government assistance to women rather than men can be quite different. For example, the PROGRESA program in Mexico is a conditional cash-transfer program that gives households economic incentives to ensure that children attend high school and receive regular health checkups. The program was set up to transfer money to women. Studies found that this policy led to an increase in the demand for goods closely affecting children's welfare, a 156.3 percent increase in the proportion of household expenditure allocated to children's clothing and a 10.1 percent decrease in the proportion of household expenditure allocated to alcohol and tobacco.[19] A Brazilian study found similar effects, including much lower probabilities of infant mortality if government economic assistance was given to women.[20] Thus, there is reason to believe that Natura's business model is generating positive socioeconomic externalities for local communities, with long-term positive impacts on society in Brazil and other countries in Latin America.

A second key positive externality from corporations is the community that they create by bringing together hundreds of people in the workplace, and the social network that is fostered as a result. Additionally, corporations can invest in communities above and beyond balance sheet considerations, nurturing social networks and contributing to the development of local infrastructure that benefits entire cities. Consider the history behind the Toyota Corporation.

The town of Koromo in Japan was a vital point in the silk trade during the second half of the nineteenth century. After a crash in silk prices that devastated its economy, it was revived in part by a local Koromo resident looking to diversify out of the family textile business, the Toyoda

Automatic Loom Works. That resident was Sakichi Toyoda and the company he founded was the Toyota Motor Corporation. Toyota constructed new infrastructure and increased employment, and its success revived the economy and the community to the point that the town changed its name to Toyota in 1959.[21] The story of Toyota is remarkable but carries a dual lesson—that a reversal of fortunes can also reverse such public recognition of a positive externality. When Toyota cut 9,000 jobs, the town responded to the "negative externality" of such significant job losses by changing its name back to Koromo.

Not only does the corporation spread its culture economically, co-workers often become friends, and the board of directors can resemble elders guiding the group to conform to the ethos of the organization. An International Labour Organization study describes how, in the 1970s, the century-long trend of shrinking number of hours in an average work week in the United States was reversed.[22] It reports that

> the share of employed, 25-to-64-year-old men who usually work 50 or more hours per week on their main job rose from 14.7 percent in 1980 to 18.5 percent in 2001. . . . For college-educated men, the proportion working 50 hours or more climbed from 22.2 percent to 30.5 percent in these two decades. Between 1979 and 2002, the frequency of long work hours increased by 14.4 percentage points among the top quintile of wage earners, but fell by 6.7 percentage points in the lowest quintile.[23]

The study also stated that "about 22 percent of the global workforce, or 614.2 million workers, are working 'excessively' long hours."[24] Women's labor-force participation has contributed to this trend. Thus, people are spending increasingly more time at work in the company of people they work with. While it may be argued that this creates more stress among the employed and adds to the numbers of the unemployed, it is also creating communities within the workplace.

Negative Externalities and "Net Value Addition"

Of course, the modern corporation is also responsible for immense negative externalities, the largest of which is, most likely, its impact on the environment.[25] Many corporations undertake processes that have regular negative impacts on the environment, such as air pollution or deforestation. Sometimes these impacts are rare, catastrophic events, like BP's oil spill in the Gulf of Mexico. One study estimates that $74.3 billion in annual damages are caused by local air pollutants in the United States each year, and these are just those pollutants for which regulation has been prevalent for years.[26]

Furthermore, a recent study estimates that "the largest industrial contributor to external costs is coal-fired electric generation, whose damages range from 1.4 to 3.5 times value added" for the United States economy.[27] That study only considered six major local air pollutants (sulfur dioxide, nitrogen oxides, volatile organic compounds, ammonia, fine particulate matter, and coarse particulate matter), and, in the case of the electricity sector, carbon dioxide emissions. If markets could account for such impacts of pollution as human morbidity, they would in theory never allow a situation in which an industry continues to operate while its costs of operation are several times the value added from its operations. Unfortunately, markets do not account for such externalities, and coal-fired electric generation, as Willie Sutton would remind us, is where the money is.

Thus, we see that because crucial externalities such as water pollution, land-use change, and climate change are not taken into account, some industries in the current economic structure actually have *lower* value added than the gross external damage they impose on society—the prices of these environmental damages are simply not set optimally, due to the absence or incompleteness of markets for these environmental goods and services.

So what is a corporation's true value, as opposed to that reflected by its current accounting measures? One illuminating measure is the True Economic Value Added, or TRUEVA (see Table 4.2).[28] This measure integrates the conventional concept of Economic Value Added with the economic valuation of the environmental impact of a corporation's activities in order to arrive at a measure that reflects its "contingent environmental liabilities and their ability to finance such exposures from operating surpluses without impairing their ability to attract and retain capital." TRUEVA reveals that off-the-books liabilities such as the abatement cost of emissions and effluents can be a substantial source of risk for industries, especially when regulation is suddenly strengthened. For instance, it could cost General Electric billions of dollars to clean up the PCBs released in the Hudson Valley, and it did cost ExxonMobil billions to clean up the damage caused by its oil spill in Alaska's Prince William Sound. The authors of TRUEVA, Robert Repetto and Daniel Dias, quote a recent estimate of U.S. emissions of approximately 7.4 billion metric tons of carbon dioxide and posit that this may create a potential off-the-books liability of about $100 billion. A corporation with such significant off-the-books liabilities clearly faces higher economic risks than one that internalizes more of these costs. Thus, the true economic value added of a corporation "subtracts from the firm's operating surplus not only its costs of capital but also the environmental damages it imposes elsewhere in the economy."[29]

Repetto and Dias have estimated the value of the airline and electricity companies, using only a limited set of environmental externalities. They included the cost of emissions of carbon dioxide, sulfur oxides, and nitrogen oxides from commercial airplanes and electric generating facilities, finding that even with this limited definition of externalities, several companies have negative true rates of return on their capital, illuminating the extent of risk exposure of these companies to regulation.

The size of negative externalities is significant, and this is reflected in these TRUEVA numbers, the largest of which are in the negative billions of dollars. The ten largest corporations from this study sample are listed in Table 4.3. These numbers illustrate the risk undertaken by some of the

Table 4-2 Summary of Economic Indicators

Economic Indicator	Abbreviation	Includes Environmental Externalities?
Net Operating Profits after Taxes	NOPAT	NO
Conventional Economic Value Added	EVA	NO
True Economic Value Added	TRUEVA	YES
Conventional Rate of Return on Capital	ROC	NO
True Rate of Return on Capital	TrueROC	YES

Source: Repetto and Dias, 2006.

Table 4-3 Ten Corporations with the Lowest TrueROC

Company Name	TrueROC (%)	TRUEVA (millions $)	ROC (%)	EVA (millions $)	NOPAT (millions $)
Allegheny Energy Inc	−14.2	−1,526.0	4.1	−13.5	341.7
Westar Energy Inc	−13.9	−642.0	5.8	48.2	203.2
American Electric Power	−12.3	−4,853.4	5.0	135.0	1429.6
Cinergy Corp	−12.1	−1,987.0	4.8	11.2	568.3
Great Plains Energy Inc	−10.8	−394.5	8.6	95.1	217.2
DPL Inc	−7.6	−429.2	6.3	53.6	218.2
Xcel Energy Inc	−7.7	−2,231.2	3.7	−135.5	680.2
Southern Co	−7.0	−3,353.3	6.3	411.0	1779.7
Reliant Energy Inc	−6.1	−1,316.6	1.0	−419.5	125.6
Ameren Corp	−5.3	−1,458.4	5.5	97.2	790.4

Source: Repetto and Dias, 2006.

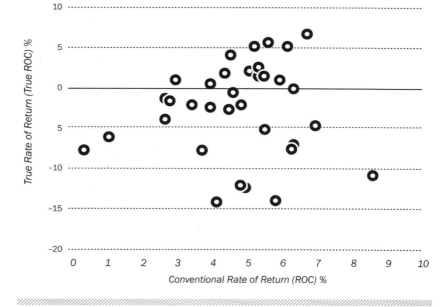

Figure 4-1   Conventional vs. True Rate of Return: Sample of US Energy Companies. Source: Repetto and Dias 2006.

largest corporations of the world, by refusing to consider the impacts of their actions for long-term welfare and eventually their profitability.

In Table 4.3, TRUEVA shows that the true value added of many energy companies in the United States in 2004 was negative, and TrueROC underscores the risk exposure of these companies to environmental regulation. For the 34 companies for which Repetto and Dias listed results, the average conventional rate of return was 4.86 percent, whereas the true rate of return was −2.44 percent. Interestingly, there is almost no correlation (0.003 in fact) between the conventional rate of return on capital (ROC) for these companies and the true return on capital (TrueROC) (see Figure 4.1). ROC versus TrueROC is truly a "scatter" diagram. Thus a company's conventional ROC provides no information regarding their true rate of return to society.

This TRUEVA study was a ground-breaking work that highlighted how exposed companies were to the risk of environmental regulation changing, and how inefficiently (from a society-wide perspective) they were operating, causing major inefficiencies and vast environmental cost externalities to the economy and to society.

Voodoo Economics and Negative Externalities

One particular industry with considerable environmental externalities is palm oil. Palm oil is an ancient commodity native to West Africa. The first oil-palm plantations in this region were established by colonial Europeans primarily to produce oil for candle making and as machine lubricant, demand for which had escalated after the Industrial Revolution. The first oil palms in Asia were planted in 1848 by British colonial traders in a botanical garden in Java as ornamental plants. They flourished in the clement growing conditions, and soon the economic logic of plantations in this region was understood. As plantations were established and then scaled up in Southeast Asia, technological advances in the hydrogenation of oils, and later in the refining and transport of oils, diversified the list of final products for which the oil was used, including margarine. Oil-palm plantations were also scaled up post–World War I as rubber plantation owners sought to diversify out of the slumping rubber market. The total area under oil palm increased from over 6,000 hectares in Sumatra in 1919 to 32,000 in 1925, doubling again to 64,000 hectares in 1930, with Malaysia experiencing similar growth spurts in area under oil palm.[30]

Today, palm oil is a commodity used in hundreds of products, ranging from soaps to processed food to napalm, with production levels rising over 115 percent in the top 20 producing countries from 1994 to 2004.[31] Indonesia is currently the world's largest producer, surpassing Malaysia in 2009 by increasing its area under oil palm from 200,000 hectares in 1967 to 3 million hectares in 2000, and then to over 5 million hectares in 2010.[32] Most of the increase in plantations in both Indonesia and Malaysia has come at the expense of the deforestation of rainforests that are on peat bogs. The result has been biodiversity loss in one of the world's most biodiverse regions; land degradation and the resulting loss of the abundant ecosystem services provided by these forests; and, when forests are cleared and the land drained to make it ready for planting, the release into the atmosphere of large quantities of carbon stored in the peat bogs.

None of these costs are taken into account by private companies when deciding whether land should be converted from rainforests to an oil-palm plantation. What *is* accounted for are the gains from timber concessions that occur when this deforestation happens, and the manner in which they are evaluated would make any economist feel as though she had been transported into *Alice in Wonderland*. The economics of palm oil seem to get "curiouser and curiouser"; the companies claim that *timber sales* make the *palm oil production* profitable. Even without accounting for all the externalities that large-scale deforestation causes (which these companies certainly do not), this is a puzzling claim. It is analogous to claiming that someone makes so much money selling hats, that their shoe business is profitable.

The gross profitability of logging (gross since it does not account for externalities) is the single largest factor that makes palm oil production profitable—this is clear in the breakdown of profits from palm oil cultivation (see Figure 4.2), where "plantation," i.e., logging profits, is said to form 50–60 percent of the profits, with "downstream oleochemicals" forming a small secondary category comprising about 10–18 percent of the profits.[33] The dark corollary of this is, of course, that continued deforestation is required for palm-oil production to be consistently "profitable," since continued cultivation on the same plot of land won't yield

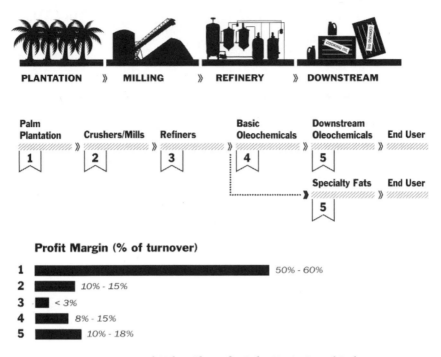

Figure 4-2   Typical Value Chain for Palm Fruit–Based Industries
Source: "MP3EI: An 'NKRI' Economic Masterplan," in Workshop
on Green Economic Corridors (2011).

their largest profit component, the timber. It is an unsustainable version of slash-and-burn agriculture on steroids, undertaken by corporations that have no stake in maintaining the land. A 2007 UNEP report projected that the unsustainable use of land would lead to the loss of most Indonesian forests by 2022.[34]

This deforestation is the reason why Indonesia is the world's third largest greenhouse-gas emitter, and unlike in most of the other top emitters, in Indonesia deforestation and peat emissions cause a large portion—80 percent in 2005—of its GHG emissions.[35] It is also the cause of large-scale biodiversity loss, including some species that are endemic to this region, such as the Sumatran tiger, Sumatran and Bornean orangutans, Asian elephant, and Sumatran rhinoceros, all of which are now classified as endangered or critically endangered.[36] In some cases, the establishment of plantations has meant displacement of local communities, which in itself causes negative externalities by adversely impacting their livelihoods and their social fabric. The list of corporations that buy palm oil produced in this unsustainable way is long; the largest such corporations include Unilever and Proctor & Gamble, and to a lesser extent, Nestlé.[37]

In 2008, Greenpeace activists, dressed as orangutans, scaled Unilever headquarters in London, Rome, Amsterdam, and several other cities, displaying banners that urged the corporation to abstain from destroying forests. This act was simple (albeit dramatic), and its effect equally dramatic: Unilever committed to sustainably sourcing all of its palm oil by 2015, and Proctor & Gamble soon followed suit, along with several other large corporations.

Corporations are increasingly sensitive to public opinion, particularly given the risks of alienating their customer base. A 2010 Greenpeace report[38] linking palm-oil supplier Sinar Mas to palm-oil sourcing derived from illegal deforested land led to losses of tens of millions of dollars in lost contracts for the company, when several companies including Nestlé, Unilever, and Burger King canceled their contracts.[39] Interestingly, though, several of these companies had contracts with Cargill, which in turn had a supply contract with Sinar Mas, which meant that some amount of their supply continued to be contaminated with unsustainably produced palm oil.

What is meant by "sustainable" palm oil is of course another matter, and the power that a corporation has over its suppliers and its ability to monitor them are key determinants of the feasibility of a sustainable palm-oil standard. The 2004 Roundtable on Sustainable Palm Oil (RSPO), an initiative to promote sustainable procurement practices, was a step in the right direction, but it has already been dubbed "Really Slow Progress Overall" by environmental activists. Corporations have cited problems with enforcing and monitoring sustainability standards with negligent suppliers, a situation exacerbated by the fact that even the largest corporations are small global buyers of this commodity.

The environmental externalities looked at so far are those imposed by corporations in day-to-day operations. A conspicuous example of a recent, catastrophic negative environmental externality imposed by a corporation is that of the 2010 BP oil spill, whose negligence regarding safety precautions contributed to not only the occurrence of one of the biggest environmental disasters in history, but also to its needless exacerbation.

I chose this example not because it is typical (corporations clearly do not routinely cause environmental disasters of this scale), but because it illustrates the immense power of the corporation and the widespread possible impacts of myopic corporate practices on industry and on society as a whole.

"The Time Has Come," the Walrus Said . . .

On April 20, 2010, there was an explosion on an oil rig in the Gulf of Mexico, killing 11 people, injuring 17, and exposing the vulnerability of ecosystems and humans caused by the deep sea drilling process. It wasn't the world's first experience with such oceanic oil spills, nor was it a first for British Petroleum, which had caused a 2006 oil spill in Prudhoe Bay, Alaska. That spill was the result of a dime-sized hole in a pipeline, and it caused a loss of about 267,000 gallons (a million liters) of oil. At the time, BP was fined about $20 million under the Clean Water Act.[40] Its Gulf of Mexico spill was, however, the worst ever in terms of environmental and economic impact, and led to BP setting aside $20 billion for the damages caused to ecosystems and coastal communities.

The numbers associated with the 2010 oil spill were staggering: over 50,000 barrels escaped every day before the well was finally capped, and the 170 million gallons of crude oil that dispersed into the ocean[41] amounted to more than the daily use of the UK, France, and Greece combined.[42] The oil reached Louisiana shores in a few days, then Mississippi and Alabama, and then Florida, decimating marine life along the way and damaging about 650 miles of shoreline.[43]

BP swung into "damage control" mode almost immediately, unfortunately concentrating mostly on the PR aspect. They brandished a 582-page emergency-response document in their official responses, which, while discussing the possibility of a spill in the Gulf of Mexico solicitously claimed the capability to save "seals, sea otters, and walruses."[44] Not a single walrus died in the oil spill of course, because no walruses live in the warm waters of the Gulf of Mexico. This appears to have been a "cut-and-paste" error in transcribing from a drilling EIA in the North Sea, where the species is relevant, and if that is indeed the case, it raises questions about the seriousness of purpose being applied in preparing these important risk-management documents.

BP's emergency response plan also listed Professor Peter Lutz, an eminent authority on sea turtles who passed away in 2005, as a national wildlife expert to be contacted in event of an emergency spill in this 2009 plan. This was in addition to listing a number of wildlife organizations that are no longer in existence, as well as "primary equipment providers for BP in the Gulf of Mexico Region [for] rapid deployment of spill response resources on a 24 hour, 7 days a week basis" which included websites that link to Japanese home-shopping-network pages.[45] And the authors of BP's plan appear to have taken the power of positive thinking to altogether new planes: the scenarios they considered were about ten times worse than the actual spill, and yet, in their scenarios, biodiversity and beaches were unharmed and water quality was impaired only marginally and temporarily.[46]

This tale of phantom organizations rescuing imaginary creatures and all of this leading to happy endings must have been a gripping read, since this plan was not only approved by the federal Minerals Management Service (MMS), but appears to have reassured the MMS so much that it even gave 27 further approvals to the industry for offshore drilling in the two weeks following the catastrophe.[47] If some of the investigated cases of gifts and favors received by MMS employees from oil companies are any indicator of the cronyism between MMS officials and oil company employees, then such untimely generosity in new approvals is not altogether surprising. For example, if gifts include a ride in a private aircraft to take an MMS official and his family to the 2005 Peach Bowl, perhaps the chances of this official approving the next proposal become somewhat enhanced.[48] The sordid saga continued: it was reported that some MMS employees accepted drugs (crystal methamphetamine) from oil company employees, and another was found negotiating a new job with an oil company while still ostensibly inspecting that oil company. All these instances were abuses the inspector general mentioned as being under investigation in a 2010 report on the MMS.[49]

In the Gulf, meanwhile, the spill had affected about 82,000 birds; about 6,000 sea turtles; nearly 26,000 marine mammals, including dolphins; and an uncountable number of fish and invertebrates.[50] Hundreds of endangered sea turtles were killed. It was sadly ironic that some of these were Kemp's Ridley sea turtles, a species that in 1979 was airlifted to the Gulf

Coast from Mexico during an oil spill caused there by the exploratory oil well Ixtoc I.[51]

Impacts on biodiversity often have significant economic dimensions, although their "economic invisibility" usually results in these dimensions being ignored—a common consequence of the way our national and corporate accounting systems fail to reflect public natural wealth.[52] Disasters such as the *Deepwater Horizon* oil spill can suddenly reveal these economic dimensions in a shocking way after the fact, as was the case with fishing and tourism in the Gulf. The fishing industry in Louisiana, in the midst of recovering from Katrina and the economic recession, took a blow in its peak season, as did the seafood-processing and tourism industries, which may well be long-term setbacks since it may take decades for these ecosystems to recuperate.[53] The National Oceanic and Atmospheric Administration (NOAA) shut down about 23 percent of the $2.4 billion seafood-production industry because of the oil spill.[54] The food-processing industries in other states were affected as well, such as the oyster-shucking plants in Virginia and Alabama.[55] It has been estimated that if the spill cut Florida tourism in half, it would cost 195,000 jobs and $11 billion in a single year alone.[56]

Such significant human and economic impacts could not but elicit a political response. Not surprisingly, the White House issued several statements to the effect that they were monitoring the situation closely and holding BP's feet to the fire. However, public perceptions that the tough talk was not being followed up by action were reinforced by some local political responses. Bobby Jindal, Louisiana's governor and a passionate advocate of "small" government who had once proudly proclaimed that he would reject $100 million of stimulus money to increase unemployment payments,[57] now gave numerous peevish interviews citing lack of funds and federal government support as an impediment for rehabilitating the coastline. Jindal was active in the recovery plans, particularly regarding construction of new barrier islands to keep the oil from reaching the wetlands,[58] an unlikely hero of the moment given that in 2006 he had introduced a bill that would open the entire US coastline to deep-sea drilling (the Deep Ocean Energy Resources Act). Indeed, a few days after the oil spill he sent a letter to President Obama decrying the new ban on offshore drilling as killing "thousands of Louisiana jobs."[59] The government put a moratorium on deep-sea drilling—for six whole months, before actually increasing the territory allocated to the same.

Once again, we need to ask: were BP's distressing actions and responses just unfortunate outliers, outrageous exceptions to a more sensible norm? Apparently not. To begin with, we cannot even give BP sole credit for the inanities in their contingency plan. Interestingly enough, Exxon-Mobil and Chevron have replicas of this particular tour de force as their contingency plans, too, including the walrus references and the contact number of the deceased Professor Lutz.[60]

BP tried to avoid responsibility for punitive-damages claims from parties harmed by the spill, but this attempt was foiled by a judge who "dismissed claims filed under state law because they were 'pre-empted by maritime law, or 'don't allege physical damage to a proprietary interest.'"[61] But in doing so, it was following a traditional pattern of behavior: working on behalf of its shareholders while neglecting its stakeholders and society at large. That is precisely what a Corporation 1920 is meant to do.

The fundamental point is that BP's actions were exactly what you would expect of a Corporation 1920. Its responses showed the doctrine of self-interest as against social responsibility as being central to its purpose. This was evident in the nature of its responses: opacity, delays in divulging information, laxity in preparing itself against a sizeable risk, and delays in seriously responding to a disaster that occurred as a result. BP did not fundamentally change its behavior by learning from this expensive catastrophe, and focused instead on trying to avoid its culpability. It remained committed to lobbying for more freedoms for offshore drilling; legislative pressure groups that oppose regulation of offshore drilling continued to be engaged.[62] It could be argued that all of these were myopic actions that gambled unreasonably with company resources and were therefore questionable even from the narrow perspective of shareholder value.

More importantly, though, these actions of BP gambled with society's resources, and even though that is not a "right" that the corporation was formally accorded by society, there is nothing in regulation today that prevents them from doing so. Forward-thinking regulation might stop companies from causing such potential losses to society, but a Corporation 2020 would consider regulatory compliance as the least effort it must make, and would look beyond that to insure itself and the society it serves against catastrophe.

For a Corporation 2020, the so-called regulatory envelope is a boundary from which to steer clear—but not so for a Corporation 1920, whose behavior is typically to explore the boundary of the regulatory envelope, constantly testing it in search of competitive advantage and more profit, occasionally breaching the envelope and bearing the fines and penalties that ensue, and then describing them as "the cost of doing business." In contrast, Corporation 2020 behavior is to not just meet but exceed prudential norms, and sometimes indeed to design new and additional constraints that reinforce the underlying purpose of such regulation. However, to achieve such behavior change, reliance merely on endogenous drivers such as profit opportunities or visionary CEOs appears somewhat optimistic. Might some form of mandatory disclosure of externalities to investors, customers, and civil society help the transition? Perhaps, as Lewis Carroll's Walrus said, "the time has come," and we must bring the term *externality* out of its hiding place in economics textbooks and into public discourse.

The Sting in the Tail

As BP's experience shows, externalizing risks and costs is not always a one-way street. The sting in the tail can sometimes be quite harmful to the body corporate. When it comes to internalizing externalities, chance can succeed where design clearly failed. Accurate policy design would have ensured that BP's risks were well covered, its contingency plans well formulated, and its potential externalities internalized. That, we know, didn't happen. Comprehensive measures to avoid the spill were not in place, and once it occurred, the contingency plans were revealed to be grossly inadequate, a situation exacerbated by its efforts to deflect blame and underplay the seriousness of the spill. Thus, it chanced that BP had to pay $20 billion to cover the damages from the spill, a move that highlighted that when design falls short, chance sometimes leads to corporations' being compelled to internalize externalities.

A too-often-observed corporate willingness to explore the regulatory envelope for competitive advantage and profits, and to apply Willy Sutton logic by seeking to exploit the benefits of negative externalities, can boomerang quite badly. The diversionary tactics employed by the tobacco industry beginning in the 1950s and 1960s did delay consensus regarding the link of smoking to cancer in the short term, but eventually resulted in class-action lawsuits costing billions of dollars. The 1980s campaign by the oil industry to keep lead in petrol was equally unsuccessful in the long term. More recently, the Indian Supreme Court ordered Hindustan Agro Chemicals Pvt. Ltd., a chemical company, to pay nearly $47 million in compensation for neglecting to pay its 15-year-old initial fine of $8.5 million, a very expensive slap on the wrist.[63]

Corporate actions that create negative externalities include not merely their passive responses to current institutional structures; corporations actively lobby and engage government to influence laws that will allow them to continue externalizing the consequences of actions on consumers and society in general. In the United States, for example, businesses contribute nearly three quarters of all political donations, with about 25 percent coming from finance, insurance, and real estate companies. The remainder comes mainly from corporations involved in pharmaceuticals, communications, construction, agribusiness (especially tobacco), energy and natural resources, transportation, and defense.[64]

Lobbying expenditures are over and above these party political contributions, and can be quite substantial. For example, in 2008, energy and mining industries spent millions of dollars on public relations to hire nearly 2,340 registered lobbyists to prevent climate legislation.[65]

Advertising expenditures to convince consumers not to change damaging behaviors, or to promote a lifestyle or products which can be value propositions only in a world of unaccounted and unaccountable externalities, can also be quite extravagant.[66] Even the funding of research is subject to corporations' cost-externalizing motivations. At present many corporations are still funding campaigns aimed at raising doubts regarding the science of climate change. However these campaigns are crumbling slowly, as it becomes increasingly clear that the experts behind such studies are very rarely unbiased. While all this effort and spending on political contributions, lobbying, and spreading disinformation and misinformation through advertising and biased research may be financially beneficial in the short term for the corporation, it rarely makes for good long-term business strategy.

A similar tension between short-term profits and long-term costs can be observed in the way risky actions are undertaken for an apparent cost saving, while exposing the company to greater long-term risks and costs. Halliburton, the company charged by BP to manage that fateful oil well, chose to forgo a $500,000 sound-activated valve that would shut down the well if an explosion occurred, a decision that policy-makers at the time supported, saying "that the switches, which cost $500,000 were too much of a burden on the industry."[67] After the oil spill, BP set up a $20 billion escrow fund to cover the damages caused by the spill, which the Obama administration clearly stated was not a "cap" on BP's liability.[68] The cost-benefit calculation of the sound-activated valve might have looked quite different if ecological value-at-risk had been calculated and factored in by Halliburton or by BP, but of course that was not done.

If misaligned or myopic incentive structures can create opportunities for corporations to arbitrage for profit, they often create long-term environmental damages that affect society as a whole. As a result, the same corporation can behave differently regarding the same issues in different economic and social environments. Hindustan Lever has widespread CSR activities partnering with local communities in India to enable water harvesting, whereas its parent company, Unilever, is one of the major corporations undertaking palm-oil production in Indonesia, an industry notorious for causing widespread deforestation, resulting in land degradation, biodiversity loss, and colossal greenhouse-gas emissions. Whole Foods, Inc., a proud paragon of the organic and sustainable food movement that reported $4.6 billion in sales in 2009,[69] nevertheless has come under fire for being staunchly anti-union to its more than 62,000 "team members."[70] Apple Inc., a darling of the corporate world, producing intuitive, user-friendly, unquestionably cutting-edge products, has scored low on company–labor relations[71] and transparency in disclosing their environmental externalities (urging shareholders to vote against resolutions that require it to publish a CSR report detailing its approach to greenhouse-gas emissions, toxics, and recycling in 2009).[72] Thus, we see that the world of corporate responsibility is often not as straightforward as one might imagine.

~ ~ ~

Our explorations of Natura, Infosys, Unilever, and BP demonstrate that the impacts of the "externalizing" that corporations undertake can be immensely far-reaching, both positively and negatively.

It is becoming increasingly clear that careful handling of externalities, and efforts to internalize them as much as possible, are hallmarks of a futuristic, intelligent, and adaptive corporation, much like considering the impact of one's current actions on the future is a hallmark of a futuristic, intelligent, and adaptive individual. These are the corporations that not only respond to expectations regarding regulation, but engage policymakers meaningfully to ensure that regulatory certainty is combined with progressive policy, instead of concentrating resources on narrow-minded and myopic lobbying that guarantees short-lived opportunities at best.

There is an increasing realization that "third-party consequences" is not a sufficient way to describe corporate externalities, as these activities often actually affect the corporations' own operations in the future. Today, the linkages of economic activity are so extensive that the effects of myopic decisions can be felt everywhere, including by the perpetrator of negative externalities. Overexploitation of natural resources compromises corporations' own supply chains; pollution shows up in employees' health bills; and lost productivity and unsustainable practices erode customer bases.

In the following chapter, I shall discuss in detail some of the next-generation initiatives engaged in by companies close to the Corporation 2020 vision, and how they and new regulation are redefining the economic landscape. These actions ensure efficiency not at the narrow scale of a firm or an industry, but at the much larger scale of the economy and society as a whole, minimizing the exposure of corporations to resource scarcities and regulatory risks.

CHAPTER FIVE

Incorporating Externalities

Using Markets, Smart Regulation, and Corporate Disclosure

Sunlight is said to be the best of disinfectants.

— *Louis D. Brandeis*

An economist and a physicist are walking down the street when the physicist points to a $20 bill on the sidewalk and exclaims, "Oh look, there's a $20 bill lying there." Without breaking his step or slowing his stride, the economist responds, "Can't be. If it was, someone would have picked it up already."

We've seen the positive and negative externalities that corporations' operations, supply chains, and investments often cause. Measuring these externalities enables us to evaluate the impact and longevity of their effects. For instance, regarding greenhouse-gas emissions: we know that the half-life of CO_2 is about 38 years; it is established that industry accounts for nearly 20 percent of global CO_2 emissions;[1] and it is possible to estimate the risks of climate-change damage to the economy.[2] Thus, the question arises: How are such negative externalities to be reduced or eliminated, in the best interest of society?

Fortunately, there is considerable scope for aligning incentives such that corporations take more responsibility for their actions. Corporations, not unlike biological species in a dynamic environment, respond to external stimuli—mainly policies and prices. They adapt and evolve, with the strongest and fittest surviving over time. Setting incentives such that corporations' costs of using natural and social resources reflect their true value to society can enable a Darwinian process by which those corporations best able to adapt would survive and facilitate the creation of more such businesses. In the long run, therefore, the social benefits and social costs of corporations' activities could be reflected in their accounts insofar as possible, realigning the corporations' profits with the goals of society. This chapter describes a set of solutions driven by responsible disclosure of externalities as well as the necessary action to lead to their reduction.

Gold at the Rainbow's End?

The feasibility and scalability of a more holistic model of economic functioning in which some corporations stay far ahead of others thanks to their sustainability-correlated bottom line has long been a matter of considerable debate. Are corporate "Wave Riders" real, or just wonders of the moment?[3] Is the observed correlation between corporations' stock performance and their environmental performance a causation or just a correlation due to both being directed by talented management? Does the fact that some corporations make money and yet generate positive externalities imply that all corporations can do the same? From a theoretical point of view, is it possible that there are economic gains to the corporation from managing its negative externalities better? Corporations need to know that the benefits they can gain are real—and not see them as an economist sees stray $20 bills. What solutions would maximize the returns of economic activity to society and to the corporation? Is regulation good or bad, or rather, *when* is regulation good or bad?

This chapter starts to develop a comprehensive tool kit of solutions that will facilitate a corporation's evolution. Some of these tools can be utilized by individual corporations, tools that include comprehensive externalities accounting and filling market gaps such as consumers' willingness to pay for sustainably and ethically produced commodities. Other tools can be utilized by corporations collaborating to create and develop markets by, for example, finding synergies where one corporation's waste is bought by another as raw material, thus reducing materials waste and increasing economic efficiency. These strategies require the emergence of economies of scale, an increased level of information in the market, and the correct pricing of resources to reflect their true economic scarcity and impact on society. (This last is particularly important. If regulation were to get prices right, corporations overall would benefit even if action by any one corporation may be insufficient.) There is a need and an appropriate role for regulation in this regard, and we'll look at instances of regulation that attempts to achieve these objectives and ensure that prices are correct, risk is explicit, and economic activity results in value added—not subtracted.

Are Those $20 Bills on the Sidewalk?

A natural question about the principles of 2020 corporations is whether those that have some of these characteristics perform better in the short run and the long run, or even whether they perform better at all, regardless of the time frame. Even if they do perform better, the causal interpretation still does not follow immediately. Are more "internalizing" companies better performers, or are better performers more able to "internalize," perhaps due to other comparative advantages they enjoy? It is interesting to consider how corporations that do undertake initiatives such as paying fair wages when not required to do so under regulation, or internalizing the cost of their environmental footprint, perform relative to their peers. While it would be worthwhile to study an entire spectrum of measures for leaders and laggards within industries, that question is beyond the scope of this book.

Some Are Leaders

There are several corporations that have turned the "internalizing" of what would normally be external damages into profit by identifying the potential to cut costs through efficiency measures or to cater to consumers who are willing to pay somewhat higher prices to ensure that the goods and services they consume are sustainably and ethically sourced at all points on the supply chain. Some corporations first created markets for sustainably produced commodities and then fulfilled this demand. The Body Shop, now a cosmetics giant, began with a single shop in Brighton, England, in 1976. Twenty years later and quite a while before sustainable and ethical production became mainstreamed into consumer consciousness, they introduced Footsie Roller, their first Community Trade product and an antecedent of today's Fair Trade products. As of December 2009, their products were in over 2,550 stores, 1,100 of them company-owned, and their sales totaled nearly $1 billion.[4] For a cosmetics company, The Body Shop has exerted enormous effort on initiatives that some would think hurt its financial bottom line. It was their "Against Animal Testing" campaign in the 1990s that contributed in no small measure to a ban on animal testing for cosmetics and their ingredients in the United Kingdom. They were the first global retailers to join the Board of the Roundtable for Sustainable Palm Oil. They have been involved in scores of other campaigns to promote environmental and social issues, collaborating with a wide range of institutions such Greenpeace International, Amnesty International, the United Nations Environmental Program, and MTV.[5] While The Body Shop was founded and run on extra-financial principles, it has become quite profitable by identifying that all in all, most consumers care about the environmental and social impact of their goods and services.

The outdoor clothing and gear company Patagonia also faced choices when it first began, and it chose to rise to these challenges. When Patagonia discovered that their early climbing tools were defacing landmarks, they replaced these products with ones that didn't cause damage. Today they are involved in a host of environmental initiatives including sourcing organic cotton for their products and, indeed, transforming their supply chain for cotton, minimizing their energy footprint, engaging with environmental organizations, and donating 1 percent of their profits to causes they support. Many of these activities are typically associated with corporate social responsibility, but Patagonia's robust growth and loyal, expanding customer base illustrate that there are significant business returns to playing nice. Their mission statement reads: "Build the best product, cause no unnecessary harm, and use business to inspire and implement solutions to the environmental crisis." They are proud to claim that "Staying true to our core values during thirty-plus years in business has helped us create a company we're proud to run and work for. And our focus on making the best products possible has brought us success in the marketplace."[6] Starbucks' efforts to build the fair-trade coffee market provides another good example of a corporation that helped create and then fill a niche market, one that continues to grow in the United States, even though it is still only a small portion of Starbucks' total sales. Imports of fair trade coffee to the United States grew at 75 percent in 2004, 35 percent in 2005, and 45 percent in 2006.[7] Despite the recession, the global fair-trade coffee market continued to grow in 2008, with sales increasing 14 percent.[8]

Some Have Leadership Thrust upon Them

Of course, not all corporations run headlong into sustainable production with genuine enthusiasm. As we've seen, many of them do create impacts both good and harmful that are not reflected in their financial accounts and often not on any of their public statements. Negative externalities are rarely accounted for unless the media picks up on them. In such cases, corporations clean up because they have to, or they risk losing customers and their reputation. Growing consumer awareness of how a product is produced often results in corporations having to clean up their act and re-duce the (often unnecessary) harm they are causing. Rainforest Alliance's campaign to highlight the fact that loans that were facilitating rainforest destruction in the Amazon persuaded Citibank and many other financial institutions to adopt the Equator Principles, a set of environmental and ethical conditions that must be fulfilled by loan applicants to qualify for loans by these institutions. Global Witness's campaign against conflict diamonds mined under dangerous and destructive conditions while fi-nancing civil war facilitated the establishment of the Kimberley Process, a government–civil-society–industry coalition to stop these diamonds from entering the market (although Global Witness left the Kimberley Process in December 2011). There are many more stories of environmental and social organizations raising consumer awareness and causing corpora-tions to clean up, and these are usually infused with the nice underdog-wins feeling. However, it's also illustrative that most of the corporations that were targeted and that changed their practices made money in the end, usually by harnessing some of the consumer's willingness to pay for ethically produced products.

Such cases can be puzzling, particularly to neoclassical economists. They are stories of the $20 bill on the sidewalk—if any advantages to cor-porations acting more responsibly truly exist, why haven't they yet picked up on them? After all, if these companies could make money from activi-ties that are environmentally sustainable and ethically sound, why aren't they acting on them already? And if this is true, why do we need regula-tion at all? In some instances, overcompliance has been very profitable indeed; BP's commitment to reduce its greenhouse-gas footprint at the time of the Kyoto Protocol netted it $630 million when it then sold gas from the oil fields that it would have otherwise flared.[9]

One reason for corporations failing to take advantage of such opportunities to do well by doing right is the absence of simple market and price discovery. Since real-world markets are fraught with information deficiencies among other imperfections, it can take time to discover that there is a market for your waste and that such a market is accessible. Nonetheless, some corporations are discovering the economic benefits of being less wasteful, and are finding that one organization's waste is another's input. Dow Chemical's energy-efficiency investments in Louisiana averaged a return of 204 percent between 1981 and 1993, and corporations with as wide a range of operations as Anheuser-Busch Breweries and DuPont profit from selling their waste.[10]

The poster child of such profitable and externality-considerate initiatives is General Electric, leading the way on "lean manufacturing techniques" that attempt to minimize resource use per unit in production, scaling up renewable energy technologies and revolutionizing ways in which energy-use systems can be made more efficient through a wide array of methods that even include social media. GE's ecomagination product sales surpassed $20 billion in 2009, and its investment fund in clean-technology companies crossed the billion-dollar mark in 2007. GE employs nearly 300,000 people in 160 countries,[11] and the company has won scores of awards for being a frontrunner in many aspects of its operations, including its ranking as one of the World's Most Admired Companies by *Fortune* magazine every year since 2005.[12]

These activities are illustrative of a process of market evolution and development, either through realizing that there is demand for what corporations would otherwise have sold as waste, or more important, for understanding increasing resource scarcity and the increasing returns to using technology that would either use fewer resources, or using available, renewable energy resources. As scarcities become more apparent, there are increasing returns to investing in technologies that address these scarcities. Despite the recession, profits from GE's ecomagination brand grew a whopping 113 percent between 2005 and 2009, to $7.1 billion, while revenues grew 200 percent.[13]

What is vital to note here is that in many instances, these corporations have performed astronomically well while playing odds stacked against them, given the taxes and subsidies in place that still favor the older market structures.

Can Accountants Save the World?

Our current understanding of the extent to which corporations cause externalities is fuzzy at best. There is a common aphorism in business management that "you cannot manage what you do not measure." Perhaps a concomitant truth is that "what you measure, you will most probably manage." Most governments are fixated on measuring classical GDP and managing GDP growth, foregoing many more holistic and relevant macroeconomic indicators such as Inclusive Wealth and Green GDP—which is what happens when you are measuring the only thing that you know how to measure.

The first solution in the tool kit for change is a better accounting framework, one that reflects both positive and negative externalities in a corporation's financial statements and thus makes transparent not only its holistic impact on the economy, society and the environment, but also its exposure to risks of resource constraints and regulation. Setting up such a framework internationally would be no mean feat, but it is in the realm of the possible; after all, there is an international accounting framework for all large corporations, the International Financial Reporting Standard (IFRS) of the International Accounting Standards Board (IASB). One complexity arises out of the diversity of externalities—freshwater preemption, human health costs, climate-changing emissions, and biodiversity losses, for example—and the diversity of circumstances in which they take place. Different industries have differing impacts on human health or ecosystems. Different ecosystems and their locations produce varying levels of public benefits, and the size of the economic losses associated with such benefits depends *inter alia* on the socioeconomic circumstances of those affected. Studies have shown that such complexities create challenges, but they are not impossible to overcome. The estimation and valuation methodology that addresses them can be researched and laid down.[14]

The next link in this chain is standardization. Although there may be a dozen ways to calculate the freshwater externalities of a cement

plant—across locations, ecosystem types, and types of cement plants—
there should not be 12 accounting standards. On the contrary, there
should be one, with clear parameters and simple enough for the industry to use. After an externalities-estimation methodology has been described and standards set, there is the need for assurance and disclosure,
the need to *audit* and to *report* on the measure of the externality. A significant movement toward one report (rather than separate financial and
sustainability results) led by A4S and GRI has formed a body of senior
experts to describe a "One Report" standard for such disclosures.[15] Recently, the Institute of Chartered Accountants of England and Wales
began hosting a "TEEB for Business Coalition" whose main task was to
calculate corporate externalities. Remarkably, within a year of formation
this coalition has been recognized and funded by the governments of the
United Kingdom and Singapore, as well as the Gordon and Betty Moore
Foundation, a large US philanthropic institution. An ambitious program
of first prioritizing and then quantifying the top 100 global externalities
is currently being launched. A mechanism of this type ensures that investors are adequately aware of the broad set of relevant risks faced by any
corporation with large externalities, as opposed to the narrower risks that
are currently reported.

There are, of course, any number of questions that remain. What
should be done about transactions that are conducted in the market but
do not reflect the actual value of the resource to society, often due to pricing policies? Clean water is a good example of a resource that is usually
underpriced on the market relative to its scarcity, mostly due to political
considerations. It is not only advisable but necessary for a forward-thinking corporation to price these resources accurately, and the tools for doing so are already becoming available in the form of better valuation techniques and geographical data on local availability. The TRUEVA study
provided an example of research that calculated the true economic value
added of several corporations, collecting data on their resource use and
establishing the frequent negative impacts. Even better examples are two
corporations well ahead of the pack, Puma and Infosys. Both corporations are leading the process of change and are well positioned to realize
the economic benefits of doing so.

The Cat That Roared

In 2011, Puma became the first company in the world to construct an environmental profit-and-loss account that mirrors regular accounting profit-and-loss accounts.

"I believe we need to move out of the era of business that causes collateral damage, and into the era of business that causes collateral benefits," says Jochen Zeitz, executive chairman of PUMA and chief sustainability officer of PPR Home, a sustainability initiative poised to move far beyond standard corporate-responsibility efforts. Puma partnered with Price Waterhouse Cooper to value their greenhouse-gas (GHG) emissions, and with Trucost for their water use. This breakthrough initiative measures, monetizes, and aggregates the negative externalities caused by Puma's GHG emissions, and thus its contribution to climate change, as well as its water use, land-use change, air pollution, and waste along its value chain.[16] Interestingly, the value of its water use was not set as the market price where it is used, which rarely reflects its true scarcity value, but through a process of modeling that accurately reflects the true social cost at its source. This straightforward, careful, no-smoke-and-mirrors approach is the product of a corporation that is forward-thinking and adaptable, which recognizes that its long-term benefit is to harmonize its operations with society's welfare and not focus on short-term arbitrage.

Puma's approach illustrates how visionary leadership can translate into initiatives that redefine the role of the corporation, advancing it to the next stage of its evolution while transforming the rules of competitive advantage. Puma carefully analyzed the direct impacts of its operations, as well as impacts at four tiers along the supply chain. Its environmental externalities are valued at $188 million, most of it from sources early in the supply chain.[17] The next step in its goal of fully integrating externalities into its accounts would be to measure social impacts such as community cohesion and diversity and gender equality, followed by positive externalities such as job creation and productivity growth.[18] These would enable the formation of a comprehensive environmental profit-and-loss account, which could be integrated into its main financial accounts. The formation of these accounts would provide vital information regarding

Puma's operational strengths and weaknesses, the company's potential to increase efficiency and cut costs, and most importantly, its sources of risk to the production and distribution processes. As Alan McGill, partner in Price Waterhouse Cooper's Sustainability and Climate Change practice, commented, "Fundamentally, this analysis is about risk management for the environment, and for business, because you cannot separate the two."

Such accounts also provide the benchmark for setting and achieving sustainability goals. A goal of 100 percent sustainable packaging and 25 percent reductions of carbon, energy, and water by 2015 would contribute to the reduction of Puma's supply-chain risk related to sudden price increases of underpriced resources due to regulation, and would prevent depletion of free or underpriced resources. Puma has already begun to engage its manufacturers (or its Tier 1 supplier levels), and aims to engage suppliers along its entire supply chain, especially since the suppliers further along the supply chain have the largest environmental impact.

Other studies that value positive externalities are also becoming available, including one conducted by GIST Advisory for Infosys, as discussed in the previous chapter. As we've already seen, Infosys generates enormous human-capital externalities as it trains thousands of employees annually, as well as when those employees leave Infosys to join other companies post-training. GIST Advisory estimated this human-capital externality using a variety of scenarios for the salary growth and attrition rates of employees who comprise this externality, as well as discount rates. It is clear that this positive externality is enormous, estimated at over $1.4 billion in 2012.

Getting to Voluntary Disclosure

Progressive programs like the international, nonprofit Carbon Disclosure Project (CDP) are a first step in getting corporations to include the full extent of their externalities in their main financial statements. Formed more than ten years ago, it now houses the largest database of GHG emissions and energy use in the world, with more than 3,050 companies voluntarily responding to its enquiries in 2010, up from 235 in 2003.[19] Its programs also include institutional disclosure regarding water use as well as a program to help local and national governments minimize the GHG impact along the supply chain of public procurement programs. In 2011, for the first time, the majority of responding companies reported that they had embedded climate-change actions as part of their business strategy.[20] Companies measure and report their GHG externality, one of the most significant negative externalities caused by corporations, as measured by the value of social damages through climate-change impacts. CDP not only creates a repository of the corporations' emissions, but it also works with them to reduce their environmental footprint, identifying opportunities for GHG reductions along their supply chain. It is an enlightened initiative, and its clients include corporations as diverse as Walmart and Dell. While it is an important step in a larger process of full disclosure, it does not require the corporation to include the value of its GHG impact or any other externality in its financial statements. Corporations engaging the government proactively would not only gain a degree of certainty upon which to base long-term investment decisions, but they also gain economic and political support to streamline these regulatory initiatives, in the form of subsidies and tax breaks.

Another recent and noteworthy development is that of private companies that evaluate the extent of corporations' externalities. Trucost PLC, a British finance-research firm has been one of the front-runners of this movement, engaging with corporations to develop mostly confidential databases that enable them to estimate a corporation's externalities and thus the extent to which their operations are at risk of regulation. A recent study by Trucost estimated annual environmental costs from global economic activity at about $ 6.6 trillion, or 11 percent of global GDP in 2008. To gauge the extent of risk exposure of companies, Trucost constructed a $10 billion hypothetical fund and "invested" it in the MSCI All Country World Index, which includes over 2,400 listed companies in countries at various levels of development. They found that the costs of externalities were over 50 percent of the earnings, suggesting that over half the earnings were exposed to the risk of regulation that would require corporations to internalize the costs of their environmental damages.

It is also becoming apparent that investors are becoming interested in the environmental, social, and governance indicators of companies. Perhaps investors perceive corporations that perform well on these indicators to be under careful management or more diversified, and thus less risky. The reasons notwithstanding, recent research from Harvard Business School shows that investors are increasingly seeking out nonfinancial information about companies and they are most interested in such indicators as these.[21]

What is also clear is that companies are increasingly listing resource scarcity such as water and regulatory risk along with their future profit-ability risks,[22] as well as concerns about increased consumer-awareness issues on broader issues surrounding corporate externalities.[23] Further-more, consumers are increasingly willing to pay higher prices for ethically and sustainably produced commodities. In a lecture titled "Doing Well by Being Green," Professor Geoffrey Heal from the Columbia Business School described an experiment conducted at the ABC Department Store in Manhattan. The study looked at two sets of towels made by compet-ing brands, both sustainably produced using organic cotton and under fair-trade conditions, though no information in this regard was initially provided to consumers. One set of towels was then so labeled, with the result that sales of the "green-labeled" brand rose by 10 percent and later fell to pre-labeling levels only when price was increased by 20 percent. After removing the labels from the first set for a period, the second set of towels was labeled as having been produced under environmentally and socially conscious conditions, which also resulting in rising sales. Clearly, there exists a demand, in some cases unmet, for goods and services that are produced under environmentally sustainable and fair-labor condi-tions. Another illustration of this can be found in the 106 percent annual average increase in the demand for Rainforest Alliance Certified coffee from 2003 through 2006.[24]

Overall, there seems to be an increasing understanding among the major stakeholders of a corporation—investors, managers, and consum-ers—that corporations' externalities can both cause a significant impact on society and can leave the corporation exposed to resource scarcity and regulatory risk. An accounting framework that takes into account these risk exposures and makes explicit the magnitude of these externalities is the obvious and necessary next step in the evolution of financial ac-counting. These frameworks are already being developed at a rapid pace by forward-thinking corporations such as Puma and by institutions such as the Global Reporting Initiative (GRI). GRI promotes the importance of developing and disseminating comprehensive reporting guidelines to enable corporations to report their impacts on numerous dimensions, including those relating to the environment, local communities, labor practices, and product responsibility. GRI is constantly updating its reporting frameworks to reflect newer knowledge of ecosystem valuation and developments on other performance indicators, and interestingly, it has seen a tremendous response from organizations in the developing world.

Reporting mechanisms like the CDP and the GRI guidelines are extremely progressive in their objective to ensure that a corporation's impacts on society and the environment are stated explicitly, and mechanisms such as these have contributed to the evolution of Puma-like profit-and-loss accounts that monetize externality. An accounting framework that accounts for this scarcity value and opportunity cost comes closer to measuring the value of the resources used to society. It also ensures that resources can be put to their most profitable use while documenting corporations' risk exposures to resource scarcity.

And What about Actuaries?

Over time, historical events have informed the processes regarding the level of disclosure that corporations are required to undertake. Risk-sharing mechanisms have been characteristic of economic and social interactions for thousands of years. In 2000 and 3000 BC, Chinese and Babylonian ship captains divided their cargoes among several ships while navigating treacherous waters in order to maximize the probability that at least some of their cargo would survive. In Ancient Iran, Achaemenian monarchs ran a form of public insurance for expensive assets. The famous Code of Hammurabi, which dates to about 1700 BC, included an insurance policy in the form of loans to attenuate losses caused to traders of goods in transit.[25] As commerce has expanded, increasingly efficient mechanisms have been deployed to reflect and mitigate risks associated with economic activities.

From its very inception, the insurance industry has been an essential actor in encouraging industries to disclose risk exposures faced by them, at least those risks that the insurance industry may be called upon to reimburse. On September 2, 1666, the Great Fire of London began in Pudding Lane at King Charles's favorite bakery. It spread across over

80 percent of London, burning more than 13,000 houses over four days and leaving 200,000 people without homes or workplaces. It also sparked the opportunity for the creation of the first insurance company.[26] It was the brainchild of a Dr. Nicholas Barebon (interestingly christened If-Jesus-Christ-Had-Not-Died-For-Thee-Thou-Hadst-Been-Damned Barebon), who became engaged in and then won a price war with the government. The company offered a limited liability contract of up to £5,000 and, in return for a premium, promised to rebuild the client's house in event of the fire, as well as employed "watermen and other lusty Persons . . . in liveries with Badges" to serve as a fire brigade.[27] Even the earliest premiums reflected the risk associated with specific building materials and encouraged the use of relatively fire-safe materials—for instance, the premium was 2 percent of the rental value for brick, but 5 percent for wood.[28] Thus, from its very inception, the insurance industry provided economic incentives for clients to undertake actions that would make them less risk-prone, or to mitigate the "moral hazard" problem. This, of course, is reflected in current premium pricing as well.

The mandate of the insurance industry to minimize risk is easily seen in the reporting requirements it requires its clients to undertake. Corporations usually need to submit detailed financial reports of activities undertaken, including assets acquired and divested, in order to ensure that their risk profile does not change drastically from one period to the next.[29] Insurance jargon refers to risks as "exposures," since they lead to loss or reduction in the value of the insured resources, typically by natural hazards or negligence. If the TRUEVA measure became an additional disclosure requirement from insurers, it could be used to deny or restrict access to valuable resources that the firms are currently using either for free or at rates cheaper than future regulations might stipulate. Such disclosure to insurers would also include positive externalities that a firm generates, such as the human-capital formation or community networks that it is responsible for but does not profit from, but which does help to secure its social licence to operate. A balance sheet of this form, one that comprehensively represents the full extent and impact of a firm's activities, forms the cornerstone of the initiatives that a dynamic and futuristic corporation must undertake.

Regulations, Taxes, and Subsidies as Enabling Conditions

Tax and subsidy structures for businesses are supposed to encourage investment and economic activity in avenues that benefit society. If there are externalities in place, the economic logic of these taxes and subsidies is quite obvious. And yet current subsidies in most countries, particularly in the energy sector, favor fossil fuels and coal-fired power plants, which, as we've seen, often have a *negative* value added. Despite these lopsided economic incentives—lopsided since they are at odds with what would maximize returns for society and the economy—some corporations such as GE have innovated and profited. Their efforts have translated into a first-mover advantage where they have used their head start in technology development to capture large market shares and define the newer directions for the development of these technologies.

Tax and subsidy structures that incorporate more of the externalities that economic activities caused would be closer to the *raison d'être* of government support for businesses and would reflect more closely the actual economic returns to different technologies and processes by changing their prices to reflect their entire costs and benefits, *inclusive of externalities*, to society.

Getting these prices right, and receiving government facilitation of investment into economic conditions that generate positive externalities, would also facilitate the development of economies of scale that occur at the industry- and economy-wide level, instead of just the level of one corporation. In other words, there are instances where something that would not have been profitable for one firm to undertake generates profits for all concerned firms if conducted at an aggregated level. This is the ethos behind the new wave of industrial parks such as the Dow Value Park in Germany and the Kalundborg industrial ecology park in Denmark.[30] Their aim is to synergize production processes by way of material flows as well as technologies, thereby facilitating economies of scale by minimizing transaction costs. Finding buyers for recyclable materials, negotiating prices, and organizing transportation logistics are all made easier by an agglomeration of industrial facilities with complementary production processes. These economies of scale also exist for knowledge, and over time R&D spillovers can have significant impacts on productivity for industries and entire economies.

Regulations

There are several recent policies that illustrate how the regulatory environment is shifting toward regarding environmental risk generated by corporations as a major source of production risk, one that should be transparently reported to all its stakeholders. There is a strong case to be made for incorporating *ex-ante* mechanisms in corporations' operations that measure, report, and minimize the net negative impact of corporations on society, instead of the current *ex-post* measures such as trying to account for the impacts caused by an oil spill. Corporations that strive only to achieve the minimum standards stipulated by policy increase their relative risk exposure to regulation and resource scarcity that can run into trillions of dollars.

There are several notable regulations that attempt to directly address negative externalities, especially those caused by obesity and smoking. The state of New York has had high taxes on tobacco in place for several years. In 2010, it increased them significantly, to $4.35 per cigarette pack,[31] proposing that the increased revenues be used to finance an expansion of the State Children's Health Insurance Program, or SCHIP.[32] In October 2011, Denmark introduced a tax on foods high in saturated fat that is equivalent to about $3.00 for every 2.2 lbs of saturated fat, enough to increase the price of a cheeseburger by about 40 cents.[33] France swiftly followed suit with a tax to raise the prices of sugary drinks, supplementing it with initiatives to limit the amount of mayonnaise and ketchup in school cafeterias.[34] The economic logic behind these taxes seeks to address classic externality effects of goods and services that cause ill health and thus impose a burden on society in the form of morbidity and mortality health costs, lost productivity, and disutility from illness. Most of these costs are seldom borne solely by the individual, especially in countries where health care has government support. This is true even in countries not usually considered to have very large government intervention in the health sectors. According to recent research from the journal *Obesity*, "The annual cost of obesity to the US health care system could now be as high as $147 billion . . . 23% of this total was financed by Medicare and

19% by Medicaid . . . [and] between 22% and 55% of the state-level costs of obesity are financed by the public sector via Medicare and Medicaid."[35] Such taxes attempt to internalize the costs of products that impose tremendous negative externalities on society and thus to ensure that society consumes these goods in optimal quantities.

There have been several instances of regulation that recognized the need to internalize environmental externalities, from the emissions-trading programs under the Clean Air Act in the United States in the 1990s to the more recent EU Emissions Trading Scheme's carbon-trading program. Opponents of such regulation often assert that "the market will take care of it." Which would be true if such a market existed. Which it doesn't. The need is to create a market, which is precisely what such regulation does. Another objection is that environmental regulation causes economic losses through labor movement across sectors. While this is likely to be true, for such regulation to be harmful to society the costs need to be higher than the benefits, which is unlikely in a well-structured policy. Recent research from Columbia University found costs of $9 billion in forgone earnings of labor in newly regulated plants under the Clean Air Act Amendments for the six years after the change in policy. While this is doubtless significant, the health benefits from this regulation are estimated at between $160 billion and $1.6 trillion, several orders of magnitude higher.[36]

Recent progressive state-level policies notably include New Mexico's environmental reporting rules that require large and medium emitters to report GHG emissions as well as those of local pollutants such as sulfur dioxide (SO_2), nitrous oxide (N_2O), and some particulates.[37] The new wave of regulation that identifies and targets externalities is very present in developing economies. China, for instance, recently instituted a ban on logging that was causing downstream freshwater losses. India is implementing a pilot emissions-trading program in several states, drawing on expertise from MIT professors and using the lessons learned during the implementation of US emissions-trading programs.[38]

Even recent regulatory proposals, coming in the wake of the financial crisis, that are aimed at better financial governance include provisions that may have significant implications for supply-chain risks of certain corporations. Section 1502 of the Dodd-Frank Act requires corporations that come under the jurisdiction of the SEC to report whether the sources of the minerals they use in their production process includes areas where conflict mining may occur, such as the Democratic Republic of Congo. Companies are also required to report on the due-diligence measures undertaken to verify the sources of these minerals.[39]

One of the primary beneficiaries of this requirement would be the semiconductor industry, whose supply chain would be extremely vulnerable to risks regarding some of these metals. Such progressive measures underscore both the fact that regulatory frameworks may begin to regulate different sources of risk and also the importance of developing forward-looking corporate strategies to avoid being locked into unsustainable investments, whether financial, environmental, or otherwise.

Regulation that targets negative externalities to supply chains would also be crucial in cases where any one corporation is unable to enforce sustainable sourcing. This could be due to its small market share as a buyer of raw material. For example, even though Unilever is the world's largest buyer of palm oil, it buys only 4 percent of global output. Such a small share means that it is less able to enforce sustainable practices on its suppliers, although it can still have an impact on regions where it is a larger buyer. Unilever has, in fact, had trouble with non-complying suppliers after its commitment to source sustainable palm oil, including one that was a member of RSPO.[40]

When a buyer's small market share impedes its ability to ensure best practices by its suppliers, the case can be made for regulation that would benefit all corporations in the industry by reducing any one corporation's monitoring costs, as well as any costs around searching and switching suppliers, creating industry-wide economies of scale.

Some regulation seeks to implement a more comprehensive accounting system that would give a truer picture of a corporation's health and future challenges. The 2005 EU Accounts Modernization Directive (AMD) mandates medium and large companies to produce an "enhanced directors' report" that would include, in addition to key financial indicators, "at least a fair review of the development and performance of the company's business . . . together with the principal risks and uncertainties that it faces," as well as, "where appropriate, analysis using other key performance indicators, including information relating to environmental matters and employee matters."[41] While the "where appropriate" clause is slightly puzzling (when is it *not* appropriate to include performance indicators regarding environmental and employee matters?), it is a positive step toward regulation that would facilitate a standardized reporting mechanism that includes the monetized value of the company's externalities, both positive and negative, into its financial accounts. It is this final step that would ensure that the economy as whole is accounting correctly for its assets and liabilities, including all forms of capital (as will be detailed in Chapter 9).

In customizing the EU AMD, the UK initially went a step further—it distinguished between reporting by listed and non-listed companies, with more stringent reporting requirements for the former, emphasizing that companies with shareholders had responsibility to provide more information. The requirement noted that "the Government believes that the shareholder base of quoted companies—typically large and diverse—has different and additional needs to that of private companies, hence the requirement to prepare more fulsome, and more forward-looking review than that required under the [EU Modernisation] Directive."[42] In November 2005, the EU watered down this requirement, citing reporting costs. (As an aside, the cost of reporting is an excellent example where economies of scale of knowledge would prevail, but were not allowed to kick in.) Interestingly, not all the business community supported this weakening of the reporting requirement. The new avatar of this regulation, the UK Companies Act (2006) was very similar to EU AMD, in stipulating that the business review must, to the extent necessary for the understanding of the development, performance, or position of the company's business, include

a) the main trends and factors likely to affect the future development, performance, and position of the company's business;

b) information about (1) environmental matters (including the impact of the company's business on the environment), (2) the company's employees, and (3) social and community issues, including information about any policies of the company in relation to those matters and the effectiveness of those policies; and

c) information about persons with whom the company has

contractual or other arrangements that are essential to the business of the company.[43]

The existence of a uniform reporting mechanism established by combining leading current research on externalities valuation and risk assessment would ensure awareness of the current and projected magnitude of a corporation's operations, supply chain, and investments' external impact on society, economy, and capital stock (defined broadly, not narrowly as is currently done). It would also enable corporations to identify sources of negative and positive impacts that they can target with ease and facilitate the economies of scale for human capital as required for reporting. Finally, it would facilitate resource allocation and regulation that would help to get the prices right—that is, to reflect true economic scarcity and externalities of commodities.

CHAPTER SIX

Accountable Advertising

*Whether or not the standard of living made possible by mass
production and in turn by mass circulation is supported by
and filled with the work of us hucksters, I guess is something
that only history can decide.*

— Leo Burnett

Advertising is a very small global business with an inordinately high share
of voice. Global advertising turnover is estimated to be around US$500
billion, less than Walmart and Carrefour combined.[1] However, everything
we buy, everything corporations sell, every commercial message that media projects into our conscious and unconscious minds every day of the
week, every week of the year, was designed and placed there by marketing and advertising companies. Marketing and advertising converts wants
into needs, sometimes creating new wants out of human insecurities,
which are then skillfully transformed into new consumer needs that must
be met. It would not be an exaggeration to say that advertising is the
single biggest force driving consumer demand today.

However, advertising agencies and practitioners of the craft generally do not see themselves as a business per se, but rather, as professional
consultants assisting their business clients. They understand the ethics or
externalities of their clients' businesses but generally do not take a stand;
they are there to carry out their clients' will. Many advertising professionals believe that they are hired guns and hence not entitled to opinions. In
other words, ethics in advertising are at best an aspiration, most often an
option to be exercised when it suits the client, and at worst, an oxymoron.

How did such a situation arise? If advertising is not a business sector, then what is it? And if it *is* a business sector, as this chapter argues, then what are its main "externalities"? If there are negative externalities, what can be done to manage or reduce or eliminate them? Does anything need to be done at all, or will the fast-changing nature of the "advertiser-consumer-business" relationship achieve the changes we seek for Corporation 2020? These are the key questions addressed by this chapter on making advertising accountable.

We begin with a telling example of how advertising influences consumption, turning human insecurity into a want, then converting that want into a need that just *has* to be met, and then profiting from the consequent surge in consumer demand and sales. This is the story of the marketing of cigarettes to women, an example of "good selling, but not selling good."[2]

The Smoke and Mirrors

With the outbreak of World War I, American women were experiencing growing responsibility and freedom in their homes, as well as a larger role in society as wartime employees. An increasing number were using cigarettes as an instrument to challenge traditional ideas about female behavior. With the right to vote in 1920 came the need to share male symbols of social behavior, and smoking in public was one of those things that signified *equality* to many women of that generation. The American tobacco industry seized upon this liberal social climate of the 1920s and 30s and exploited its themes of emancipation and power in order to recruit an untapped female market.[3] The cigarette, a social liability until that time, was turned into an acceptable and desirable commodity for women to indulge in openly.

The opportunity that the women's market presented was recognized by Percival Hill, the president of the American Tobacco Company. Hill's innovation was to market cigarettes as an extension of femininity—characterized in those days by bobbed hair, short skirts, and, most important, slim waistlines.[4] Lucky Strike's campaign ("Reach for a Lucky Instead of a Sweet") was successful in getting women to see smoking as a means of weight control.[5] After one year, this campaign led to more than a 300 percent increase in sales for the brand.[6]

Almost 100 years have gone by but some things have not changed. Women still want to be slim and therefore desirable, and this idea is at the heart of most claims targeted at women. However, while brands such as Camel and Lucky Strike had advertising that was targeted at women, the key demographic nevertheless continued to be male.

Noticing further potential, in 1968 Philip Morris launched "Virginia Slims," the first cigarette designed *specifically* with the female consumer in mind. From a slimmer cigarette to a pack design that was slim and pastel and meant to slip easily into a purse, Virginia Slims were targeted at women. It is reported that the company spent close to a year and millions of dollars on research and development to get the right mix of marketing elements. The proposition for the brand—"for the independent woman of today"—was brought alive with the tag line "You've come a long way, baby." The brand's first test market was a six-month trial in San Francisco, California. It was soon apparent that Leo Burnett, the Chicago-based advertising agency which designed this campaign, had hit a bull's-eye. In less than two months after Virginia Slims was first released, the brand had already achieved a 1.1 percent market share in San Francisco, which a Philip Morris internal document refers to as "nothing short of a smashing success."[7] Thus, the decision was made to roll out the brand countrywide across the United States.

During the 1960s and '70s, feminism and female liberation were common themes in these advertisements. Often a reference was made to women who in the '20s had faced censure from their menfolk for having been caught smoking in public.[8] Usually these ads compared women's smoking to ideals such as the right to vote, thereby creating a strong positive association in the minds of women who had just discovered their freedom. The advertising industry certainly knew which buttons to press. Market research, diagnostic research, psychologists, sociologists, anthropologists, and every possible stream of science would be called upon to understand the consumer and build communication that addressed or exploited their fears and inadequacies.

Studies have shown a direct link between tobacco advertising and consumption. In 1990, New Zealand banned tobacco advertising and sponsorships, and sales dropped by 7.5 percent.[9] This statistic may seem superfluous, as it may appear to confirm what is obvious, but it is relevant.

It illustrates the remarkable resistance of tobacco advertising to buckle in the face of half a century of mounting evidence of tobacco's damaging impacts on human health.

Ensuring that cigarette advertising did not mislead consumers would have been an obvious strategy to contain public health damage and costs. However, it is salutary to learn how hard the tobacco industry fought to misrepresent the impacts of tobacco on human health, and for how long they succeeded in preventing any action to constrain misleading advertising. Since the 1930s, tobacco advertising had actually laid claims to health *benefits* from smoking, a stance that concerned the Federal Trade Commission (FTC). But it was not until 1957 that the US Public Health Service took a stand on this issue, with Surgeon General Leroy E. Burney announcing that there was a causal relationship between smoking and lung cancer.[10] Even so, no legislative action followed. It was not until four years later, in 1961, when four major health NGOs wrote to President John F. Kennedy on the subject, and won his concern and support, that a commission was called to launch an investigation on the matter. Finally, in 1964 a report on smoking and health was published by an advisory committee to US Surgeon General Luther L. Terry, after a 14-month-long evaluation by a team of 150 experts of over 7,000 scientific papers and articles on the subject. On the basis of this report, the FTC concluded that cigarette advertising that did not disclose the health risks of smoking was "unfair and deceptive."[11] The tobacco industry beseeched Congress for protection and further delayed legislation on tobacco advertising.

At last, on January 2, 1971, almost 40 years since the matter had become a concern of US national agencies, tobacco advertising was finally banned from television and radio in the United States.

Despite the ban, and thanks to smart advertising and trademark extensions, big tobacco brands continued to occupy center stage. Creative ingenuity flowed from the best brains in the advertising business, and at each stage, the advertising industry stayed one step ahead of legislation, bending the law but never quite breaking it. In 1997, many years after the United States had banned tobacco advertising, the United Kingdom was all set to legislate a similar ban. At this critical moment, the advertising firm Saatchi & Saatchi created a campaign for a tobacco brand called Silk Cut. These ads pictured scissors cutting through purple silk with the Silk

Cut logo on it. Once the ban was announced, Silk Cut removed their logo from the advertisements, leaving only the image of the silk with an artistic cut through the middle. Even without the logo, a staggering 98 percent of surveyed consumers associated these product-less advertisements with Silk Cut.[12] Advertising had followed the letter of the law but not its spirit—one of the oldest tricks in the book of unethical business conduct.

In 2006, tobacco companies spent around $34 million per day in marketing their products in the United States.[13] Today, advertising and marketing expenditures (so-called ad spends) have reduced because the avenues available have been reduced. When advertising on mass media was banned, agencies responded by raising the bar on sponsorships. This period saw the rise of the sporting event built around the concept of lifestyle marketing. Specialized units were set up to push the regulatory envelope and get marketers to spend more and more, despite the advertising ban. The advertising industry is known for its ability to balance on the fence. Agencies are only too happy to spend tobacco dollars. The justification is that cigarette manufacture is a legitimate business, and therefore its promotion is equally legitimate.

But when we look deeper, cigarettes are certainly not as legitimate as they would have consumers think. When the medical payments for the health effects of smoking are tallied, the result is about $72.7 billion per year, according to health economists at the University of California.[14] Dorothy Rice, the coauthor of the report pointed out that the 1993 bill for smoking-related disease costs in California alone was $8.7 billion. New York followed closely with an estimated $6.6 billion in costs. Overall, the health effects of smoking accounted for 11.8 percent of total medical expenditures in the United States. Estimating (conservatively) that the rest of the world added another $72 billion to the annual cost of caring for tobacco related health problems, we are looking at a global spend of close to $150 billion per annum, and this based on 1998 costs. This is more than four times as large as the total profits of the top six tobacco companies.[15]

The question begs to be asked: if the cost of a cigarette reflected the true cost of the impact of that cigarette on the lives of those who smoked it, their families and associates, and the taxpayers who pay for some of these health bills, who then would make cigarettes, and who would want to smoke?

In the Master Settlement Agreement (MSA) established in 1998 between the attorneys general of 46 states and the four largest US tobacco companies (Philip Morris USA, R. J. Reynolds Tobacco Company, Brown & Williamson Tobacco Corp, and Lorillard Tobacco Company), these companies agreed to pay a minimum of around $206 billion over the *first 25 years* of the agreement.[16] In doing so, they were not only accepting their liability but also affirming that the sale of tobacco products remained lucrative business. But this amount pales in comparison to the estimated health costs, which, even if one conservatively assumes no increase in the extent of health care for smoking-related diseases over 25 years, and inflation at current low levels, would amount to $2.35 *trillion* during this 25-year period, or over 11 times the amount committed by these four big tobacco companies. When discounting is also taken into account, this ratio of costs to payments grows to over 14 times.[17]

Big Tobacco could never have popularized cigarette smoking without the help of advertising. Images linked to smoking cigarettes have always been carefully composed and orchestrated. The post-coffee cigarette, the postprandial cigarette, the postcoital cigarette, the pre-interview cigarette, the post-interview cigarette—the time was always right for a smoke, and advertising ensured that you knew it. Generations of advertising executives have built these associations in our minds, and they continue to do so.

The narrowed gaze, the subtle pout, smoke curling lazily from the end, a symbol of freedom and desire—all these are images from advertisements. It was the advertising industry that built gratification into the very core of tobacco. It made Marlboro a symbol of machismo and Virginia Slims a mark of femininity. This ability to give nearly identical products completely different identities is a demonstration of the power of advertising, as well as its ability to shrug off any responsibility for the consequences.

Babies Make Good Business

There are many stories about advertising and its ability to turn a blind eye to the negative side effects of selling products to people who do not need them or indeed for whom they could be harmful. An iconic example is advertising for infant formula, a category that has unashamedly exploited the most visceral of emotions, the love of a mother for her child.

In West and Central Africa, 56 percent of child deaths could be avoided if children were not malnourished.[18] One of the best means of infant nourishment is breast milk. It is a widely accepted fact that an infant who is exclusively breast-fed for the first six months of its life builds immunity and the ability to withstand infections.[19] Breast milk is available to most infants regardless of economic circumstance. Many communities have wet nurses to help out when a mother has problems lactating, thus ensuring that the infant gets the proper nourishment required to build antibodies. However, the rate for exclusive breast-feeding in the region, according to a 2007 UNICEF report, was a mere 20 percent, among the lowest in the world. This downward spiral started in the late–1960s and early '70s, when baby-food manufacturers aggressively promoted infant formula on the grounds that it made babies healthier! Mothers would spend money that they could ill afford on buying infant formula. Because of poverty, expensive infant formula was often diluted more than was recommended, using water of unreliable quality. Poor hygiene and lack of bottle sterilization compounded the problem. Water-borne bacteria and germs added to the building catastrophe. The risk of malnutrition, disease, and death gets magnified if babies are deprived of the nutritional and immunological properties of breast milk and simultaneously exposed to the dangers of artificial feeding. Not surprisingly, infant mortality rates went through the roof, not only in Africa but also in other lesser-developed nations. A UNICEF estimate places the risk of diarrhea death to a formula-fed child in unhygienic conditions as seven times greater than the risk to a breast-fed child.[20]

In the 1970s, policy makers internationally began to recognize the link between the decline in breast-feeding worldwide and the marketing of commercial breast-milk substitutes. Dr. Cicely Williams, a pediatrician in Singapore in the late 1930s, was among the first to see the connection. In a 1939 speech to Singapore's Rotary Club titled "Milk and Murder," she pointed out that infants were dying because of inadequate feeding practices. She asserted that "misguided propaganda on infant feeding should be punished as the most criminal form of sedition, and those deaths should be regarded as murder."[21]

In 1970, in Sierra Leone, a survey counted 246 radio commercials for three infant formulas in one month. And billboards in Nigeria still

featured a chubby smiling baby and a can of SMA formula with the tag-
line, "Welcome to Nigeria, where SMA babies are healthy and happy."[22]

In 1981, the landmark International Code of Marketing of Breastmilk
Substitutes was established by the World Health Assembly to regulate infant formula marketing, including strict restrictions on advertising.[23] Unfortunately, many companies continued to advertise infant formula milk.
The resultant low level of breast-feeding accounts for an estimated 1.4
million deaths in children under five every year.[24] These mothers who
stopped breast-feeding thanks to infant formula advertising would not
have known that, according to advertising doyen David Ogilvy, "Advertising reflects the mores of society, but does not influence them."[25] For they
had certainly been influenced, and their babies were paying the price.

It is probably no coincidence that, as with the ban on tobacco advertising, it took modern society *40 years* to move from recognizing the harms
from Corporation 1920–style advertising of infant formula milk to any
actual legislation to ban such advertising.

Small but Shrill

As the examples of tobacco and infant formula both demonstrate, advertising may be a very small industry, but it is disproportionately loud,
powerful, and pervasive. Advertising executives love to read about themselves and their industry. In a developing but small market such as India,
where advertising turnover in 2010 was around US$5 billion, or just about
1 percent of the global total, the industry has eight print magazines and
over fifteen e-magazines![26]

The world of advertising is full of stars and divas. These men and
(a few) women are known the world over and enjoy a disproportionate
amount of presence and power in the public space. For example, there is
significant media attention to an interminable slanging match between Sir
Martin Sorrell and Maurice Levy, heads of the world's leading media and
advertising titans, WPP and Publicis Groupe. Do the top two houses in
any other industry engage in so much controversy or get so much media
coverage? And Sir Martin Sorell's economic predictions (e.g., his descrip-
tion of the recession as "bath-shaped" with a "corrugated bottom") may
be of little more than conversational value, but they still feature prominently in the financial press. The question begs to be asked: How much

does such coverage correlate with the influence of these advertising titans on the revenue generated by media?

And moreover: What is it about advertising that makes it such a hot topic, and a subject of general interest? Why does the whole world, even those not involved in the sector, think they know a lot about advertising? Perhaps it is because this is one activity that touches the lives of each and every human being on the planet—with no exceptions. Advertising, in some form or fashion, is part of our daily lives no matter who we are, or where. Even tribal communities living far away from the modern consumerism of the city dweller are exposed to advertising. Seeing what the Jones have, and desiring it, is human nature. Markets and business enterprise are cornerstones of human endeavor, and advertising has a role to play in both. From prehistoric barter to modern-day manipulation through mass media, the essence of selling your wares is the ability to make them desirable. Indeed, the whole industry is cloaked in an aura of desire. It is this universal appeal of advertising that ensures it gets more than its fair share of coverage and attention, and helps deliver its visible success.

On the positive side, when advertising is consciously used for social good, the power of this allure is not forgotten. Adam Werbach, the CEO of Saatchi & Saatchi S, when interviewed for this book emphasized that their mission was "making sustainability *irresistible*." He wants "to make [sustainability] something that people cannot resist having in their companies, in their daily lives, in the way they work, in the way they play. To make them understand that this is not just something that we *have* to do, like accounting, [but rather] something we *want* to do, because . . . it makes our lives better, it's something that's critical to the future, and it's something that we do because we're proud of it."[27]

The other factor ensuring that advertising gets center stage is its ability to provoke. Modern society has become increasingly intolerant of nonconformists, and the "middle path" (a phrase from Buddhist philosophy) has become the norm, though not quite in the manner intended by Lord Buddha. Advertising, however, is one area where provocation is not just tolerated but is indulgently encouraged. Clients want their advertising agencies to think out of the box. Sometimes they may pay the price for it, as happened in the case of the anti-tobacco advertisement "No More Killing" that was created by a Chinese agency and which ended up offending everyone, including nonsmokers. Or the advertisement for breast cancer that was considered too horrifying and so was banned by the authorities.[28] On the other hand, the Benetton campaign ("*Un*hate") is a great example of how advertising can shock and provoke and get people to talk and focus not just on a brand, but on issues that otherwise would have been lost to the man on the street.[29]

Thus the industry can provoke debate and direct attention in whichever direction it chooses to. Advertising is an incredibly powerful tool that can be used to either build or to break. This is why there is a crying need for advertising to be accountable and for the advertising industry to drive accountability among clients and marketers.

As we saw from the tobacco case, advertising knows which buttons to press. There have been many instances when this ability to mold opinions and change behavior has been used for the greater good of society. One of the more-recent examples was the campaign run by the local authorities in Beijing to curb spitting on the streets prior to the Olympic Games.[30] The campaign was developed by Ogilvy Shanghai and is reported to have had significant impact on the citizens of Beijing.

Advertising: A Waning Power?

The advertising business is becoming more and more cutthroat and seems to be staring at a bleak future. Commission income (the dominant model of charging clients a percentage of media spending) is decreasing. Many advertisers have switched from commissions to fixed fees. Furthermore, big advertisers are looking at a higher percentage of the agency revenue coming from performance-based fees. "Perform or perish" seems to be the mantra of the day.

It is this very visible segregation that helped companies such as Proctor & Gamble, Unilever, Coca-Cola, and Anheuser Busch lead a sea change in advertising agency compensation systems in 2009. P&G is reputed to be the first major advertiser that moved away from the traditional commission system to performance-linked compensation. They are a highly innovative consumer-products company that has over the years changed the rules of the game both within and without. Out of their total sales in 2009 of $79 billion, $7.6 billion was spent on agency fees and media expenses.

From among its roster of agencies, the Publicis Groupe alone receives around $900 million annually from P&G,[31] which represents about 15 percent of Publicis's annual revenue.[32] It is thus understandable that P&G would have considerable impact on the advertising agencies it employs.

In early 2009, Unilever also made significant changes to its agency compensation model, led by its new CEO, Paul Polman.[33] In 2008, Unilever had spent $7.2 billion globally on advertising and promotions. Agencies were informed that the new upfront profit margin of 5 percent, instead of the previous rate of 10 percent (with the possibility for bonuses), was not negotiable.[34]

According to Emma Cookson of the global advertising firm BBH, the advertising industry has for years been "approaching and avoiding" a change in how it is paid, but may not be able to do so much longer. In 2009 Coca-Cola announced that it would use a "value-based" compensation system that pays agencies for results achieved, rather than inputs and media costs.[35]

Unfortunately, many agencies frown upon such performance-linked remuneration because this makes them accountable. While agencies believe they build businesses and brands, they would ideally like to de-link remuneration from performance. When P&G decided to implement their sales-linked compensation structure, the agencies were up in arms. Ironically, there was even argument about whether sales had more to do with distribution than advertising. The lack of tested metrics was also voiced as a concern with the proposed system. P&G stuck to their guns and wisely used common industry platforms to gain traction for their revolutionary ideas. A number of other advertisers decided to follow suit. Today many of the large corporations across the globe pay as much as 50 percent of their total fees on performance-linked parameters.

This focus on effective message-delivery to consumers has an unpleasant side effect, which is probably best described as having a "tiger by the tail." In home, out of home, at work, at play, in sickness and in health, advertising messages chase you wherever you go. For many consumers, advertising is becoming the bane of modern existence. Consumers are finding advertising more and more intrusive and so there are opposing forces at play. Consumer resistance has built up and in some cases vocal consumer resistance has resulted in legislation to control advertising, if not ban it entirely. Telemarketing companies have had to face consumer ire in market after market. Controls have been imposed in most developed markets and consumers have the opportunity to opt out with schemes such as the Do Not Call Registry in the United States.

Advertising is constantly looking for new avenues to talk to consumers, but increasingly consumers want to shut down the cacophony or at least "talk back." A wonderful example of this two-way interaction is the Bubble Project. For this project, conceived in 2002, artist Ji Lee printed 15,000 blank stickers that looked like "speech bubbles" from comic strips, and pasted them on advertisements throughout New York City, thus allowing passers-by to write in their reactions, thoughts, and witticisms.

The manifesto of the Bubble Project talks about how "communal spaces are being overrun with ads. Train stations, streets, squares, buses, and subways now scream one message after another at us. Once considered public, these spaces are increasingly seized by corporations to propagate their messages. We the public, are both target and victim of this media attack."[36] As a result of the project, consumers became engaged in reclaiming the public "commons" and converted "corporate monologues into open public dialogues."[37] The Bubble Project grew popular and found imitations springing up in Argentina, Italy, and other countries.

In other parts of the world, legislation has intervened to keep public spaces "public." In 2007, São Paulo (one of the world's largest cities) became the first major city outside the communist world to ban almost all outdoor advertising.[38] In a city with two conflicting identities—it is both the commercial capital of Brazil and the epicenter of gang violence and extensive slums—São Paulo's Lei Cidade Limpa ("Clean City Law") is now considered an unexpected success. As part of this law, nearly all outdoor advertisements, including billboards, outdoor video screens, and ads on buses, were all torn down, and the size of storefront signage was regulated. The law was enforced with nearly $8 million in fines, and despite protests and legal challenges, more than 70 percent of city residents welcomed the move. In fact, even the head of Brazil's largest advertising company, Grupo ABC, said, "I think it's a good law. It was a challenge for us because, of course, it's easier to simply throw garbage advertising all over your city."[39]

Advertising Accountability and Corporation 2020

Advertising carries enormous significance in distinguishing a Corporation 1920 from a Corporation 2020 because of its power to persuade people to consume in ways that they would not have done if they had not been enticed to do so. Simply, advertising fuels consumption, turning previous "wants" into new "needs," but the ecological *footprint* of the products that meet these needs can and should be carefully considered by a Corporation 2020. Irresponsible consumerism cannot be a recipe for well-being, but the age-old question of "who will bell the cat?" is often raised. The Corporation 1920 response would be to hide behind the belief systems of free-market fundamentalism and proclaim blind faith in "market forces." However, as Jochen Zeitz (Executive Chairman of PUMA and CEO of the Sport & Lifestyle Group of PPR, interviewed for this book—see www.corp2020.com) points out, "Consumerism has been invented by the corporation, so it's our responsibility to change consumerism and make it more sustainable." He considers protestations of consumer unwillingness as "lame excuses," and he seeks innovative ways to make consumers excited about the opportunities for responsible consumption that "businesses—in particular, the branded-goods businesses—have to take as a challenge."

This challenge is to a significant extent a *measurement* challenge, because a product's footprint through its life cycle is not easy to measure. However, such measurement is being attempted in earnest by several large corporations. If a company can provide a net positive impact on society (holistically measured after accounting for externalized costs) by producing a particularly popular product, then that is a Corporation 2020 reason for doing so.

It should be noted that advertising is also the means to inform the public not only of a product's existence, but also of its benefits and its harms. Corporation 2020 advertisers ought to follow the principles that underpin many of the ethical advertising standards in existence today and should not misinform an audience of a product by showcasing its benefits alone, but should instead communicate the risks involved in the use of the product. However, in a Corporation 2020 context, advertising must be more accountable for the ways it fuels consumption and for the real outcomes that this consumption has in the long run—both in individual people's lives and in society overall.

Rising Consumer Power and the Changing Balance

On the March 15, 1962, President John F. Kennedy made a speech to Congress equating the rights of the ordinary American with national interest. He said, "If a consumer is offered inferior products, if prices are exorbitant, if drugs are unsafe or worthless, if the consumer is unable to choose on an informed basis, then his dollar is wasted, his health and safety may be threatened, and national interest suffers."[40] He claimed for the American consumer four basic rights:

1. *The Right to Safety*—consumers should be protected against the marketing of hazardous goods.
2. *The Right to Choose*—competition is necessary for consumers to have access to a variety of products and services. If this is not possible in a given industry, government regulation will provide adequate quality and service at fair prices.
3. *The Right to Information*—consumers should be given the necessary facts for an informed choice and protection against fraudulent or misleading information.
4. *The Right to Be Heard*—consumer interests should receive full consideration in the formulation of government policy.

By introducing these consumer rights, President Kennedy reflected the reality that US consumers were the economy's main driver, and yet, they lacked coherent voice or visibility in Congress. The 1980s and '90s saw the consumer movement take hold across the world. Consumer activism took off, supported by legislation and civil-society organizations.[41] Even the developing world saw an upsurge of activism. Many corporations realized that being perceived as a company committed to consumers' interests could become a competitive advantage, and this was the period when "guaranteed money back if not satisfied" become a standard marketing ploy. Unfortunately consumers were getting more and more confused with the plethora of choices and the claims and counterclaims. How do you decide which product is right for you?

Enter the Internet, and its ability to get information across to all strata of society.

It is fascinating to see how "the Net" has changed the way consumers react to brands. There has been a clear and demonstrable change in the power equations between corporations and consumers. In a single minute 694,445 search queries are launched on Google alone![42] Consumers no longer need to take advertising or the products they use at face value. The Internet has changed the way people select their brands, and it has provided a platform for exchange of news and information and opinion. It has liberated consumers from the burden of selection based on manufacturers' sales pitches. Increasingly, consumers seek peer reviews before purchasing products. The impact of peer opinions is felt most when one looks at products that are targeted at youth, the demographic that spends the most time on the Net and constantly uses the Net as a decision-making tool. Every 60 seconds, 1,200-plus ads are posted on Craigslist. These advertisements are a clear indication that consumers are talking to each other.

The speed with which information is shared among like-minded people is amazing. The Net has become an instrument of transformation—witness the "Arab Spring" of 2011, which demonstrated the power of the Net to facilitate communication at all levels and across all channels.

The Net has empowered consumers and given them the ability to talk back to corporations and indulge in occasional arm-twisting. One of the best examples in the recent past was the Verizon backflip. Verizon decided to charge its customers a $2 "convenience" fee on all payments that were made online and on the phone. The policy was to go into effect on January 15, 2012, and was announced on December 29, 2011. In less than 24 hours, thanks to the flood of negative feedback from consumers, Verizon had to withdraw the proposed charge.[43]

Today's consumer is not willing to put up with manufacturer mumbo jumbo or advertising that is misleading. The ability to talk back empowers two-way communication and cocreation. Imagine a situation where a company made just the packaging and a basic product, and then encouraged consumers to decide what it contained? That is exactly what Apple has done. The majority of the applications ("apps") that are available for

Apple gadgets are created by consumers and companies that have absolutely no connection with Apple. This ensures that Apple users get access to a talent pool that would have never been possible had it all been done by the company itself. Consumers, in turn, give feedback on the apps, based on their personal experience of the application. This level of cocreation is not common but increasingly smart manufacturers are seeing the value that they can generate by harnessing the power of the consumer as a creator.

We are seeing the impact of cocreation on the advertising industry and it is not a pretty sight. In a first-of-its-kind move, in August 2009 Unilever—the giant consumer products company—dumped its agency of 16 years, Lowe London, and put its brand Peperami in the public domain by inviting creative solutions from thousands of people rather than the handful who would have worked on the brand at Lowe.[44] A prize of $10,000 was offered to the winner. By April 2010, bolstered by the success of the initiative with Peperami, Unilever put another 13 brands out into the public domain for crowdsourcing.[45]

Bob Garfield—journalist, advertising commentator, and author of the book *The Chaos Scenario* (2009)—put it brilliantly when he said,

> The yin and yang of mass media and mass marketing—so marvelously, mutually sustaining for 400 years—have decoupled. The digital universe that pried them apart is itself a marvel, shifting power from the few to the many and altering human behavior, not to mention economies, on a grand scale. The question for business—as well as government, religion, science, politics, academia, and every other institution hitherto operated from the top down—is what to do now.[46]

Garfield coined the term "listenomics" to describe the trend toward businesses using open-source techniques to find ideas for product development, marketing, production, and many other activities that have traditionally been controlled by isolated departments. These companies can alternatively be viewed as encouraging or co-opting these forces, depending on one's viewpoint. "Listenomics" is part of a set of principles that enabled traditionally organized society and industry to take advantage of the shifts that threaten the powers that be.

A market like India epitomizes the new reality of the digital age. It is estimated that there are 112 million Internet users in India, although only 12 million with access to it through broadband connections.[47] In 2010, more than 35 million Internet users accessed the Internet via mobile phones instead. This number is pegged to grow to more than 250 million by 2015.[48] India's recent crusade against corruption in public life was fueled by the mobile phone and the Internet. Twenty million calls were received in support of the anticorruption fight.[49] Consumers have changed. Technology has given them the ability to interact with brands, services, and corporations. The smartphone is changing the world as we knew it, one user at a time.

Corporations have to learn that what was traditionally the target consumer is no longer a passive recipient of communication. She is paying attention not only to corporate advertising for a product, but also to other consumers' views, and contributing her own. Today's consumer is *creating* advertising—positive and negative. "Listenomics" is changing the way consumers accept messaging, and it is time that corporations understand the nuances of this changed dynamic. Both streams of communication are important—and that is the fundamental change in the environment. This is something that goes completely against the grain of the advertising industry, which for the longest time was used for one-way communication. Could it be that the time has come for corporations to seek protection from the consumer?

Recipes for Accelerating Change

This book argues that serious change in advertising will come endogenously—through the changing balance of power between consumer and producer. However, this is an evolutionary process, and will take time—several decades perhaps. But what can be done over the next decade, out to 2020, given the urgency of reform in the corporate world? This section outlines a set of recommended recipes for change: two principles and four strategies.

The first principle for advertising that is founded in equity, one that goes beyond what any industry self-regulation or governmental standards require, is that corporate advertisers treat all consumers as equal irrespective of which markets they are in, developing or developed. As developing countries grow into emerging markets in which many multinational corporations see growth opportunities, less-sophisticated industry and governmental standards usually mean that there is more opportunity for shaping consumer behavior in ways that are not considered responsible in more-developed markets. The story of selling baby milk food in Africa is a telling example. Accountable advertising means not exploiting such "opportunities."

Second, as with other aspects of Corporation 2020, transparency and disclosure are key principles in its advertising, too. A robust practice of disclosure around advertising can improve the comparison between corporate bodies and also push them to be more accountable. An annual "Accountable Advertising Report" would reveal which relevant industry standards have been used, provide a place to share newly created corporate principles on responsible advertising, and most importantly, be a vehicle for companies to differentiate themselves from, and be better than, their competitors. Formalizing the practice helps make it a priority. Ideally, this would be published as a policy disclosure statement in annual statutory reports, although one can see why companies would prefer to club this with the corporation's CSR report.

In parallel to these two principles, using information to inspire changes in behavior—this time from the consumer side—is also critical to Corporation 2020 advertising. Advertisers can use their unique assets as adept communicators to provide additional information to consumers, nudging them into making more responsible consumption decisions.

1. **Disclose *life span* on the product and in all advertisements.** This tactic has the potential to reduce overconsumption driven by people not using their products to their fullest potential. It would drive individuals to question whether they really need a new version of an item or whether they should purchase an item that has such a short life span in the first place. By communicating this information to consumers directly, companies are also incented to compete on the life span—in which consumers are bound to think that more is better.

2. **Disclose *countries of origin* on the product and in all advertisements.** On the product itself, this should be a simple visual that highlights all of the countries in which any part of the product was produced. Consumers would be able to discern from such a simple visual representation just how global a footprint that specific product has, and while this simplifies a more formal life-cycle analysis process, its simplicity is what makes it effective in getting people to avoid products that are too global in nature and have too many "airmiles" in their assembly.

3. **Recommend on the product itself how to *dispose* of it.** One of the more recent trends in sustainability is product take-back programs. Building on their value, advertisers should communicate how to dispose of a product when advertising it, so that consumers recognize the residual or waste value of the product they are purchasing and the responsibility they have to dispose of it properly. This action essentially brings previously unrecognized costs to the forefront, and it also would encourage companies to make take-backs easier.

4. **Voluntarily commit a "10 percent development donation" on total advertising spend in developing countries.** This recommendation for Corporation 2020 advertisers is specific to the developing world, in which the exponential growth in consumers signals unprecedented levels of market potential for multinational corporations. To offset "footprint" expansion in local economies, advertisers could support local sustainability projects through a 10 percent "ad dollars to development dollars" commitment. Similar to the "1 percent for the planet" standard that many companies have adopted in recent years, this 10 percent for development would be based purely on ad spend. The benefit of a proportion like this is that companies might be incented to spend less on advertising, which in some cases may reduce consumption. More importantly, however, it is an action that links back to the "Accountable Advertising Report," giving advertisers another platform to showcase how they are acting as responsible corporate citizens.

Whither Advertising?

In August 2011, Gallup polled 1,000 Americans ages 18 and older to check their view of 25 different industries. Those surveyed could provide three different responses: positive, negative, or neutral. The PR and advertising industries were combined for this research, and the results were shocking: 37 percent of those polled had a negative view of advertising, as compared to the computer industry, of which only 10 percent had a negative view.[50]

An early-December 2011 press release by Gallup shows that only 11 percent of those polled rated the honesty/ethics of advertising professionals as high. Advertising is sandwiched between stockbrokers at 12 percent and telemarketers at 8 percent. Accountants, on the other hand, were at 43 percent![51]

It is rather unfortunate that the practitioners of advertising are themselves immensely critical of the industry, and with good cause. David Ogilvy has said, "Advertising is a business of words, but advertising agencies are infested with men and women who cannot write. They cannot write advertisements, and they cannot write plans. They are helpless as deaf-mutes on the stage of the Metropolitan Opera."[52]

The advertising industry has been a very inward-looking business with two key drivers, profit and passion, in equal measure. With the increasing consolidation of the business, the profit motive is taking the lead, and passion is left adrift as an additional extra. The psychology of the Advertising Animal is that s/he knows it all. This is partly fueled by the nature of the industry. People in advertising are supposed to know not just their business but their clients' business too. An agency often has just 30 days in which to build a campaign for a brand that it previously knew nothing about! This creates a huge sense of superiority. Balance this with a huge sense of insecurity experienced by the industry, thanks to the fact that close to 90 percent of a creative person's ideas get turned down. Often advertising accounts move to a new agency when the team handling the business moves. Client dissatisfaction with their agencies is at an all-time high. It has become common for marketers to review their agency relationships every two years. Business moves when people move and accounts are more often than not on the verge of being pitched. As a result, most people in advertising have a schizophrenic existence. This is partly a defense mechanism that stems from the insecurity caused by most of their ideas being turned down. On the other hand, because they believe they are at the cutting edge of style and technique, big egos abound in advertising, and their self-confidence is rooted in results.

Advertising can and does mold attitudes and opinions. It has the ability to change human behavior and has been used as a means of social engineering. Recognizing this fact, David Ogilvy has said, "Political advertising ought to be stopped. It's the only really dishonest kind of advertising that's left. It's totally dishonest."[53]

It is this power of advertising that needs to be rediscovered by practitioners of what Bill Bernbach calls the art of persuasion. Unfortunately, many practitioners of this art regard advertising as just a handmaiden of the corporation. It pursues and enacts the vision of the corporation, creates demand, drives brand values, builds imagery, facilitates consumer engagement and involvement—but all of this at the behest of the corporation, regardless of the impact on society or consumers. Advertising is largely agnostic—even amoral, if required—in the execution of its duties, as we see from innumerable examples, foremost among them being tobacco and infant formula. An extended arm of a large organism, whose brain is the corporation, advertising needs to reflect the views and objectives of the corporation. But this model is broken and it needs to be fixed.

The reality of today's world is one of cocreation, co-ownership, and collaboration. No longer does media just carry messages to consumers. Consumers have begun to create their own messages and content. One of the most fascinating developments in recent times has been the consumer's ability to shut down the influx of messages, whether it is on TV through TIVO or on the Net by blocking pop-ups or outdoors through consumer activism. This is going to increase as consumers get bombarded more and more. An average American is exposed to over 3,000 advertising messages per day.[54] No wonder consumers want to block irrelevant messaging. Instead of continuing to bombard people with ads, the advertising industry has an opportunity to reinvent itself and the business by turning to the populace for inspiration

In short, it comes down to this: advertising has not changed much over the past 100 years; why should it change now? Because if it does not change, it faces extinction—that's why.

The tobacco lobby never thought that a day would come when smoking would be banned in public places and even on the streets. Baby milk food manufacturers never thought that they would have to face controls brought about by legislation. Milk producers across the states never thought that Walmart would stop buying milk that came from cows that had been given growth hormones. Advertising agency partners of P&G never imagined that P&G would ask them to report their own carbon footprint and use this as a metric for rewarding performance.

The advertising industry is mature. It is time for it to start breaking free from Corporation 1920. Hiding behind the coattails of Corporation 1920 was only natural, but Corporation 2020 has no coattails. The time to break free is now—because the consumer and social media will empower a new form of advertising.

"Curiosity about life in all of its aspects, I think, is still the secret of great creative people," said Leo Burnett, the man who created many advertising icons that we all know: the Jolly Green Giant, the Marlboro Man, the Pillsbury Doughboy, and Tony the Tiger.[55] It is time for the advertising industry to be curious about its own future.

CHAPTER SEVEN

Limiting Financial Leverage

*If I owe you a pound, I have a problem; but if I owe you a
million, the problem is yours.*

— *John Maynard Keynes*

The advent of limited liability was a key driver of the success of corporations and for economic development, as it allowed entrepreneurs
and their financiers to test new business ideas without taking unlimited
financial risks.[1] Limited liability alone, however, would not have powered
the last century and a half of economic progress if it were not for the
power of leverage, which was provided competitively to corporations by
a financial sector of increasing depth and sophistication.

Of course, financial leverage has also fueled all of the last four major
economic crises in the world, including the Latin American debt crisis, the
savings and loan crisis in the United States, the Asian debt crisis, and the
recent housing-sector-led global financial crisis. It has also served to force-
multiply the "brown economy" and increase the vulnerability of economies to asset bubbles.[2] Used appropriately, leverage can balance financing
risks and support the steady growth of enterprises and economies. Used
in ill-advised ways, leverage overexposes organizations to downside risks
and creates or magnifies negative returns for corporate stakeholders as
well as creating systemic risks and costs for society at large.

This chapter explores the risks associated with leverage, the current
framework for managing financial leverage, and ways in which we can
improve corporations' use of leverage in order to reduce systemic risks.
The key questions addressed are, Has unconstrained leverage been a
driver of systemic failures? Can leverage be limited by better regulation,

and if so, who should be regulated—only bankers, or also corporations? Should freedom from leverage limits, a global norm for the private sector, also apply to the public sector and to companies considered "too big to fail" despite their de facto recourse to the public purse? Could limits to leverage reduce systemic risk and better align corporate interests with societal goals? At present, many regulators are shying away from addressing these questions and their related challenges, leaving the better interests of society to be resolved by the "invisible hand" of markets. In other words, investor behavior is expected to determine how much leverage is appropriate, with fund managers becoming the unlikely conscience-keepers of society. Unfettered markets were never meant to solve social problems, and yet society's responses (and sometimes even regulators' responses) seem to assume that the opposite is true.

Capital-adequacy rules currently apply only to banks and financial institutions, with the global deregulation binge of recent decades weakening an already sensitive last line of defense. Large corporations are able to take on aggressive risk positions in everything from commodities at the core of their business to structured derivative bets at or beyond the periphery of their business model, thanks to free markets and the ready availability of bank financing. However, two steps can be taken to improve corporations' use of leverage. First, we can reevaluate and rebuild the financial sector's regulatory infrastructure to better monitor systemic risk and control of leverage. Second, we can explore regulatory options for nonbanking corporations that include reasonable limitations on leverage for organizations with substantial exposure to financial leverage. Any corporation (be it a bank, a mortgage lender, an insurer, or a car maker) that is considered "too big to fail" is in effect placing public capital at risk, and, for that privilege, it must at least set aside some of its own capital funds as a cushion against unexpected losses. Achieving these two steps will also encourage efficient management of capital raised and will reduce the market economy's exposure to runaway asset bubbles.

The Benefits, Risks, and Costs of Financial Leverage

We can define financial leverage, in general, as any contract-based mechanism through which an entity gains access to assets *by using funds provided by others or by putting at risk a lower amount of its own equity capital.* For the average institution, financial leverage includes taking out loans, issuing bonds, and leasing assets. However, more sophisticated variations of financial leverage include executing bank repurchase agreements (repos), issuing insurance policies or guarantees, and entering structured derivatives transactions. All of these activities greatly magnify the impact of a given amount of equity capital. The downside of leverage is that it also increases the amount of risk and the size of potential losses, because the provider of funds will usually take security or ensure that it has first preference in claims (sometimes referred to as "seniority" of claim) on the assets acquired, if things indeed do go wrong.

Leverage enables a corporation to make investments or incur expenses it would not otherwise have been able to undertake, based on its existing resources. Apart from the general advantage of allowing businesses to use resources beyond their subscribed capital and earned reserves, financial leverage has some additional positive effects: it expands consumers' purchasing power;[3] it enables entities to finance projects that they otherwise would not have been able to execute; it helps corporations grow their scale of operations in order to lower production costs; and it fuels economic expansions through the collective increase in expenditures that it has enabled. From the perspective of an investor, "plain vanilla" debt instruments (bonds and commercial paper—that is, relatively simple forms of leverage) also provide investment vehicles that have lower risk as compared to equity, and so leverage using debt issuance also contributes to investment diversification.

However, despite the aforementioned positive attributes, the use of high financial leverage also imposes a negative externality on parties not involved in a given transaction when financial distress or default sets in for the levered entity. Employees lose jobs, suppliers and vendors lose sales or collections and possibly face default, governments lose revenue, other enterprises feel the effects of reduced economic activity, and even foreign institutions are affected through trade. Ben Bernanke, current chairman of the US Federal Reserve, has observed that "firms' leverage decisions create externalities at both the microeconomic and macroeconomic levels" that will not be taken into account in private capital-structure decisions.[4] The unravelling of Enron, for example, had much to do with its excessive use of leverage.

Enron was originally born in 1985 out of the merger of several natural gas production, transmission, and marketing companies. Enron borrowed heavily in order to finance the merger, despite the fact that deregulation and increased competition in its markets was already putting pressure on the company.[5] Under the leadership of CEO Kenneth Lay and executive Jeffrey Skilling, Enron developed an extensive energy-trading business over the late 1980s and 1990s that became a platform for Enron's growth into new areas. Driven by fierce internal competition, a single-minded focus on current earnings, and high expectations from Wall Street, Enron's executives and managers pursued risky investments under high-leverage structures in order to grow their revenue and profits without regard to the long-term viability of these deals. In order to keep their leverage ratio down and potential liabilities and losses out of view, Enron's executives used "special purpose entities"—which were not consolidated into the company's financial statements and about which little was disclosed—to stash away many such deals and contracts.[6] As the company secretly levered up, it wasn't subject to capital constraints and, thanks in part to its murky accounting practices, it grew to be the seventh largest company in the Fortune 500,[7] with total revenues rising from $31 billion in 1998 to $101 billion in 2000.[8]

During 2001, Enron's leveraged con game unraveled as analysts started to grow skeptical of the company's lack of transparency. Skilling, Enron's CEO at the time, resigned abruptly in August; the company announced a significant quarterly loss in October; and the SEC opened investigations into Enron's accounting practices. Enron restated its prior-year financial results in November, reducing its income by $591 million and booking an additional $628 million in liabilities as of December 31, 2000. It eventually filed for bankruptcy in December 2001.[9] Enron's misdemeanors ended up costing more than 19,000 employees their jobs and many creditors a significant portion of their receivables, as financial claims were expected to be settled at roughly one-fifth of their original value.[10] Many stockholders lost a large portion of their investment, with Enron's stock tumbling from a high of just over $90 in 2000 to less than $1 by December 2001.[11] With 62 percent of the assets held by Enron's 401(k) employee retirement plan consisting of Enron stock at year-end in 2000, and employees restricted from selling their 401(k) plan's shares in Enron during fall 2001 as the stock's price collapsed, many employees lost their retirement savings. The effects of Enron's excesses rippled throughout the economy, as energy prices increased because of reduced trading liquidity, and power development projects were put on hold due to transparency concerns and the rising cost of credit.[14] Enron is a case study not only of reckless and fraudulent behavior, but also of the externalized damages that a corporation's leverage seeking can impose on society.

Because high leverage enables institutions to grow their balance sheets significantly beyond constraints on their ability to raise equity capital, it also facilitates institutions' growth to a size that can be considered "too big to fail" (TBTF). Some of the factors that contribute to TBTF status include size, interconnectedness, and degree of public visibility.[13] A TBTF institution *usually* refers to a bank or other financial institution that federal regulators determine is too important to fail in a disorderly manner without the federal government intervening to protect its creditors and stave off ripple effects on the financial system and the wider economy. However, in practice, an institution from any industry can grow to become TBTF. The following is but a small sample of institutions that have received TBTF support or bailouts from the US government: Fannie Mae, Freddie Mac, AIG, Chrysler, General Motors, Citigroup, Bank of America, Goldman Sachs, Bear Stearns, most of the airline industry (in 2001), Long-Term Capital Management, Lockheed Corporation, and Penn Central Railroad. Beyond presenting an increase in systemic risk for the economy, the implicit TBTF status of very large institutions also creates a problem of moral hazard, because the managers of those institutions have increased incentives to take on leverage-related risk if they know their worst-case scenario losses will be socialized. In addition, the expectation of government bailouts for a TBTF firm could effectively lower the firm's cost of borrowing, further encouraging risk-taking behavior. High leverage is a dominant enabler of TBTF status.

Excessive leverage feeds the market manias that lead to asset-price bubbles by enabling overconsumption of goods and services when they are in high demand. Access to this allegedly "cheap" capital can drive skyrocketing asset prices initially, but eventually the market adjusts, often triggering an abrupt correction or, worse, an economy-wide recession. Research from the McKinsey Global Institute suggests that rising leverage is a good proxy in detecting asset bubbles, and for good reason.[14] McKinsey reported that long periods of deleveraging typically follow financial crises, which usually exerts a drag on subsequent economic growth. Another McKinsey study found that recovery in US employment levels after recessions is taking longer and longer: 15 months for 1990, 39 months for 2001, and a projected 60 months for 2008.[15] In other words, the cost to society of asset bubbles (and the leverage that fueled them) is getting higher in terms of the increasing length of time it takes labor-market dislocations to heal.

Crises and Leverage Are Common Bedfellows

Financial leverage has represented, at the least, an amplifier of financial and economic crises around the world and, at the most, a primary driving force behind some of them. The power of leverage to turn economic stability into ruin when pursued in excess has been proven time and again by corporations, sovereign governments, and individuals alike. Many a financial crisis and ensuing economic recession has been either triggered— or its effects significantly worsened—by financial leverage. This includes all of the last four major financial crises experienced around the world, those being Latin America's debt crisis (caused by excessive lending to sovereigns to tide over balance of payments gaps caused by the 1970s oil price shocks), the savings and loan crisis in the United States (driven by unsound and overextended lending and poor supervision of savings and loan institutions), the Asian currency crisis (resulting from indiscriminate and risky leverage by Asia's private sector), and the so-called Great Recession of 2008 (a real estate price bubble driven by rampant credit-risk taking by mortgage lenders and further amplified by highly leveraged financial instruments). In all of these cases, leverage played a central role in contributing to asset bubbles that subsequently burst and in prolonging recessionary impacts as a result of the process of de-leveraging.[16]

Latin America's "lost decade" of the 1980s was amplified by leverage, in that instance not by corporations but by sovereign governments. Latin America's debt-service load grew significantly as the US dollar appreciated and interest rates skyrocketed, leading to more borrowing just to pay high interest, a common problem created by excessive debt. Banks, in pursuit of profits, continued lending despite warnings by experts and regulators. Along the way, regulation that would have prevented banks from reaching certain concentrations of risk in foreign sovereign loans was written flexibly to favor the existing lending practices.[17] Mexico defaulted on its obligations in 1982 and many other Latin American countries, seeing the writing on the wall, approached banks to restructure their debts. Altogether, 27 countries owing a combined $239 billion attempted to reschedule their loans. Banks suffered significant losses, but with regulators' aid they were recapitalized over that decade. The idea of "too big to fail"—born as a policy option during the early 1980s during the debate over Continental Illinois's imminent collapse—grew deeper roots in the response to the Latin American debt crisis.

The savings and loan (S&L) crisis in the United States was also driven by unsound and excessive lending practices, coupled with lax regulatory oversight and exemption from more stringent banking standards. S&L institutions were small, innocuous, depositor-owned banks that accepted deposits and made home loans to their members at low cost. However, with the high interest rates of the 1970s and early 1980s, depositors began to withdraw funds. The combination of increasing interest rates and an increasing maturity mismatch between loans and deposits resulted in large losses for the industry, with many S&Ls failing in the early 1980s.[18] Regulators and legislators came under pressure to keep the industry alive and improve its profitability, so S&Ls were gradually given powers to invest in a widening array of financial products, and to lower their capital requirements. Legislation sponsored by the Reagan administration in the 1980s eliminated statutory limits on the loan-to-value ratio, thus allowing investment in commercial mortgages, commercial and consumer loans, and leases. Some state jurisdictions, looking to compete with federal standards in a regulatory race to the bottom, allowed S&Ls to invest 100 percent of their deposits in any kind of venture. S&Ls were thus encouraged to grow in size and defer closure as they pursued high-leverage strategies in the false hope that doubling their bets would enable them to recoup previous losses. It was the classic gambler's trap, ironically aided and abetted by regulatory relaxations that encouraged *more* risk rather than less. The final cost of resolving failed S&Ls was estimated at $153 billion, including $124 billion from federal taxpayers.[19]

Asia's debt crisis provides yet another case study in the dangerous effects of unconstrained leverage. Asia's 1990s asset bubbles were created by "hot money" that was drawn into the "Asian Tiger" economies and then used to incur significant private debts. Often those private debts were effectively subsidized by implicit guarantees from sovereign governments, creating significant moral hazard.[20] In the absence of depth and liquidity in local money and debt markets, corporations and banks were borrowing cheaply in US dollars and relying heavily on the expectation of stable currency pegs to the US dollar. Over the period 1991–97, the average rates of growth in bank lending across Malaysia, Indonesia, Thailand, and the Philippines were as high as 25 percent per year. Bad debts piled up, and the collapse of finance companies in Thailand led first to an equity market shock in Thailand, and then a ripple effect that led investors to lose confidence and withdraw investments, fueling currency speculation and depreciation and a negative spiral that brought these soaring economies unpleasantly to the ground for years.

And finally, leverage was at the heart of the largest financial crisis of our times, which triggered the so-called Great Recession of 2008, the most serious economic setback since the Great Depression of 1929. The 2008 financial crisis can be traced to the emergence and collapse of a real-estate price bubble that was driven largely by rampant credit risk-taking by lenders. This risk-taking was amplified by highly leveraged financial instruments such as mortgage-backed securities, collateralized debt obligations, and credit default swaps. Low interest rates, easy and available credit, and benign regulation were some of the key factors that caused the asset bubble.[21] Calls by critics to rein in debt or regulate the markets while the bubble was being created were unfortunately ignored. Institutions involved in mortgage markets (Fannie Mae, Freddie Mac) grew to proportions that afforded them TBTF status. Once heavily indebted homeowners started falling behind on payments and facing foreclosure, the price bubble in the housing market began to deflate and unravel. As payment defaults hit the web of financial instruments that the financial sector had created, write-downs and losses started piling up and soon unhinged the entire financial system. Credit markets seized up.

And what started as a housing/financial sector problem became a broad economic one. Real gross domestic product declined significantly, job losses ensued, and in the United States the government was forced to pass into law a $700 billion financial bailout bill in October, 2008, to protect institutions it deemed "too big to fail." A further stimulus package of $787 billion was enacted to help turn around a downward-spiraling economy, and even more support has been provided since. Despite all this, at the time of writing, economic recovery still eludes us and the unemployment rate still hovers around 9 percent—further illustrating the point that the societal costs of leverage-fueled crises fall heavily and for a long time on third parties who are not the ones who caused the problem. And as pointed out earlier,[22] setting the stage for the 2008 crisis was an increasingly globalized and rapidly growing financial sector, increasing liquidity in preceding years, and increasing complexity of financial instruments (driven by innovation and deregulation in the closing decades of the twentieth century),[23] all of which contributed to the rampant use of leverage, and finally, to a short and cataclysmic period of de-leveraging that became the greatest financial crisis of all time.

With such close links between crisis and excessive leverage, one would not exaggerate in suggesting that where there is one, the other is usually nearby.

Controlling Leverage

In a market-driven capitalist economy, the business enterprise is generally tasked with making its own financial and operational decisions as part of the process of providing goods and services in the pursuit of profit. Financially speaking, the firm's managers are influenced only by self-imposed corporate-governance mechanisms, by the mandate provided by the firm's owners, and by the market's perceptions of the firm's ability to provide a return to its investors. Naturally, there are always regulations that a corporation must adhere to, including issuing financial statements if the entity is listed in public exchanges or submitting to the oversight of agencies if it engages in specified regulated activities. However, only in selected sectors—finance in general, banking in particular—are a firm's finances actively monitored and *somewhat* constrained by a more rational, external arbiter—governmental institutions.

The theory behind banking- and financial-sector regulation stems from the correct assumptions that these sectors are crucial for stable economic growth and that systemic risk in the financial system needs to be regulated by constraining leverage. The recurrence of financial crises, however, points to continued deficiency in the institutional management of systemic risk and leverage. Capital adequacy requirements at banks have not prevented financial crises and conflicts of interest, and a lack of transparency has created hidden coves for risk to accumulate. Additionally, since nonfinancial corporations are subject to almost no leverage constraints, managers are able to make leveraged bets, and if statutory disclosure requirements and investor scrutiny are a problem, managers can utilize off-balance sheet transactions and structured derivatives to disguise transactions that in fact generate even more leverage. We must first examine leverage as it is controlled in financial institutions, and then also assess how it is monitored, if at all, for nonfinancial corporations. It should be noted that regulatory schemes vary by country and can sometimes be quite complicated. Thus, the aim here is to provide just a brief overview of common regulatory frameworks and selected illustrative regulatory schemes, as well as their impact on private-sector leverage, and not to account for every regulatory system in the world.

Banking is a sector of critical importance for the economy due to its functions as both payment-clearing mechanism and repository for a significant proportion of individuals' and corporations' liquid assets. It is a relatively uncontroversial proposition that banking institutions need to be actively supervised to ensure the solvency and liquidity of the financial system as a whole, both being prerequisites for economic prosperity.

Reserve Requirements

Central banks are the primary but not the only vehicle through which governments supervise their banks. One of their mechanisms for constraining bank lending is to impose reserve requirements on them. Cash-reserve requirements represent the fraction of banking deposits (demand deposits and interest-bearing accounts) that are required to be retained either as cash in the bank's vault or as a balance directly with the central bank. In addition, there may be liquidity reserves (government securities and treasury bills), also expressed as a fraction of deposits. Reserve requirements help limit the leverage in the banking system as a whole. They also help reduce the risk of liquidity problems. As a frame of reference, the US reserve requirement was 10 percent for deposit amounts over a specified balance,[24] while the European Central Bank's was 2 percent.[25] Due to their far-reaching economic effects, however, reserve requirements are usually not high overall, and they are infrequently changed by major central banks. The Reserve Bank of India, a conservative and active manager of banking-system risks and money supply, is one of the exceptions: cash-reserve ratios (CRR) in India have been in the range 3–10 percent, and liquidity reserves (SLR) have been as high as 25 percent for decades. Their prudence has often been criticized as excessive, but India was one of the very few countries whose financial system was neither affected by the Asian debt crisis nor by the financial crisis of 2008.

Capital Adequacy Ratios

Whereas cash-reserve ratios are akin to using "brute force" to preempt bank liquidity away from markets, capital adequacy ratios are a more subtle device, in that they use the economic disincentive of raising the capital costs of leverage to achieve similar ends. A capital-adequacy ratio limits an institution's financial leverage by requiring the firm to have a minimum amount of capital—including ownership equity and other forms of long-term capital—based on a specified percentage of the firm's assets. In the United States, simple forms of capital adequacy ratios, such as requiring capital to be, say, 5 percent of assets, were used by various regulatory agencies during the 1960s and 1970s, with more complex forms of capital ratios defining the multiple tiers of capital arising over the ensuing decades. Similar trends occurred in parallel in the European countries. Seeking greater regulatory coordination, the central bankers of the G-10 nations that formed the Basel Committee on Banking Supervision produced the first Basel Capital Accord in 1988 for banks to conform to guidelines on capital adequacy.[26]

The first Basel Accord ("Basel I") required a minimum ratio of 4 percent for Tier 1 capital (composed mainly of ownership equity) to risk-weighted assets and 8 percent for Tier 1 plus Tier 2 capital—which includes subordinated debt and other capital. Basel I assigned risk weights to different types of loans and assets depending on each asset class's risk; a higher risk weight would imply higher required capital, with most "held-for-sale" or statutorily held government debt having a risk weight of 0 percent. This system was implemented during the early 1990s in many countries around the world. However, there were and still are concerns about "regulatory arbitrage" by banks. More and more structured asset categories got the benefits of being classified as "government" to attract the lowest regulatory capital provisions, and risks shifted to *off-balance sheet* instruments. These and other imperfections prompted an overhaul.[27]

A revised "Basel II" framework was released in 2004 with a more sophisticated (and less open to regulatory arbitrage) system of risk-weighting, providing banks with three optional approaches to calculate risk-weighted capital, ranging from simple and prescriptive (for small banks) to an internal ratings-based approach with regulatory approval for sophisticated banks. It also included stress testing and supervisory oversight as well as emphasizing disclosure and market discipline, relying on market efficiency to punish institutions for excessive risk-taking. Many criticisms were levied against the Basel II framework: that it was portfolio invariant (that is, it did not adjust for diversity of risk across institutions) and called for a "one-size-fits-all" approach; that it did not account for concentrations of risk; that it allowed the use of subjective risk inputs by banks; that it depended on regulators having near perfect foresight; and that it did not account for market imperfections, among other issues.[28]

The 2008 financial crisis, which came about just after Basel II was implemented in Europe, seemed to justify these criticisms and implied that Basel II was ineffective. This prompted calls for development of new Basel guidelines, generally referred to as Basel III. Among the changes sought, not surprisingly, were requirements for more equity capital. Basel III also asked to strengthen the capital treatment of securitizations; supplemented the risk-based capital requirement with a "leverage ratio" that included off-balance-sheet exposures; provided measures to limit excess credit growth; required stronger risk-management governance at institutions; required additional disclosures to increase transparency; and introduced new liquidity and funding ratios, among other initiatives. Leverage and its systemic risk implications were at last being recognized as a harsh reality that needed serious corrective attention, after decades of international financial deregulation.

National and local bank regulatory authorities also often implement other restrictions or regulations on banking institutions. Many countries levy fees on banks to fund deposit-insurance systems to protect unwitting depositors in the event of bank failure. In the United States, Federal Deposit Insurance Corporation (FDIC) insurance reduces the risk of bank runs even as it creates moral hazard, given that banks' downside risk is, in effect, subsidized and that depositors have less incentive to monitor banks' activities or riskiness. Banks are also often regulated in terms of ownership structure and in what financial products they can offer. A case can be made that risky capital markets and investment-banking products should be offered from separate legal entities, and not from clearing banks (those involved in deposit taking and lending, and more central to the functioning of the mechanics of clearing and settlement). The United States had such regulation in place (the Glass-Steagall Act),[29] but the trend toward deregulation in the 1980s and 1990s—exemplified by the Financial Services Modernization Act of 1999 in the United States (commonly referred to as the Gramm-Leach-Bliley Act)—greatly weakened the grip of regulators over bank risk-management, setting the stage for worldwide crises in the 2000s.

Other types of financial institutions are also regulated to differing degrees, including investment banks, hedge funds, mutual funds, and insurance companies, to list a few. The extent of control and oversight exerted for these market segments, however, is much lower than it is for banking, and it varies considerably by type of firm and/or instrument, depending on how the regulatory boundaries are established. For example, investment banks' brokerage operations in the United States were subject to the oversight of the Securities and Exchange Commission (SEC), and there was a delicate balance of voluntary processes that were acceded to by the investment banks to avoid full-blown regulation. In 2004, the SEC allowed the five largest investment banks to expand their leverage ratios beyond the previously existing leverage-ratio limits. This allowed Bear Stearns and other banks to quickly attain leverage ratios of 33-to-1 and higher before the troubles started.[30] Thus, investment banks had much looser capital-adequacy requirements than commercial banks. Hedge funds were even less regulated prior to the 2008 crisis, bearing out pundits' continued criticism of their lack of transparency and volatility-inducing speculation. Mutual funds and insurance companies have requirements that vary significantly by jurisdiction, but many of the regulations affecting them relate to fees, operational processes, and disclosure.

Regulation of Nonfinancial Corporations

Nonfinancial corporations are generally not subject to regulation of their financial decisions or fiscal condition. The rationale for not regulating the finances of nonfinancial corporations is the premise that free-market participants can make more efficient capital-allocation decisions in their pursuit of maximum profits. Measures that we could very loosely refer to as "financial regulation for nonfinancial firms" are therefore surgically aimed at a few areas like financial disclosure, corporate governance, financial reporting, and the like. There are few examples of jurisdictions where comprehensive financial regulation of nonfinancial companies is practiced.

One interesting case of nonfinancial corporations' leverage being monitored actively is that of India's "consortium banking" or "multiple banking" arrangements. Under these schemes, banks form lending groups that share key financial information about their corporate borrowers, including information about their credit ratings, financial exposure, securities outstanding, and compliance with financial covenants. This sharing of information enables the group to reduce the information asymmetries that sometimes plague lenders as well as minimizing the possibility that a borrowing firm can play banks off one another in order to take on more risk than is advisable. The Reserve Bank of India, which cooperates with the Indian Banks' Association, issues circulars that outline banks' responsibilities in consortium-banking arrangements. Ultimately, these arrangements serve to reduce the risk of corporate and bank failures.

In a 2011 interview with the author, Mr. Romesh Sobti, managing director and CEO of IndusInd Bank, talked about the success that India's banking regulatory approach had in preventing the 2008 financial crisis from significantly affecting its economy.[31] Mr. Sobti credited India's central banking controls on leverage, but also the existence of consortium banking, for the stability of India's financial system. As Mr. Sobti emphasized, "the premise of this [consortium banking] structure is need-based financing," meaning that the bank consortium actively assesses the capital needs of a corporation and constrains leverage to what is necessary. The corporation must adequately explain what the money is for, and the consortium does transaction-based auditing to see where the money goes. Unfortunately, Mr. Sobti observed, "as India became more globalized, bankers started criticizing this scheme," adding, "but I think a strong case has come back that [consortium banking] was the way to go." It is clear that consortium banking had proven to be an effective model in a large emerging market for cost-effective leverage control in nonfinancial sectors.

Barring such notable exceptions, nonfinancial corporations are relatively unconstrained in how they use and manage leverage. Corporate charters, articles of incorporation, and bylaws determine the legal capacities of corporations, but they tend to be structured as general documents that do not spell out the intricacies of how a firm will finance itself or whether certain types of financial transactions will be barred or constrained. Mature corporate jurisdictions do not prescribe any given capital structure or limits on leverage. Rather, these legislative architectures outline corporate capacity and how it may be exercised by delegating authority for various purposes and functions depending on the nature of transaction. As such, managerial discretion is applied to proposed financial transactions at every level of the enterprise, and the question of incurring leverage at a nonfinancial corporation is really a function of managerial judgment subject to external commercial constraints imposed by investors.

Given the scarcity of internal hard limits on leverage at nonfinancial corporations, external stakeholders play a role in influencing a firm's leverage. Shareholders, banks, counterparties to contracts, and other creditors continuously pore over the details of publicly available documents outlining the enterprise's financial condition in order to determine its financial health and potential borrowing capacity. Participants in the capital markets, as well as the firm's other stakeholders, decide whether a corporation is worthy of additional lending. Free-market evangelists would argue that those external stakeholders acting in their own self-interest should serve as an effective control on leverage. There are reasons why market discipline, while it sounds nice in theory, often fails in practice.

Modern welfare economics and the First Welfare Theorem tell us that the private market provides a Pareto efficient outcome under four strictly applied conditions:

1. There are no externalities.
2. The market is for private (not "public") goods.
3. Market participants have perfect information and the market is not incomplete.
4. There is perfect competition.

Failure to meet any of the conditions enumerated above enables the possibility of market failures, yet even a cursory look at these four conditions suggests they are seldom met in the real world. The economy is replete with large externalities in many areas of public goods. Many categories of "public goods" are large and central to human well-being and economic development (law and order, communal harmony, a bearable climate, ecosystems that maintain soil fertility and freshwater availability, etc.), and are by no means so small or peripheral that they can conveniently be ignored. Market players are often neither perfectly informed, truly independent, nor perfectly competitive. We can add to the mix of departures from theory the existence of "individual failures" when people act irrationally, which happens often and serves as the focus of the thriving field of behavioral economics. From a financial-leverage perspective, particularly thorny problems can arise in two of these areas: imperfect information and individual failure.

Information asymmetries are said to exist when one party has more or better information than the other. In the context of financing decisions, the managers of a corporation have a distinct information advantage over the firm's lenders and counterparties due to managers' intimate knowledge of the company and its prospects. It is notable that this information asymmetry also exists between the firm's managers and its owners, creating what is known as the principal-agent problem. The current legal and regulatory framework tries to address information asymmetry by providing for a system of consistent accounting and reporting rules that require fair measurement and disclosure. It also requires financial auditors to provide independent attestation on management's financial reporting in order to reduce the risk of error and misrepresentation. Separately, credit-rating agencies perform financial risk-assessment that helps reduce the information-asymmetry problem in the private market. Credit-rating agencies provide meaningful signals about the health of an enterprise to potential counterparties.

These systems of monitoring and control are not without shortcomings. Accounting standards have often failed to provide enough transparency around risk when it comes to complex financial transactions, derivative exposures, and off-balance-sheet vehicles. Enron's financial exploits come to mind as a glaring example of such limitations, and even when accounting guidelines are updated, some new financial innovation will surface that evades their purpose. Further, although most financial audits achieve their objectives, auditors can occasionally miss red flags if they become complacent about a client company or face budget pressures that motivate leaner audit procedures. As such, auditors can fall prey to the same biases that affect corporations.

Credit-rating agencies were previously assumed to be independent sources of information that helped lenders and counterparties assess financial risk. However, one of the critical lessons of the 2008 financial crisis was that credit-rating agencies failed at providing an unbiased, objective assessment of risk, as they handed out AAA ratings on toxic mortgage instruments in exchange for more business and/or higher fees. Thus, the holy grail of transparency—itself a precondition to the market's effective management of leverage—seems to be a moving target. Moreover, as financial innovation continues to increase the complexity of transactions, it often (as a corollary) reduces transparency, given that more complex instruments are more difficult to understand. Even the most brilliant minds and experienced financial experts failed to properly appraise the risks that accumulated in the financial system leading up to the 2008 financial crisis. Such information asymmetries played a central role in the crisis's creation and unfolding.

The other significant factor mentioned above is individual failure, which refers to the fact that individuals sometimes act in ways that can be considered irrational or seemingly against their best long-term interest. Irrationality in human behavior is a well-established fact that has been researched by many economists, psychologists, and social scientists. How can irrationality affect financial decisions? One way is when a herd mentality takes over an industry or, worse, an entire economy, leading corporate managers to be biased for or against certain strategic or financial transactions in a way that defies common sense.

Two illustrative examples of irrational thinking (which are especially relevant to the leverage–financial crisis connection) are the assumed impossibility in models used by mainstream rating agencies of the US housing market ever declining in value, and the conclusion by market professionals that mortgage-backed securities in subprime loans to people with little or no equity in their homes deserved a AAA rating. Irrational thinking can lead managers to take on excessive risk and leverage. When we combine these forces with the challenge of aligning incentives, we have a recipe for disaster.

The principal-agent problem arises when a principal (for our purposes here, the shareholders or owner of a firm) hires an agent (corporate management) to advance the principal's interests, although the principal will necessarily have incomplete information about the agent's motivations and actions. Under these conditions, moral hazard or conflicts of interest can arise that will be detrimental to the principal. The corporation cannot guarantee that the employee's interests are completely aligned with its own. To address the situation, corporations try to use different mechanisms to align employees' interests with stockholders'—bonuses or commissions, performance reviews, prospects for promotion or firing, stock-option plans, etc. Nonetheless, corporate managers can sometimes game these incentive systems in order to maximize their short-term payoffs without considering the damaging long-term effects of their decisions, as is often the case with risk taking and leverage.

Although we can presume that corporate managers do not wish negative financial consequences to befall their firms, the problem of moral hazard in the context of leverage is acute because the manager is at least partially insulated from the risks to which he or she commits the enterprise. In other words, the losses faced by managers when they make bad bets (i.e., damaged reputation, demotion, firing) are dwarfed by the financial losses faced by their enterprises. It is quite possible that corporate managers take risks on behalf of their firms that they wouldn't take on themselves, or with their own money. Thus, the incentive problem can only be partially addressed, at best, by corporations' legal contracts with their employees, and this results in a breakdown of the efficient-market theory. It's worthwhile to note that this breakdown can and does occur on both sides of a transaction: the borrower takes on debt that it might not be able to pay and the lender makes a bad investment.

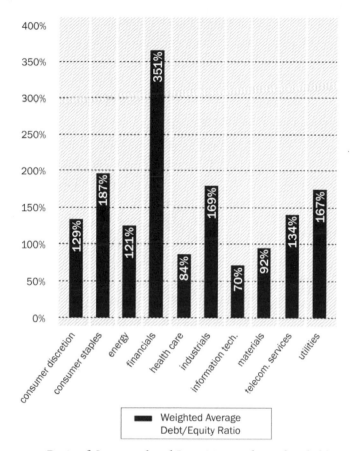

Figure 7-1   Ratio of Structured and Long-Term Debt to Shareholders' Equity
Note: Data was obtained in April 2012 for most recent fiscal year, for
global public companies with over US$1b in assets and US$1b in revenue
(nearly 5,000 companies). Source: Thomson ONE.

A related problem with financial leverage is that when a firm increases the proportion of its assets funded by debt it lowers its share of equity at stake. This distorts incentives further by encouraging more risk-taking behavior. After all, if you have very little skin in the game, you feel better about betting big. If you lose, you stand to lose a small amount compared to the outsized gains you would have made if you had succeeded. This is how leverage has been managed at some large corporations that have failed—like a betting game on margin.

It is well known that certain industries tend to be predisposed toward utilizing higher financial leverage than others, although there is always variation among individual firms within each industry. Some industries, such as utilities, tend to exhibit higher levels of debt not only because of their large needs for long-term project financing but because their quasi-monopolistic business models afford them relative stability and security of cash inflows. Other industries, such as pharmaceuticals, tend to rely much less on debt, reflecting the higher risk profile of their investments. Any discussion about appropriate levels of leverage should incorporate these sectoral differences in companies' borrowing capacity, given that not every firm, and indeed not every industry, is created equal. Figure 7.1 shows the average leverage ratios by industry sector, giving us a sense of the variation in leverage across industries.

Since leverage is hardly managed or controlled in any significant way for nonfinancial corporations, it is only limited by managerial discretion and creditors' willingness to lend, with the lending process fraught with pitfalls. In the United States and many other countries, leverage is actually incentivized via the tax deductibility of interest and other types of financial losses. This tips the scale all the more toward nonfinancial corporations seeking leverage and, to the extent there are regulatory gaps, by financial institutions. Despite some controls on leverage found in particular sectors, corporations are given relatively free rein to incur leverage as they see fit.

Toward a New Leverage-Management Framework

Current approaches to managing leverage have resulted in corporations overextending themselves financially and contributed to significant instability in the global economy. Economists recognize the destabilizing effect that leverage can have on the macro economy, and we have seen the negative externalities that it imposes on third parties not involved in the transactions. Our global frameworks for managing leverage at the systemic and corporate level need to change fundamentally. Excessive faith has been placed on the skill and intentions of corporate managers across all sectors, from finance to manufacturing. Markets can provide an efficient first-best solution to many problems, but they often fail when conditions are suboptimal and they do not address disparities in income or wealth distribution. Policy is necessary to address market shortcomings, and the tools to improve our risk-management performance are within reach. More solutions are being contemplated and implemented at this time, while others have not yet reached policy-makers' drawing boards.

The global financial regulatory landscape is changing in response to the 2008 financial crisis. Basel III is but one example of the evolution of global banking regulatory standards, and in the United States a strong push for reregulation of the financial system was made with the passage of the Dodd-Frank Wall Street Reform and Consumer Protection Act in 2010.

The Dodd-Frank Act holds that nonbank companies can be subject to regulation if they are deemed to pose a risk to the financial system. It pushes for stricter rules as companies grow in size and complexity, and prohibits banks from engaging in significant proprietary trading on their own account. It requires large and complex financial companies to submit plans for orderly shutdown, which is a way of recognizing the negative externalities of too-big-to-fail companies that pursue high-risk strategies. In the same vein, it prohibits Federal Reserve lending to individual companies, as a way of mitigating moral hazard. It provides the SEC and CFTC with authority to regulate over-the-counter derivatives, requires central clearing and exchange trading for them, and provides regulators the ability to impose margin requirements on their trades.[32] Dodd-Frank also enacts other regulatory changes for mortgage lending, brings hedge funds and credit-rating agencies under the oversight of the SEC, and improves rules on executive compensation and corporate governance. These changes are steps in the right direction to better monitor and control leverage, addressing the market failures in finance. However, such regulation is needed across national boundaries; otherwise, it will at best create competitive disparities or at worst encourage the most affected corporations to reengineer their global business models in order to avoid US regulation.

In a return to older wisdom, there may need to be put in place new banking controls that restrict banks from engaging in transactions peripheral to the primary purpose of banks as lenders and financial clearers. Banks should be precluded from engaging in investment banking and insurance activities—which are inherently riskier than ordinary lending and can prove destabilizing to the credit system. This used to be the case in the United States before the Gramm-Leach-Bliley Act of 1999 eliminated those barriers, under pressure of intense lobbying and in the aftermath of Citicorp's initially illegal merger with Travelers Insurance Group just one year earlier. The Glass-Steagall Act of 1933 that had obliged the separation of banking activity from trading and capital markets activity did have sound roots in systemic risk-management thinking, and such regulation needs to be reconsidered.

In addition, constraints should be enacted to prevent banks from transacting in inappropriate or risk-multiplying derivatives in the guise of risk management. Similarly, constraints are needed to identify and reconsider leverage ratios and to disclose derivatives whose fundamental purpose is large unrecorded financing. This could be achieved by highlighting the purchase or sale of derivatives that generate such forms of risk, and by requiring banks to submit risk analyses to their respective regulators for ratification within a certain number of days after engaging in a derivative transaction. Failure to comply could result in fines, and any transactions not so ratified and recorded could be unwound. To prevent the adverse-selection problem that played a role in bringing the world economy to its knees, additional constraints should be placed on securitization transactions. To that end, regulation could require banks to sell securitized assets (other than some classes of exchange-listed and traded securities) only on a "with-recourse" basis, such that they retain a significant portion of the downside risk and are therefore disincentivized from relaxing their lending standards to make a quick buck.

Capital requirements for banks also need to be made more stringent in order to recognize event risk and to enforce the use of capital as backing for unexpected events. The proposed framework of Basel III appears to begin addressing this need. Decisions about capital adequacy need to be taken out of the hands of banks, which in many places around the world define their own risk-measurement standards, a fatal flaw of the Basel II regulatory model. Such a model has proven ineffective, as banks have either failed to recognize their own biases in risk-weighing their assets or deliberately understated such risks.

Measures also need to be taken to actively monitor and limit bank-credit growth, which also plays a role in money creation. A study should be conducted to determine what levels of credit in an economy are excessive, and triggers should be put in place for regulators to require additional bank capital in periods of high credit. Both would help to reduce the pro-cyclicality of the current banking regulatory system. Further, the use of an absolute leverage ratio regardless of risk-weights of assets—as proposed in Basel III—is a productive idea, as banks can currently game the asset mix to increase their leverage by engaging in offsetting transactions that shift risk to other nonregulated sectors. An absolute leverage ratio represents a simple and effective solution to prevent manipulation of the more complex capital-adequacy measures.

Banks should also be required to share basic credit and counterparty information with other banks that are part of the central banking system, so that the market for credit is free of the information asymmetries that enable large corporations to play banks off one another. This is akin to the formerly thriving "consortium banking" arrangements of the United Kingdom and India, in which banks shared such information about their borrowers, collectively enabling themselves to assess credit risks more effectively. The central bank of each country could serve as a clearing house for this information within its banking system, and the central banks could further consolidate this information to create a global database that could be consulted in order to gauge the credit risk of multinational corporations. These mechanisms would help increase transparency and reduce systemic as well as corporate-level risk.

Significant improvements can also be made to manage leverage more effectively in the nonfinancial sector. Nonfinancial corporations have increased their use of debt instruments and derivatives over the last few decades, increasing the risks for themselves and their stakeholders. Many such institutions have used leverage as a growth mechanism, potentially reaching "too big to fail" status in terms of their size and interconnectedness. We need to take measures to control leverage at nonfinancial corporations in order to ensure they remain healthy and viable.

Eliminating Perverse Subsidies: Tax-Deductibility of Interest

One of the significant incentives for corporations to increase their use of debt is the tax deductibility of interest expense in many jurisdictions, which effectively subsidizes debt at the expense of equity capital. Interest payments are a return to the providers of debt capital, just as dividend payments are a return to the providers of equity capital. However, interest payments are deductible for tax purposes in the United States and many other countries, whereas dividend payments are typically not deductible. This creates a clear incentive for companies to lever up, with the government effectively subsidizing a portion of the cost of debt. Ironically, this creates a distortion in the capital markets. The Modigliani-Miller Theorem, first introduced in 1958, posited that in well-functioning markets the market value of a firm (debt plus equity) depends only on the income stream produced by its assets, and that such market value is not affected by the firm's capital structure.[33] This holds in theory because increasing the proportion of debt in a firm makes equity capital riskier, which raises the equity capital's required return without affecting the firm's weighted average cost of capital. When debt is tax-advantaged, however, the firm trades off between the benefit of the tax subsidy and the risk of firm default when selecting its capital structure. Too often, managers are tempted to use "cheap debt" to enhance returns at the expense of higher risk.

A relatively attractive and simple solution would be to impose limits on the tax deductibility of interest expense for nonfinancial corporations by phasing out or capping the total amount of interest deductible. This would at least reduce the distortion in the market that favors and finances heavy indebtedness. An alternative would be to impose a surcharge or tax on the amount of a firm's total liabilities that exceeds a certain threshold. For example, a surcharge of 1 or 2 percent could be levied on the amount of a firm's total liabilities that exceeds $25 billion. Proceeds from the surcharge could be used to reduce the public debt of the sovereign nation that imposes it. They should not be used to establish a "bailout fund," which would create a moral hazard should corporate managers come to expect its use to support failing firms. It is also important to recognize that once a firm has attained TBTF status, no government can make a credible promise not to intervene if it runs into financial difficulty, because forbearance will only result in wider economic distress. Thus, it is probable that the prospect of a large firm defaulting will result in government intervention, making it preferable that the often untidy democratic process is used to transparently provide support to the firm through laws or statutes, and under public pressure and scrutiny not to insulate managers and owners from loss. In such a system, moral hazard is reduced.

Moreover, given that it is likely that public debt will be incurred later on to support the failing firm or provide countercyclical Keynesian stimulus to a sagging economy, it is desirable to reduce debt before leverage-induced calamities hit.

Making It More Difficult to Become "Too Big to Fail"

Another available option would be to mandate minimum capital-adequacy ratios and leverage reporting requirements on all such firms above a certain size, perhaps $50 billion in market capitalization, so that corporations considered too large or too interconnected do not jeopardize the economic system should they fail. The minimum capital-adequacy ratios can be tailored to different industries, considering that some industries that are natural monopolies—like utilities—can manage a higher debt load than other entities whose risk profiles are more skewed—like biotechnology or pharmaceuticals. For example, regulators would consider the inter-industry variations in leverage that we saw in Figure 7.1. These requirements would only apply to entities above the predetermined size so as to not overburden small businesses or businesses whose potential individual default would have no measurable impact on the economy.

Strengthening Disclosure Requirements

Improved disclosure requirements need to be enacted for off-balance-sheet obligations and derivative transactions. Proper measurement and reporting of leverage is critical to the effective control of leverage at non-financial firms. One essential disclosure that should be required in corporations' financial reports is the maximum amount of loss or exposure on derivative contracts to which the firm would be subject in a worst-case scenario, as well as a probability estimate of such a worst-case scenario. Since corporations sometimes enter into and exit or unwind financial transactions within a given reporting period (thus avoiding period-end disclosure), firms could be required to file simple information reports for all derivative transactions with notional or potential future cash-payment amounts over a certain threshold amount. This would improve the timeliness of disclosure of this critical information, which is often delayed until quarter- or year-end, and sometimes not disclosed at all.

Constraining Leverage from Acquisitions

Mergers and acquisitions, commonly referred to as "M&A," represent an important source of leverage around the world, especially when they take the form of leveraged-buyout (LBO) transactions, which involve the heavy use of debt. Companies are acquired for a variety of reasons relating to operating and financial synergies—including the desire for economies of scale, diversification, and greater market power. Each of the last three decades has witnessed a distinct wave of mergers characteristic of their time. In the run-up to the 2008 recession, syndication, structured finance, and collateralization, combined with easy credit, fueled a massive M&A wave. Global M&A volume peaked in 2007 at an all-time high of $4.7 trillion,[34] then decreased in 2008, and was in the process of rebounding in 2010 to $2.4 trillion (see Figure 7.2 for previous decades' data).[35]

Although the majority of M&A transactions are financed with cash or stock or a combination thereof, merger-related leverage can be quite

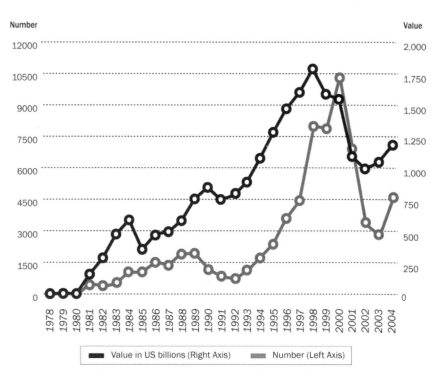

Figure 7-2   M&A Activity in the United States
Source: SDC Platinum by Thomson Financial Securities Data.

large in absolute terms. Approximately 14,000 LBOs took place in 2007, up from 5,000 in 2000 and 2,000 in the mid-1990s.[36] LBOs typically have leverage ratios of at least 4 or 5 and higher. In some cases, LBOs have been financed with up to 97 percent debt, such as Campeau's acquisition of Federated Department Stores in 1988, which ended in bankruptcy.[37] It is sometimes the case that LBOs are undercapitalized from the outset and later file for bankruptcy, with lawsuits being filed by aggrieved creditors based on allegations of *fraudulent conveyance*, such as was the case with the 2007 LBO of the Tribune Company.[38] LBOs often use complex capital structures, including senior secured debt, subordinated debt, unsecured debt (often high-yield, sometimes "junk bond" status), bridge financing, and preferred equity.[39] Even in non-LBO M&A activity, studies have indicated that the financial leverage of combined firms increases significantly following mergers,[40] and that mergers increase default risk.[41] Figure 7.3 shows the increase in debt that typically occurs in firms post-merger, implying a propensity to take on more leverage, and hence more risk, in order to deliver the stated goals of deal and to meet the expectations of new owners.

Given all this, it would be sensible to ensure that very large acquisitions do not result in excessive leverage that creates excessively large negative externalities and market shocks. We should not wait for such a shock to occur before we begin to take precautions. M&A transactions that exceed a given transaction amount—such as $10 billion—should be subject to review and approval by that country's central bank (the Federal Reserve, in the case of the United States) in order to ensure the amount of leverage used is not likely to sink the company in debt and create downstream economic ripples. The central bank could propose modifications to the transaction's capital structure in order to achieve a better balance of risk and return if it deems the transaction to be too risky as drafted. If the transaction happens across borders, multiple central banks could coordinate their reviews. One reason why the central bank should perform the review is that, in many countries, central banks have a level of independence from political processes and industry influence that is difficult to achieve or replicate elsewhere. Another is that the central bank is primarily concerned with the stability of the economy and should temper market participants' sometimes overly optimistic projections.

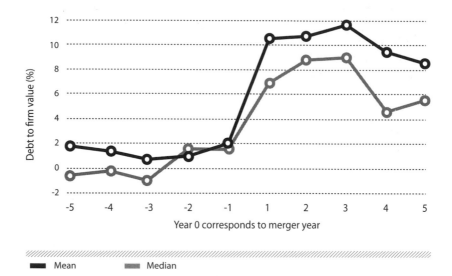

Figure 7-3   Industry-Adjusted Debt Analysis
Source: Aloke Ghosh and Prem C. Jain, "Financial leverage changes associated
with corporate mergers," Journal of Corporate Finance *6 (2000).*

Incentive and Compensation Systems

Finally, changes need to be made to corporate incentive and compensation systems in order to address the issue of misalignment of incentives and the pressure that managers face to produce short-term results.

The relative rise in compensation in the financial sector seen in Figure 7.4 is largely due to the rise in investment banking compensations. Wall Street and City investment banks epitomize a culture of large performance bonuses that regularly attract the attention of the press and civil society. Precrisis, it was the sheer size of their bonuses, not only for CEOs, but also star traders and deal-makers. Now society's shock is directed more at the resilience of this culture in the aftermath of the financial crisis and the too-big-to-fail support that the financial system enjoys. The realization that investment banks offer significant rewards for financial entrepreneurship on the upside but do not penalize it on the downside is proving difficult for society to accept. This asymmetry sits oddly with market philosophy as well, where risks and rewards tend to be correlated.

There are three important drivers of this asymmetry, which should be discussed more openly by central bankers and financial regulators as

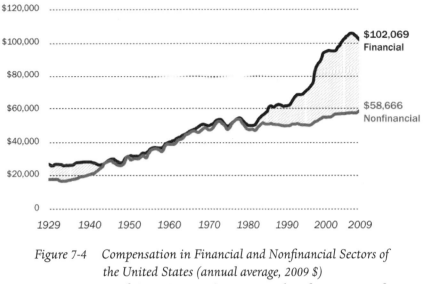

$120,000

$100,000 $102,069 Financial

$80,000

$60,000 $58,666 Nonfinancial

$40,000

$20,000

0

1929   1940   1950   1960   1970   1980   1990   2000 2009

Figure 7-4   *Compensation in Financial and Nonfinancial Sectors of the United States (annual average, 2009 $)*
Source: Financial Crisis Inquiry Commission, data from Bureau of Economic Analysis, Bureau of Labor Statistics, CPI-Urban

a means of injecting more fairness into incentive and compensation systems. They relate respectively to the profit-inelasticity of bonus pools, the inadequate provisioning for derivatives risk, and the ethical issues around the nature of these bonuses.

Investment banking bonus pools—the amount to be allocated from earnings toward total annual bonuses—are typically negotiated with the boards of directors in advance, usually as a percentage of divisional earnings. The logic is to encourage entrepreneurship and an "equity" culture by aligning the objectives of the firm and its employees. In good times, such percentages create a bounty that is spread among deserving high-performers. When times are bad, however, it is not necessarily the case that poor performance receives punishment. Through years of delivering profit and reinforced habit, the high-performer has become a "million-dollar guy," a "five-million-dollar guy," etc. If an investment banking firm "pays him down" in a bad year, the palpable fear is that he'll pick up his boots and join the one next door, taking his team with him. Such fears, preying upon not just managements but boards as well, are the reason that bonus pools are not as performance-elastic on the downside as they ought to be in a fairer world. Attitudes need to change, but it will not just happen; it will require openness, criticism, public debate, and both good and bad press. Even if only gradually, leading bankers and their regulators can and should bring about an industry-wide attitude change in the principles and practises of setting and carving up their bonus pools.

Second, the measurement of performance that is rewarded by investment-banking bonuses is often less scientific at the unit, desk, or individual level than an outsider might imagine, especially when it comes to the accounting around derivatives. Provisioning for the future costs and risks of derivatives is both an art and a discipline that is not widely known or implemented, resulting (in the worst case) in performance being recorded without ever being realized.[42] Moreover, performance is often double- or even triple-counted toward team and individual evaluations. For example, structured-derivative-deal profit is often "triple-counted" when it comes to bonus rewards—toward the salesperson who persuades the client to buy the derivative, the derivatives structurer who designs the trade in the first place, and the trader who has to book and risk-manage risks from residual mismatches that are commonplace for any complex structured derivative. If the derivative that was structured and sold carries regulatory risk—the risk of the derivative being torn up or forcibly unwound at a loss because it was post-hoc found to be inappropriate or it fell afoul of a new financial regulation—whose bonus pool should reflect the reputational and actual costs of such an unwinding? The trader in such a situation might argue that his profit write-off is sufficient punishment. Would structuring performance, or sales performance, account for this loss as well? Or would they hide behind the fact that, at the time of trading, the transaction had passed muster with the bank's compliance process? There are no industry standards for such issues, which therefore adds to the "ad-hoc-ism" that plagues bonus culture at investment banks. It is high time these issues were brought out into the open, discussed, and resolved in order to move the industry forward to areas of real challenge. In addition to regulatory risk and its related trade unwinds and reputational impacts, there can be other impacts on society that are not accounted for in reward and compensation. For example, whose performance will reflect third-party costs (the negative externalities) if a company engaged in socially valuable work ceases operations thanks to being sold an adventurous, but mislabeled, risk-management product that caused an unmanageable loss?

The final area of improvement aims at the heart of the ethics of bonus culture. Is a bonus a prize, a reward offered after the event for the *past year's* good performance in the interest of the firm? Or is it a bribe, an inducement to deliver another great year of performance and seek your next bonus? My observation is that, over the last two decades, the "prize" nature of bonuses has increasingly given way to the "bribe" nature of bonuses, with senior managers increasingly buying peace, team stability, and future performance by offering an inducement in the guise of a reward to their top performers. In other words, it becomes somewhat academic what you actually made last year and in what context, for what the firm needs is performance next year, and here is evidence that we consider you the person to deliver that performance. Once again, these are very real issues with not enough public visibility. Recently, in spring 2012, we have seen a shareholder backlash against top-executive pay, with a few CEO resignations as a result of their compensation packages not being approved.[43] However, the malady runs a lot deeper than just at CEO level, and for it to be cured, we need industry dialogue, disclosure, and transformation of scale that mere shareholder objections at some AGMs may not be able to achieve.

Incentive and compensation systems have a lot to do with the kind of culture one finds oneself in. Consider Spain's Mondragon Cooperative Corporation and you will find that the ratio of CEO pay to lowest-paid employee is not over 500:1, as it often is in London investment banks, but somewhere around 15:1. This is not an argument for investment-banking bosses' packages to be equal to those of other industries and across borders, but it is an argument for them to come out and openly engage in systemic change, rather than hide behind curtains of confidentiality in the dark shadows of short-term self-interest.

Moving Beyond Markets

Our global economic system appears to have premised economic growth on the incurrence of leverage upon leverage upon leverage, at the financial, corporate, and consumer levels. When de-leveraging finally comes during crises, the consequences are disastrous and the system collapses under the weight of organizations that were allowed to become overleveraged. Often they are defended from collapse because they are considered too big to fail. In the end, taxpayers and citizens bear the consequences as bailouts, layoffs, and bankruptcies cleanse the system of imprudently incurred risk. Many corporations today have come to suffer a collective amnesia regarding the license to operate that is granted them by society, and they have forgotten how to create value by truly innovating. Instead of seeking returns by developing new products and services or opening new markets, many corporations today incur excessive leverage solely to boost their returns. Their increased return comes at the price of increased risk. In essence, leverage has become the lazy manager's tactic for increasing short-term share prices. This is why we must remain ever vigilant of corporations' overuse of leverage.

Leverage is not well-monitored, well-managed, or well-controlled in our current economic system. Financial and nonfinancial institutions have used their political might effectively over the last few decades to ensure that governments the world over stay out of businesses' financial matters, and they succeeded in turning back or staving off regulation in a variety of areas. Unfortunately, global efforts at financial deregulation have seldom ended well, and we have witnessed the repeated failures of financial markets that were always supposed to arrive at the right balance. We must realize that markets alone cannot solve all of our problems. We must seize the opportunity to make changes to the regulatory system and ensure leverage is not misused by corporations to the detriment of society. Achieving better control of leverage will dramatically reduce its negative spillovers and result in a growth trajectory that will be much more stable, sustainable, and just.

CHAPTER EIGHT

Resource Taxation

Taxing the Bads, Not the Goods

Taxes, after all, are dues that we pay for the privileges of membership in an organized society.
— *Franklin D. Roosevelt*

In the midst of significant efficiency gains from the continuing revolutions in information technology, consumers forget easily enough to look up from the screens of their rapidly improving (and rapidly replaced) computers, laptops, smartphones, and tablet devices to realize that our complex modern existence ultimately stems from the same old basics: cutting, burning, and digging.

Global consumption of almost every principal industrial commodity increased dramatically during the second half of the twentieth century, driven mainly by a quadrupling of household consumption between 1960 and 2000. World energy production has skyrocketed, as access to energy served as a critical input behind the 242 percent economic expansion of the last four decades. According to the International Energy Agency, between 1973 and 2009, world energy consumption nearly doubled from the equivalent of 4.6 billion to 8.4 billion tons of oil.[1] Fossil fuels—coal, petroleum, and natural gas—represented over 80 percent of global energy consumption over this period.

Growth in energy consumption is forecast overwhelmingly from developing countries (see Figure 8.1). The energy profile for projected world consumption is increasingly carbon-intensive and ecologically intrusive (Figure 8.2). As a result, CO_2 emissions from 1970 until 2008 doubled from

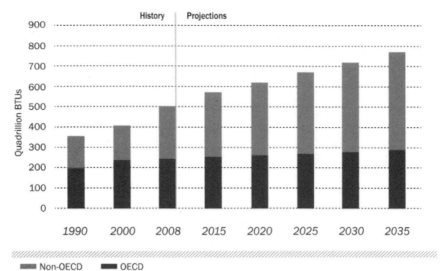

Figure 8-1   World Energy Consumption (1990–2035)
Source: U.S. Energy Information Administration, "International Energy Outlook,
2011," www.eia.gov/forecasts/ieo/more_highlights.cfm#world.

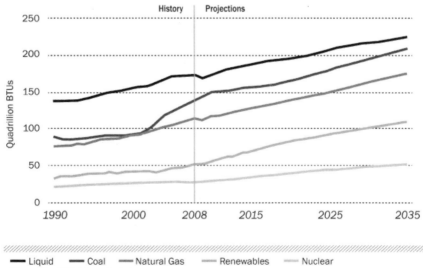

Figure 8-2   World Energy Consumption by Fuel (1990–2035)
Source: U.S. Energy Information Administration, "International Energy
Outlook, 2011," www.eia.gov/forecasts/ieo/more_highlights.cfm#world.

Figure 8-3   Global CO2 Emissions (kt) (1970–2008)
Source: World Bank World Development Indicators.

15.6 million to 29 million tons (Figure 8.3).[2] Most of this increase in energy use has occurred and will continue in the developing world, where, if material living standards were equal to those of the average American, the natural-resource inputs required to enable this consumption would exceed five Earths' worth of additional raw materials.[3]

Global mining production follows similar increase patterns as energy and materials use. Extraction of the precious minerals seen in Table 8.1 has nearly tripled globally from 1.1 billion to 3.1 billion tons between 1970 and 1999. Even if the economy has become more resource-efficient in the production and utilization of minerals, the increases in absolute mining volumes are staggering, as shown in Table 8.1. Mining of copper, lead, zinc, and iron ore have increased dramatically between twice and three and a half times.[4] Nearly all of these minerals come from virgin ore. Even though the price of recycling commodities has decreased with technological advancements, virgin ore largely remains cheaper, and in the case of copper, for example, the proportion obtained from recycling has actually dropped from 20 percent (1980) to 13 percent now. As with energy resources, vast increases in absolute volumes of minerals produced means that mines have shifted increasingly towards areas with valuable ecosystems and rich biodiversity, thus adding to the cost externalities of resource extraction.

Table 8-1   Global Mineral Production (1970–2009)

Mineral	1970 Extraction (Tons)	2009 Extraction (Tons)	Absolute Increase (Tons)	Relative Increase (%)
Copper	5,900,000	15,900,000	10,000,000	269%
Bauxite	57,800,000	199,000,000	141,200,000	344%
Zinc	5,460,000	11,200,000	5,740,000	205%
Iron Ore	769,000,000	2,240,000,000	1,471,000,000	291%
Tin	232,000	260,000	28,000	112%
Nickel	628,000	1,400,000	772,000	223%
Tungsten	32,400	61,300	28,900	189%
Lead	3,390,000	3,860,000	470,000	114%
Silver	9,360	21,800	12,440	233%
Lithium	73,100	301,000	227,900	412%
Mercury	9,790	1,920	-7,870	-180%
Gold	1,480	2,450	970	166%
Platinum	132	445	313	337%
Graphite	393,000	1,090,000	697,000	277%
Lime	97,000,000	299,000,000	202,000,000	308%
Potash	18,200,000	20,800,000	2,600,000	114%
Salt	146,000,000	280,000,000	134,000,000	192%
Zirconium	399,000	1,160,000	761,000	291%

Source: United States Geological Survey, "Mineral Commodity Summaries," minerals. usgs.gov/minerals/pubs/mcs/.

Resource taxation is about targeting materials and energy efficiency; it aims to rewire corporations to use fewer resources while delivering the same or higher levels of products and services. For years economists have de facto justified perpetual consumption on the assumption that the market will naturally revalue finite resources according to scarcity, in effect, slowing or preventing resource exhaustion while promoting technological innovation for alternatives. In so doing, they have generally ignored the externalities of resource extraction, especially the loss of ecosystem services from hitherto preserved natural areas where mining occurs. Once again, the familiar theme of private profits and public losses raises its head, and one sees ample evidence of the Corporation 1920 penchant for internalizing incomes and externalizing costs. Research repeatedly demonstrates that we have failed to allocate natural capital effectively in the economy, ignoring or obfuscating scarcities and risks until it is too late. We don't want to find out what "too late" means for the potential crises from climate change, freshwater shortages, or fishery losses.

Indeed, while conventional reserves of everyday energy and mineral resources are peaking, instead of shifting energy and raw-material extraction or production increasingly toward "unconventional" resources, we see the same old resources getting extracted at greater and greater social costs. Remote but ecologically precious areas, such as Alaska and the Arctic for oil, or the Niyamgiri Hills of Odisha for bauxite, continue to get opened up for the simple reason that society lacks the institutional capacity to properly value ecosystems and biodiversity.[5] The economic invisibility of nature becomes the unwitting battleground of blind business-as-usual profit seeking on the one hand and eclectic conservation-sensitive public economics on the other. It has become largely a matter of chance leadership and geopolitical circumstance as to which side wins any particular battle and where. The war, however, is still clearly being won by business-as-usual.

Perverse Subsidies and Resource Extraction

For decades, governments have repeatedly injected monetary steroids into the perpetual-consumption economy.[6] Instead of allowing consumers to bear the true costs of the energy and raw materials they consume, politicians have thrown the public wallet at extractive industries to keep consumer prices low. This market distortion has addicted consumers to low product prices, and substantially weakened the business case and innovation for low-resource-use technologies.

A joint study between IEA, OPEC, OECD, and the World Bank estimated that consumption subsidies related to fossil fuels amounted to

$557 billion in 2008.[7] IEA analysis found further that removing all subsidies by 2020 would reduce primary energy demand 5.8 percent, with a subsequent drop in carbon-dioxide emissions of 6.9 percent compared to a baseline in which the subsidies in place today remain constant. Such a reduction equals the current emissions of France, Germany, Italy, Spain, and the United Kingdom combined.[8]

In addition to consumption subsidies, nearly $100 billion was provided to producers of fossil fuels in 2008, meaning that over $650 billion—nearly 1 percent of global GDP—was spent on subsidizing the energy resources that account for the vast majority of the world's greenhouse-gas emissions, conventional air pollution, and water pollution.[9] While subsidies are largely politically motivated and intended to be handouts to the poor in developing countries, the reality on the ground is often different. The chief economist of the International Energy Agency, Fatih Birol, reports that of global energy subsidies for fossil fuels, only 8 percent of funds reaches the bottom 20 percent of income groups; over 80 percent of subsidies end up supporting those with medium and higher income levels.[10] A case in point can be seen in the gasoline subsidies in Mexico, one component of an estimated $25 billion fuel-subsidy program in 2008,[11] only 5.9 percent of which benefited the bottom 20 percent of the population that year, while 41 percent reached the top two deciles.[12] These market distortions have had profound impacts on the global environment while locking these countries into a resource-intense economic pathway.[13]

As documented by the World Bank, 35 countries receive at least one-fifth of their GDP or government revenues from natural-resource extraction and related exports.[14] Companies that use these cheap resources hardly need subsidies. In the United States, a gallon of gasoline is cheaper than a gallon of orange juice or even, in some instances, bottled water. As these companies race to the top of the market hyped up on economic steroids, society and the environment sink along with any financial incentives that would stimulate technological and policy development to decouple resource consumption from economic growth.

The case for investigating, disclosing, and reducing fossil-fuel subsidies could not be clearer, stronger, or more urgent. Recent G-20 communiqués (London, Pittsburgh), UN reports (UNEP's "Towards a Green Economy") and a growing number of serious voices from civil society have argued that this must be done. It is to be hoped that momentum for action on this front will build further at Rio+20. However, removing subsidies for fossil fuels is only part of the picture, and for only the "energy" side of the challenge of resource extraction. Subsidy removal alone will not reverse the climate-change impacts of fossil-fuel use, and big challenges will remain with minerals. The need to examine other mechanisms urgently such as resource taxation is therefore especially pressing.

The Rationale for Resource Taxation

Taxing the resource base of our predominantly brown economy—coal, petroleum, and many other minerals—can steer the market away from resource-intensive growth and toward smart-technology industries in renewable energy, clean water, new and better materials, and waste management. Resource taxation would force a revaluation of resources, in turn allowing us to manage, not simply extract, natural assets. Resource taxation will not only reduce the resource-intensity of consumption, but it has the additional potential to generate new revenues and save the expense of perverse subsidies, and to generate additional financing that can be used for high priority areas such as education and health care—or it can be applied against the rising cost of nature's resources.

Such a "double dividend" taxation framework is needed now more than ever. In the wake of the 2008 financial crisis, global government debt has ballooned to nearly $40 trillion.[15] The uncertain investment climate has US corporations alone holding over $1.2 trillion in cash.[16] Public trust in business is badly shaken. As Robert Shiller aptly points out in his book *Animal Spirits*, capitalism is a powerful vehicle for change, but one with significant blind spots if not properly guided. As corporations look to reinvest and rebuild, it is essential that market signals and market governance decouple profit maximization from resource consumption if we are to transition to a "green economy" and aim for sustainable development. For governments, this points toward a transformation in the tax system, taking the burden of taxation away from profits and toward resource use. For corporations, this places emphasis on the most progressive source of consumer surplus and customer satisfaction: innovation.

The central nervous system of Corporation 1920 undoubtedly feels costs, but until ecological capital is properly valued, it is virtually blind to the costs of our ongoing environmental losses. We are not going to value natural capital by depending on grants from charitable donors and government sponsored research; we must build a business case for private enterprise, the most powerful problem-solving tool in the history of humankind, to conserve, recycle, and innovate instead of cutting, digging, and burning. Revaluing natural resources can connect their costs to the corporation's bottom line and transform private business into a problem-solving entity compatible with the needs of the twenty-first century.

The philosophy of free markets and small government has long demonized taxation as a job-killing, "socialist" redistribution tool that robs from the rich in order to feed the inefficiencies of "big government." Like any tool, however, taxes are only good or bad depending on how they are used. Using taxes to revalue natural resources positions an innovative Corporation 2020 as a successful protagonist of twenty-first-century capitalism.

Pricing Public Wealth

Setting prices for natural-resource extraction is by no means simple, not least because it raises issues of ethics and equity. Natural resources are usually "public wealth" before they are leased or licensed or encumbered by governments in favor of corporations. What, then, is a fair price for such a contract between the government as society's agent on one hand and the corporation on the other, one that balances private profitability with a fair return to the citizen? Should it be set on a long-term basis, as a fixed royalty rate oblivious to the paths of inflation, supply, and market prices, or should it be variable based on these drivers of profitability? Can "free markets" ever determine fair prices that satisfy the principles of ethics and public equity? These are difficult questions, but they must be tackled and answered in order to create any semblance of a balance among corporate profitability, public financing, and fair returns to the citizen for whom every extra dollar of royalty or resource tax can be a dollar of personal taxes reduced.

First, though, it would be appropriate to size and understand the nature and dimensions of our global resource-extraction challenge.

The Size of the Pie

Taxes are part of the costs consumers pay for products, but they are usually levied either at the point of sale (a value-added tax) or importation (through duties and excise taxes), or as the general tax on a producer's profits (as corporate tax), or some combination thereof. They are much less often levied at the point of extraction of any public wealth, at the mine (as mining royalties).

Let us imagine that the minerals most used in our daily lives, such as petroleum, coal, iron, copper, and bauxite, were taxed as a percentage of their total value.[17] How much revenue could be raised? The "Global Resource Tax Assessment" (Figure 8.4), presents one calculation for 32 minerals, levying a theoretical 4 percent tax on their 2009 global commodity value. It suggests that $104 billion annually can be raised. While this analysis assesses a tax based on percentage of total value, other approaches are possible. Taxes might, for example, be based on specific social or environmental damages associated with the extraction or use of the mineral.

A closer look into one sector—coal—provides several insights into the necessity and the feasibility of shifting taxes from profits to resources. Coal is one of the most geologically abundant global fuels, with sizable deposits geographically distributed across the globe. In the mid-1970s, international trade in coal amounted to less than 300 million metric tons.[18] According to the World Coal Association, global coal trade since then has grown sixfold to over 1.8 billion tons in 2009.[19] Moreover, coal's prominence in the current and projected Asian energy mix emphasizes the need to revalue this fuel according to human and ecological damages.

In 2009, the ten largest US public coal companies produced nearly 720,000 short tons of coal. For the same year, these firms paid a total of close to $530 million in US federal income taxes. These aggregate numbers, however, mask key details. First, these companies' 10-K reports reveal that three of them—Arch Coal, Alpha Natural Resources, and Westmoreland Coal—didn't pay any taxes at all that year; rather, on net these firms received *payments from the US federal government*.[20] Thus, we see that the actual taxes paid by these companies, as a percent of the estimated value of the coal at the average world price, varies from −2.1 to 11.5 percent.[21]

It is therefore possible that a flat resource tax of 4 percent on coal extraction, free of loopholes, could actually reduce the total tax that some
coal mining companies pay. It should be noted that the 4 percent rate
chosen for this analysis is not the only rate that could be decided upon by
policymakers; the actual rate chosen might depend upon the details of
each jurisdiction. Overall, that 4 percent tax would nevertheless increase
total tax revenues from $528 million to $947 million.[22] The placement of
this flat tax on the coal mined, instead of on corporate profits, would
encourage development of cleaner energy consumption in the upstream
economy, and the tax revenue could go toward reducing income taxes for
upstream industries or providing funds to remediate coal's damages to
human health and the environment, or indeed it could be returned to the
citizens of the United States as a tax rebate.

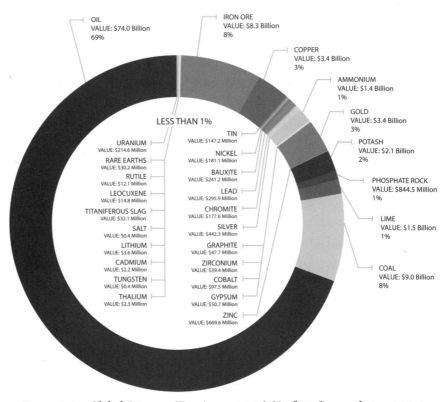

*Figure 8-4   Global Resource Tax Assessment (4% of 32 Commodities at 2009
Prices) Source: Data from US EIA, World Coal Association, and USGS.*

Linking specific ecological or societal damages to resource taxation largely encourages companies to shift production toward more socially responsible extraction. As a crude example of translating such measurements into practice, taxation could incorporate the fact that petroleum sourced in the rainforests of Ecuador has the potential to inflict significantly more ecological damage than petroleum drawn from the deserts of the Middle East.[23] Similarly, resources could be taxed according to a global pollution index linked to a resource's production and use in relation to, for example, climate change. The exact nature of such policy frameworks, however, is less important than our understanding that environmental and economic science provides us with tools to attach ecological and environmental value to our consumption.

Toward a New Economic Model

Contrary to popular perception, reconstituting our economy from one based on perpetually increasing resource extraction toward one of resource conservation does not require a sacrificed standard of living. This is a myth propagated by decades of postwar consumerism, which established a belief system that posits unconditional faith in free markets and the corporation as society's champion.

The market needs to move from failures to freedom. Opening innovation means liberating the market from interference—Adam Smith's "invisible hand" has for decades been locked in all too tight a handshake with corporate lobbyists who ensure that entrenched interests are protected. Imagine Bill Gates trying to launch the personal computer revolution in a world where the mainframe computer manufacturers received over $100 billion annually in government subsidies.[24] Taxing key resources emphasizes the need for efficiency and accelerates the retirement of inefficient technologies, stimulating the innovation and deployment cycle. Raising living standards while avoiding the consumption of "five Earths" for a population of 9 billion people in next 30 years will require Joseph Schumpeter's notion of "creative destruction" to reach an unprecedented scale. Without it, we cannot secure the constant innovation necessary to address the economic invisibility of natural and social capital.[25]

Some of world's largest and most profitable companies rooted in the extractive economy will no doubt continue to defend society's bad consumption habits and to argue in favor of business as usual and against any tax reforms. They do have a point, because no matter what the threat from our culture of perpetual consumption, policies of taxing natural resources have to be implemented with care, precision, and a deep understanding of national contexts, or they risk harming the economy. The story of the consumption of coal and resource-extraction policies regarding coal in three countries with different political systems, different levels of subsoil resources, and different economic and social behaviors, is telling. For reasons which will become clear, I will label the United States the "consumer," Australia the "producer," and Germany the "manager."[26] These three powerful societies are responding to the present challenges very differently. Let us begin with the consumer.

The Capital of Consumption

With less than 5 percent of the world's population, the United States consumes more of many natural resources, particularly energy resources, than any country, consuming over 23 percent of the world's coal, 21 percent of the natural gas, and 24 percent of the world's petroleum.[27] Yet the United States raises the second-lowest amount of environmental tax revenue as a percentage of GDP, including energy taxation, in the Organization for Economic Co-operation and Development (OECD), second only to Mexico.[28] Its electricity and gasoline prices are well below European levels. US consumption of raw materials reached 23.6 metric tons per American in 2000, a level 51 percent above the average consumption in Europe.[29] Compared to 1970 averages, the typical US home has increased in size from 1,500 to nearly 2,400 square feet, despite a decrease in total home occupancy rates, meaning that Americans must consume more and more energy to heat, cool, and power their homes.[30] The iconic American "McMansion" defines the enormous extent of US consumption, which is unprecedented in any period of human history.

Few resources tell the US story of consumption and the need for taxation better than coal. Coal-fired power generates approximately 50 percent of US electricity supplies.[31] Coal production is driven by the electric-power sector, which accounts for over 90 percent of US coal consumption today, compared with only 19 percent in 1950.[32] Coal's prominence remains largely unchecked, even if coal-fired power projects have lately experienced significant delays.[33] US regulatory process continually fails to price coal at levels reflective of the fuel's damages to human health and the economy. Senior economists recently found that the economic damages of coal-fired power exceeded value-added by a factor of 2.2, meaning coal-fired electricity's current prices are vastly too low.[34] A study from the Harvard Medical School suggests that these hidden costs of coal might add an additional $0.17 per kilowatt-hour to an average cost of residential electricity, rendering the full costs of coal-fired power around $0.25/kWh.[35] The study also found that the human health effects from coal-fired power emissions of particulate matter, sulfur, nitrogen oxide, mercury, and other toxins, cost the US economy from $65 billion to $217 billion a year.[36] In addition, the public-health burden associated with coal mining in Appalachia alone totals more than $74.6 billion per year.[37] A comparison of these estimates with data from the US Center for Disease Control makes it clear that the externalities of coal-fired power kill more Americans annually than drunk drivers.[38]

Despite 100 years of technological innovation, the US power industry remains strongly centralized around coal, even if this paradigm has slowly shifted in recent years. Alexander Graham Bell would hardly recognize the modern telephone, but Thomas Edison would find today's centralized power system relatively similar to that born in 1882 at his Pearl Street Station. Over two-thirds of the energy content of coal is wasted as low-grade heat, radiated into the atmosphere. US power companies delivered electricity at 30–33 percent efficiency from inputs to consumers during the 1960s—virtually the same efficiency found today.[39] Advanced coal-fired boilers in Germany and increasingly in developing countries, such as China, routinely achieve efficiency levels near 44–45 percent.[40] How can such a massive industry with such financial power experience almost zero efficiency gains and sit outside international norms?

A large part of the answer is fairly simple, as the Waxman-Markey Bill's short political life aptly demonstrates. Since Samuel Insull and John D. Rockefeller, the United States has been the land of Big Energy. Commonly referred to as a "natural monopoly," the electric-power industry comprises a patchwork of mining, electricity generation, and transmission operators that produced annual sales of around $260 billion.[41] This translates into influence, and the result is that the power industry has too rarely been forced to undergo change. Legislative processes for the Waxman-Markey Bill, the first serious US legislation proposed to address climate change and energy security, provoked over 770 business and interest groups to lobby Capitol Hill in 2008.[42] These groups spent millions of dollars on public relations to hire approximately 2,340 registered lobbyists to shield against this climate legislation that intended, in part, to price energy according to externalities.[43]

Unregistered lobbying efforts also occur through more overt subterfuge—for example, through "astroturfing" campaigns (lobbying through the guise of a grassroots movement), which, in the age of electronic media, have become extremely successful.[44] A notable example is that of a conservative PR/lobbying firm's creating a YouTube video entitled "Al Gore's Penguin Army," produced to look like an amateur video spoof coinciding with the release of Al Gore's 2006 documentary *An Inconvenient Truth*.[45]

Between 1998 and 2011, electric utilities as well as oil and gas companies spent almost $3 billion on lobbying,[46] four times as much as on research and development (R&D). Coal industries' R&D expenditure accounted for only 0.1–0.3 percent of sales, outranked by nearly every other industry.[47] Traditionally, electric utilities have retorted that, as regulated entities, they are unable to justify R&D expenditures in their ratemaking. Yet, for an industry that considers itself indispensable, the notion that utilities have plenty of cash on hand to influence Congress but come up broke on R&D lacks credibility. Power-company leaders often complain that cooperation on large-scale research projects across such a historically fragmented sector borders on the impossible, but most utilities have been strongly and consistently able to coordinate their lobbying in opposition to climate legislation.

The American Coalition for Clean Coal Electricity (ACCCE), a specialized lobbying group that addresses climate policy on behalf of the coal industry, uses its $45 million annual budget to inform every American that coal is the optimal fuel for electricity generation.[48] Influence spending has led to outrageous and even insulting violations of public trust. The ACCCE became embroiled in a scandal in which a subcontractor sent falsified letters pretending to be from grassroots stakeholders to Representative Edward Markey, a principle author on America's first legislative climate initiative, to portray the bill as disadvantaging the poor and minority groups.[49] Public campaigns have not stopped at targeting politicians. Groups such as the "Friends of Coal" in West Virginia, a top US coal-producing state, even produced a coloring book for distribution in local elementary schools, and the ACCCE funded a commercial in which lumps of coal sang Christmas carols. The commercial received such ridicule from the press that it was eventually removed from television.[50]

The Benefits of Taxing the Bads, Not the Goods

What if coal were priced even in part according to its externalities? What would this mean for the average global citizen, or the average American? Such questions are complex, and test the limits of economic and environmental understanding, but reviewing the numbers is important if we want to size a future for natural resources. The global resource pie shown in Figure 8.4 provides the revenue available from taxing coal mined, which, if set at even 4 percent of its 2009 market value would raise $9 billion per year. For the United States specifically, it would raise about $3 billion annually. Although these sums hardly compensate for the economic damages caused by coal, they would surely contribute to accelerating the adoption of more efficient energy resources.

Levying taxes on resources upstream (at the mine) or downstream (in manufacturing and consumption) offers potentially different levels of economic efficiency. Taxing coal-fired power instead of coal itself offers further insights. During 2009, American coal-fired power plants produced approximately 1.7 trillion kilowatt-hours, the standard measurement of electric power.[51] Electricity taxes on coal-fired power of even an arbitrary $.02 per kilowatt would raise $35 billion for the American public. At a tax rate of $.17, which is the value of coal-fired power's damages per kilowatt-hour calculated by the Harvard study, it would generate closer to $300 billion.[52]

In 2008, the approximately 8,300,000 energy consumers of "Middle America" filed income taxes with an adjustable gross income between $75,000 and $100,000.[53] Their taxes raised almost $66 billion, with an average payment of $7,802.[54] Taxing coal-fired electricity even at the $0.02 rate would enable an income tax refund of over $4,000 to every one of them, or could be used to benefit those in lower income tax brackets.[55] Since the average American consumes approximately 12,000 kilowatt-hours a year of electricity,[56] the tax could impose a direct cost to consumers of at most $250, which is easily refunded in lower property or income taxes.[57]

Of course, this direct-consumption premium admittedly ignores cost increases for products manufactured in the United States that heavily rely on underpriced coal-fired power. Firms often rely on razor-thin margins to manufacture profitably, and they remain sensitive to the price of electricity. So instead of allocating the entire tax benefit from coal-fired power to consumers, the tax could help manufacturing pay for efficiency improvements and worker-training in new, efficient technologies. This has been done in high-cost manufacturing countries such as Germany, which has improved the financial health of energy-intensive industries subject to aggressive climate policies. Instead of coal being a barrier to the clean technologies that will redefine the twenty-first century, taxes from coal can pay for the transition.

Australian Finders, Keepers

"Today is a significant day for Australians and the Australians of the future who want to see a better environment," remarked Prime Minister Julia Gillard on the narrow passage of Australia's first government program to price carbon dioxide emissions. Parliamentary opposition leader Tony Abbott responded immediately, "We can repeal the tax, we will repeal the tax, we must repeal the tax. This is a pledge in blood. This tax will go."[58]

Abbott's blood pledge reflects the deepening political polarization of Australia's natural-resource and environmental policies. How could such a rich, modern country see such extreme views on resource and pollution management? How do Australia's resource policies affect the business community and social welfare?

The answers lie at least in part with former Prime Minister Kevin Rudd. The story of Rudd's term as prime minister of Australia is one of the democracy's great twenty-first-century dramas. Following a long tenure of conservative leadership, Rudd and his Labor party swept into office in 2007 on a "Yes, We Can" message comparable to the one that propelled Barack Obama's ascent to the White House. The Rudd government's first act was to sign the Kyoto Protocol and pursue domestic policies to reduce Australia's greenhouse-gas emissions. To enable that goal, Rudd sought to renegotiate the social contract between Australia's extractive industries and the public by increasing corporate taxes on mining companies. Liberalism seemed at last to march across Australian politics, but Rudd did not look back to gauge how many were following his green policy parade. Few political spectators at the time could have imagined that the most popular prime minister in Australia's history would soon be removed from office by his own party and have his policy initiatives watered down by his successor, Julia Gillard, at the behest of large corporate interests.

If the United States is the world's fossil energy "consumer," Australia is its "producer." Australia is essentially the world's mine; few countries have struck the geological lottery as richly. Where it once lamented being tucked away in the corner of the Asian-Pacific region, Australia now finds itself at the center of a massive natural-resource economy that feeds rapidly developing Asia with energy and minerals. With 38 percent of the world's nickel, 33 percent of the lead, 28 percent of the zinc, 25 percent of the brown coal, and 38 percent of the uranium, Australia commands an immense mineral-resource base that has caused its economy to boom. Australia also has 20 percent of the world's silver, 16 percent of the industrial diamonds, 15 percent of the iron ore, and 13 percent of the gold.[59] According to the Department of Foreign Affairs and Trade, natural resources account for well over A$50 billion in trade annually and represent Australia's largest single sector by export value. Of Australia's top 25 merchandise and service exports, twelve are minerals.[60]

Ever since Australia's nationhood in 1901, the prevailing attitude toward mining mineral resources can largely be described by the old adage "finders, keepers." Private extraction companies have operated with general disdain for the idea of paying for access to resources that belong to the people of Australia.

A case in point is gold. Incredibly, gold was not taxed in Australia until 1991, depriving the Australian people of hundreds of millions of dollars in tax revenue.[61] Gold production in Australia exploded from 27 tons per year in 1982 to 157 tons in 1988, earning A$2.7 billion from exports in 1988 across a market increasingly focused on exports. As gold prices appreciated considerably in the 1980s, the Australian newspaper *The Age* published an influential editorial stating that "Australian taxpayers are theoretically subsidizing gold mining companies to the tune of millions of dollars each year. . . . Economically and morally there is no reason for the tax-free status to remain."[62]

As *The Age* went on to state, such a pattern of public risk and private gain sends the wrong message to business about resource consumption. Corporations should not access public resources as though they were limitless geological ATMs. In the face of a rising Asia, the constraints of the world's natural-resource markets accelerated a boom-and-bust cycle in global commodity markets. A government review of taxation in Australia, known informally as the Henry Review after Rudd's Secretary of Treasury, Ken Henry, found a vast difference in the taxes levied and corporate profits from extracting Australia's natural resources, as shown below in Figure 8.5. BHP Billiton reported half-year profits of in excess of $23 billion in 2011.[63] Similarly, Rio Tinto showed profits for 2010 over $14.3 billion, and Xstrata, the world's largest coal exporting company, revealed profits over $5 billion.[64]

Global mining companies operating in Australia have made exceptional profits by mining and selling Australia's mineral wealth, but have refunded only a small fraction of these earnings back to the Australian citizen. While the Australian government received only an additional A$9

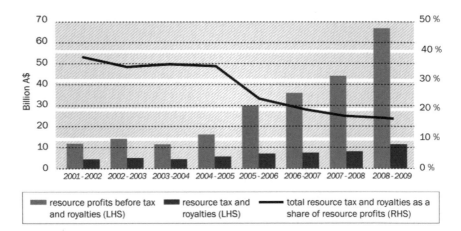

Figure 8-5   Australian Royalty and Tax Revenues
Compared with Resource Profits (2001–9)
Source: Commonwealth of Australia, "Australia's Future
Tax System: Report to the Treasurer" (2009).

billion in taxes from mining companies over the past ten years, profits were nearly A$80 billion.[65] Compared to taxes in Norway, Great Britain, and other OECD countries, Australia appeared to be giving away its natural resources virtually for free. Rudd's government sought to correct this imbalance. Under the direction of Secretary Ken Henry, the Department of Treasury put forth an analysis that suggested that the government propose a 40 percent tax on resource "super profits," along with a redistributive cut in corporate tax rates from 30 percent to 28 percent. The mining companies' response was deliberative and sharp—it included misleading advertising campaigns and intense political lobbying, all of which resulted in Kevin Rudd losing his party's support and his premiership. Rudd's failed tax was a defeat for the people of Australia, and a lesson on the difficulties of renegotiating the social contract involving private extractive industries and publicly owned resources. In the final analysis, it remains a sobering reflection on the significant challenges of taxing resource extraction.

Germany: Conserving, Recycling, and Innovating

If the United States consumes resources, and Australia produces them, Germany manages them. Home to the world's fifth-largest economy with an annual GDP over $3 trillion, Germany produces automobiles, chemicals, machinery, and power-generation equipment iconic of the world's best-quality industrial goods. Germany typically ranks as the world's fifth- or sixth-largest emitter of greenhouse gases. Beyond only modest deposits of coal and natural gas, Germany is devoid of nearly all energy and mineral resources. Feeding the German economy requires significant imports of natural resources. Around 60 percent of Germany's primary energy supply is imported.[66] Having lost out on the geological lottery, the entire German economy is focused on producing high-value goods from ever-fewer inputs—in other words, it is focussed on efficiency.

Despite energy-intensive industry representing 44 percent its economic output—compared to only 30 percent in the United States[67]—Germany produces $6,300 per ton of oil equivalent, over $1,000 more than the United States for the same energy input.[68] The official motto of the German Energy Agency is *Effizienz Entscheidet*, or "Efficiency Decides," a slogan that captures the essence of Germany industry. How Germany has translated efficiency into resource management provides an example as to how business, public policy, and environmentalism combine to maximize corporate, natural, and social returns.

Since the 2011 tragedy at the Fukushima reactor in Japan, the eyes of government policymakers the world round have focused on Germany. Chancellor Angela Merkel's government led the country toward permanently phasing out nuclear power immediately following Fukushima.[69] She has recommitted Germany to an energy future organized around renewables and a national target of reducing greenhouse-gas emissions by 40 percent within the next 20 years, easily the most aggressive low-carbon path of any industrialized nation. Walking away from fission and the internal-combustion engine, both products of German science, the country is embarking toward a low-carbon energy future that, according to CEO Heinrich Hiesinger of ThyssenKrupp, is "an effort comparable to reunification"[70] in terms of financial costs and political dedication.[71]

The key to Germany's energy transition rests on how the country will manage natural, financial, and social resources. Taxation continues to play a starring role in this story, as Germany has relied on it to address many of its complex resource problems. In 1999, faced with a fiscal crisis, the Germany legislature passed the Ecological Tax Reform Act, which imposed gradually increasing surcharges on petroleum products and electricity.[72] As a result, Germans continue to pay among the highest prices in the world for energy. In 2011, gasoline in Germany cost approximately $8 a gallon[73]—more than twice American prices—with taxes representing about 63 percent of the total.[74] Compare this to the United States, where taxes represent only about 16 percent of the total price of a gallon of gasoline.[75] In addition, German electricity prices are generally three times the rate a typical American would pay. A second bill, the Germany Renewable Energy Law, adds $10.50 in annual costs for feed-in tariffs in support of alternative energy sources, particularly solar and wind power.[76]

The German government has strategically invested its revenues back into the economy. In 2003, tax reform raised nearly $24 billion, most of which went toward reducing pension contributions by some 1.7 percent.[77] Funds boosted employment by reducing the payroll tax rate from 42.3 percent to 34.6 percent of gross wages.[78] After consulting with industry, the government funneled tax funds into areas considered critical for the German economy. Between 2001 and 2006, the Kreditanstalt für

Wiederaufbau (German Development Bank, KfW) Program for Energy Efficiency in Buildings issued over 450,000 loans totaling approximately $36 billion.[79] Over $1.2 million housing units were offered subsidized loans based on resource taxation.[80]

The results of such investments are powerful. The program is credited with helping to create a million new jobs while cutting home energy consumption in half. Budget analysts estimate that for every euro of government subsidy, the program attracted over nine euros in loans.[81] Although at high costs, German renewable electricity production increased from 6 percent of the electricity supply in the 1990s to over 10 percent in 2009.[82] Meanwhile, German companies and research institutions submitted between 30 and 40 percent of global patent applications in efficiency-product development.[83]

Assuredly, Germany's approaches to taxation are not without faults, or political controversy. Even still, the country offers an example of how tax revenue—if spent strategically—can enrich both public and private interests.

Reconciling Economic and Ecological Efficiency

The ecological realities of the twenty-first century necessitate a reorganization of the production and consumption of natural resources. Designing sound and fair taxation polices is a huge challenge, and political solutions are rarely perfect. Yet we cannot let the desire for perfection become the enemy of the greater good in designing programs to revalue resources. Time is of the essence. Moving from cutting, digging, and burning toward conserving, recycling, and innovating is not free or frictionless. Warren Buffet once remarked that price is what you pay, value is what you get. The ability to obtain value is available to us.

Three main facts justify increased taxation of natural resources. First, resources are rarely priced according to the damages caused by the resource's extraction or use. For example, coal mining causes damages to local water and air resources, while the combustion of coal results in damages to human health and the environment far beyond the monetary value of the electricity produced. The externalities of extraction and production are underwritten by the public.

Second, resources are finite, and while technology has improved access to new resources, ultimately demand and supply mismatches for critical resources such as petroleum, coal, natural gas, copper, and other minerals can cause severe economic shocks. Swings in the prices for petroleum and other commodities over the past years provide ample evidence that companies cannot forecast business effectively without certainty in resource markets. Regulatory certainty plays as great a role as geology in economic stability. Resource taxation prepares the economy for volatile commodity markets. In Northern Europe, where gasoline is taxed up to three times more at the pump than in the United States, volatility in petroleum markets is much less of a political or economic crisis. Assuredly, high oil prices are a drag on the European economy. Still, decades of high gasoline prices have conditioned Europe to produce substitutes to oil-based transportation, mainly in the form of public transportation and well-planned, walkable cities. Countries and corporations that prepare for resource-price variability add versatility to their bottom line.

Third, well-designed taxation drives innovation, and that should be a key goal of any reform. Shifting the tax burden from "taxing the goods" to "taxing the bads" aligns taxation with rewarding resource efficiency and not resource use. This is not to say that the extractive industries have not found cost-effective innovations to deliver resources faster and more cheaply to consumers the world wide. The aim of such innovation, however, has been value-addition through higher and more efficient extraction, rather than value-addition through less extraction. This has impeded innovation into lower-resource products and services. GE's "ecomagination" initiative and other large companies' efforts to address the constraints presented by the twenty-first century capture the essence of innovating a way out of serious challenges. We might be cutting, digging, and burning decades into the future, but at least we can do so with a focus on resource conservation. Taxation can tip the pricing threshold such that recycling is more profitable than mining and the negative externalities on the environmental and human health are properly accounted for by business.

CHAPTER NINE

Corporation 2020

The New DNA of Business

*Power and machinery, money and goods, are useful only as
they set us free to live. They are but means to an end. For instance, I do not consider the machines which bear my name
simply as machines. If that was all there was to it I would do
something else. I take them as concrete evidence of the working out of a theory of business, which I hope is something
more than a theory of business—a theory that looks toward
making this world a better place in which to live. . . .*

— *Henry Ford*

So much has been written by so many excellent authors on "tomorrow's
corporation" that it may appear surprising that anyone would imagine
that still more is needed. Three reasons tell us otherwise. The first is that
change won't just happen. There is too much optimism built around examples of forward-looking corporate CEOs and incomplete models and
anecdotal observations of correlation between corporate sustainability
and corporate success. Second, there are no elegant or easy solutions.
There are too many single-themed or dominant-themed theses describing
how we can transform corporate purpose and behavior. Too many people
tell us that transformation is already well under way, often arguing that it
is all about transparency, or all about ownership, which underrepresents
the complexity and extent of the challenge we have on our hands. No one
institution alone, be it government or civil society or the market or the
corporation itself, can overcome this challenge. Third, the challenge is

too often presented as an environmental challenge or a social justice issue or both. But it is in fact a challenge of survival for the corporation itself, for the modern economies that corporations constitute and operate, and indeed for human civilization as we know it. This is urgent: significant transformations must begin within this decade.

It Won't Just Happen

My first point of disagreement with the recent wave of discussion is that it relies too much on a conviction about the imminence of revolution or redesign or reform of today's corporation, drawn from correlations between improved corporate performance and an increased corporate focus on sustainability. Usually, this correlation is a result of some combination of lower costs, higher efficiency, product innovation, and business model innovation, thanks to the business following a more sustainable path. Sustainability is viewed by some as "the key driver of innovation."[1] Others promote a movement described as a "green wave" in which smart corporations or "wave riders" catch on early and profit from better practices.[2] These convictions are all informed by well-considered theses and evidenced by iconic examples of "new corporate DNA," but at the same time, the weakness of such theses is reflected by the "wave riders" that have not come through the last decade with flying colors.

Those hoping for such kinds of endogenous change appear to be declaring victory too early. The reality is that despite these correlations between sustainability and corporate success, endogenous change (the idea that corporations can and should drive sustainability "from within" because it is good for them) may not be enough. It is too dependent on the continuing inspiration and initiative of a few corporate leaders playing on a field heavily tilted against them and still dominated by tens of thousands of firms that are sustainability laggards. And there are still a trillion dollars of subsidies supporting fossil fuels, intensive agriculture, and trawler fishing, even though governments are well aware of the risks and social costs of climate change, have ample information on pesticide and fertilizer impacts on human health, water bodies, and biodiversity, and can see the impact of open-access pelagic fisheries on the remaining stocks of fish in the seas.

Second, corporate ownership—which in theory determines the

direction taken by companies—is less and less in the hands of individuals or communities and increasingly in institutional hands (an estimated 70 percent),[3] mostly mutual funds and pension funds for whom performance means quarterly returns. The culture of "twos and twenties" (2 percent commission, 20 percent share of capital gain) fostered by mutual fund managers and hedge funds has taken a deep hold on the psyche of the entire landscape of investment management, so much so that even institutional investors who have "natural" reasons to be thinking long-term and measuring long-term performance (such as life insurers and pension funds) are instead overly focused on their short-term performance.

As a result, most corporations are still powering ahead and feeding a brown economy, one that does not increase social equity and does not decrease the persistence of poverty and does not reduce environmental risks and ecological scarcities. Most corporations are still hard-wired to deliver their best performance in a brown economy. NGOs, change agents, and deep thinkers may rail against such corporations and call them "dinosaurs" or "monsters," but the reality is that they comprise most of the economy, and there have not been large enough changes in the operating environment for them to either evolve and survive, or quietly go extinct.

There Are No Elegant Solutions

There are too many elegant and well-argued theses for corporate evolution, redesign, or reform which underrepresent (and thus avoid addressing) the complexity of the challenge on hand. This complexity is deeply engrained in the legal history of the corporation, in postwar economic history, and in the ascendancy of democracy and free-market capitalism. It is also inextricably linked to our prevalent systems of subsidies and incentives for a brown economy, an economic model which has delivered progress for a century and a half in the Western world, and is now providing growth and development worldwide but exposing the whole planet to unacceptable social and environmental risks.

In *The Naked Corporation*, Don Tapscott and David Ticoll make the case that the Internet and social media are forcing businesses into an age of transparency toward shareholders, customers, employees, partners, and society.[4] Financial data, employee grievances, and internal memos regarding environmental disasters, product weaknesses, and scandals are all publicly available if one knows where the information is held. Tapscott and Ticoll argue that transparency is revolutionizing business and forcing it to engage with and demonstrate values-based decision making, as against just a short-term-profit focus. Transparency is indeed a vital development and it is a theme that touches some key planks of change that this book advocates. Disclosing corporate externalities in statutory accounts is about increasing transparency, as is control and disclosure of lobbying and "revolving door" hiring, for example. Transparency alone, however, is not going to transform the way business is done. Penalties for a lack of transparency are too few, regulations are still needed, and taxation and subsidies need urgent reform.

The changing face of consumer choice is a vital driver of change. As a result, advertising may not have the privilege of remaining values-neutral and unaccountable for much longer. Corporate culture is certainly in the cross-wires of society, although I hesitate to go as far as Dov Seidman's *How*, which argues that consumers are increasingly driving sustainability by being sensitive to the values and culture of the corporation which produces what they consume—the "how" of business.[5]

There Is Real Urgency

Until the problem of the redesign of economic agency is resolved, we cannot hope to see a "green economy" emerging around the world. Put simply, the earth's surface is a bundle of complex interacting systems that nurture humanity and feed our economies. The rapid growth of the postwar years and its resultant onslaught of "cutting, digging, burning" is pushing against this complex system at many levels.

To put it bluntly, Corporation 1920 cannot and will not deliver a green economy. And without a green economy, there is every risk that we shall breach planetary boundaries, or safe operating limits for human society to inhabit the biosphere.

As Johan Rockström from the Stockholm Resilience Centre and his colleagues explain, there is not one planetary boundary (greenhouse-gas emissions are the boundary most prominent in the public mind nowadays) but several planetary boundaries to consider, and to complicate matters, they are not independent but connected. Such limits might already have been crossed in the realm of atmospheric emissions and biodiversity loss.

And there are already many examples of the onset of these large-scale changes, including the death of coral reefs, widespread desertification, and extreme weather events.

At the same time, there are risks in other directions: excess nitrogen, shortages of rock phosphorous and potash (both key fertilizers), freshwater scarcities, ocean acidification . . . the list is long. It has become clear that 2020 is about as long as we have before we must embark on a wave of reforms that collectively can bring the economy and humanity back on a safe trajectory. In 2009 Dr. Pachauri, chair of the IPCC, wrote:

> We [in the IPCC] have estimated that to stabilize global temperature increases at just 2° to 2.4° Celsius, we have only about seven years to turn around global emissions of greenhouse gases like carbon dioxide. By 2015 they'll have to peak. By 2020, we'll need to put in place a 25–40 percent reduction in greenhouse-gas emissions. That's a huge challenge. . . . But I believe these emissions reductions are possible. We've carried out assessments of the sort of mitigation strategies needed and find that the costs are really minimal. The necessary technologies are here. . . . There will be some discomfort during the transition to lower-carbon technologies, but at the end of the day, we'll be better off. And our children will be much better off.[6]

Thus, if it won't just happen, and as there are no simple or elegant solutions, and if it is indeed an urgent survival challenge, then what is the change agenda that will get us the green economy that our survival requires, and the emergence of Corporation 2020 that will be its main agent?

Business needs a new DNA—but what is it, and how can we all collaborate in order to engineer its ascendancy in the very real context of today's ownership patterns, market systems, and democracies in the very short time we have on our hands?

The New DNA of Business

J. N. Tata, the nineteenth-century industrialist and founder of India's corporate behemoth, the Tata Group, believed that "in a free enterprise, the community is not just another stakeholder in business, but is in fact, the very purpose of its existence."[7] This philosophy continues to be part of the corporate credo of the Tata Group to this day, reflected in a comment from Ishaat Hussain, Finance Director of Tata Sons, the group's holding company: "The narrow shareholder definition will allow you to grow fast but will have you fade just as fast. If you look at stakeholder value, then you are taking a long term view of the business." Hussain's view is that the change that is needed "has to come from within. It has to be part of your DNA."[8]

The need to redesign the corporation to make it fit for the future— to make it operate by the dictates of a different DNA—has been felt by many corporate leaders, corporate houses, and thinkers over the last few decades. Corporation 20/20, a recent initiative by the Tellus Institute to promote the need and importance of corporate redesign and to devise solutions, is a vision and a set of six principles for corporate design for the corporation of the future and its enabling institutions—governments, market regulators, industry bodies, and civil society. Allen White and Marjorie Kelly of the Tellus Institute have assembled insights from over 300 leading thinkers in business, civil society, finance, labor, and law on how the tenets of sustainability, equity, and good governance could be worked into a new design for the corporation.[9] Their first and foremost principle for corporate repurposing and redesign is that *private enterprise should be harnessed for public benefit*. This is the antithesis of the cost-externalizing behavior of Corporation 1920, whose DNA often leads it to reap private profits from converting or preempting or destroying public wealth, through public costs in the form of its negative externalities.

For almost a century now, like a recessive gene, the "social purpose" of a corporation has been visible only sporadically, in the strategies and cultures of a handful of forward-looking corporations. The aberration in the history of the corporation is not found early in its 2,800-year-old history, but rather, in the nineteenth and twentieth centuries (to be precise, the period 1819 to 1919, the "crucible" period from the first introduction of limited-liability corporations in the United States). During this century the corporation, empowered by its legal history and encouraged by a postwar global alignment of the forces of deregulation and innovation in trade and capital markets, broke away from its community moorings, freed itself from social purpose, and reinvented itself as the perfect agent of free-market capitalism. Its successor, Corporation 2020, needs to allow this recessive "social purpose" gene to express itself once more, with corporate goals being aligned with the goals of society.

There are many examples of this "social corporation" already beginning to happen. Banking might nowadays appear to be an unlikely business with which to demonstrate corporate good behavior, but here is some evidence. Banco Santander, a multinational bank based in Spain, is a veritable giant in Brazil. Over the past decade, Santander has merged with or acquired several other banks, including Brazil's Banco Real, and it now has over 50,000 employees in Brazil, with a total global headcount of 170,000. Fabio Barbosa was Banco Real's president for 16 years, then served another three as president of the merged entity Santander, before moving on to lead the Brazilian publishing house Abreo. The sustainability philosophy of Santander in Brazil has evolved from performing acts of corporate social responsibility to seeking social change.[10] It grew from Fabio Barbosa's vision of a "social corporation" with social motivation beyond mere profit. He asked the company to answer two questions: What type of human being do we want to develop? and What type of society do we want to build? Barbosa introduced to Banco Real the concept of "protagonism," or promoting behavior change in the society in which the bank operates. "Be a Human Protagonist" is the slogan adopted by Santander's managers, who are trained by their Human Resources Department to weave sustainability into the fabric of the business. Santander clearly walks the walk: 57 percent of their middle managers and 39 percent of senior managers are women, breastfeeding facilities are provided in two buildings, and maternity leave includes a considerable 39 weeks of maternity/statutory pay.[11] Their risk-management function recognizes "socioenvironmental risk" as a formal risk category, and socio-environmental performance is used as an indicator for credit concessions as well as client and supplier acceptance, a practice implemented across the entire wholesale bank by 2010, for their client-adoption due-diligence. They take exceptions very seriously; since 2009, relationships with six clients were interrupted on the grounds of poor socio-environmental performance following a full review of their 3,900 corporate relationships.

Such integration of socio-environmental performance is indeed rare in the international banking world, but it has enormously positive implications. Just imagine what would have been the impact of Wall Street and City investment banks holding 100 percent reviews of their corporate client base for socio-environmental performance? How might "relationship interruptions" of the kind implemented by Santander, Brazil, have affected the liquidity raising and credit ratings of BP, Texaco, Vedanta Resources PLC, and other corporations that have evidenced questionable socio-environmental performance? And how might that have directed a change in their behavior?

Itaú Unibanco, the largest private bank in Latin America, has also made sustainability a cornerstone of their business strategy. IndusInd Bank, one of the leading Indian private-sector banks, has done likewise—across all customer segments, covering private and corporate banking customers. The power and potential of targeting consumers through their bankers is a relatively new idea, and it is not visible broadly enough in international retail banking other than in a few firms.

Aligning corporate goals with those of society, or "social purpose," never really left some very old corporate houses (e.g., the Tata Group) despite evolving corporate legal history, and it has resurfaced in some new ones. In addition to the banks named above, this book evidences such a realignment of goals in many corporations that were created in postwar years, including Natura and Infosys. But no commentary on this phenomenon would be complete without a mention of this vital strand of Corporation 2020 DNA to be found in the Ford Motor Company in its early days.

Henry Ford and Goal Alignment with Society

Early versions of Ford's original Model T ran on both ethanol and gasoline. Henry Ford considered biofuels to be the energy of the future, and his vision was that farmers could grow and use their own corn-based ethanol for their Model-Ts. In 1925, during the height of Prohibition in the United States, he said,

> The fuel of the future . . . is going to come from fruit . . . weeds, sawdust—almost anything. There is fuel in every bit of vegetable matter that can be fermented. There's enough alcohol in one year's yield of an acre of potatoes to drive the machinery necessary to cultivate the field for a hundred years.[12]

Even though price and supply considerations led to ethanol being phased out as the Model-T's fuel (instead becoming an octane-enhancing additive to gasoline), Ford never fully abandoned his belief that sustainable fuel sources would one day be viable. He continued to promote alcohol fuel even while its viability was being sapped by the temperance movement (that is, Prohibition, 1919–33). Henry Ford could see then what it has taken humanity another three-quarters of a century to realize: that there is a difference between sustainable and unsustainable fuel, and that gasoline cannot be the fuel of the future. Imagine the history of energy and the course of human and planetary history if Henry Ford's vision had prevailed, and gasoline had *not* become the main fuel option for almost all cars today?

Though we have already seen (in Chapter 3) that the early Ford Motor Company had an enormous footprint, Henry Ford was zealous about eliminating waste. He wanted his company to make something out of everything that would otherwise be "scrap" or "waste." During the 1920s and '30s, Ford's River Rouge plant in Dearborn, Michigan, recycled and reused coke, scrap wood, blast-furnace slag, pellets, and crates. Wooden cartons in which batteries were packed by suppliers were made to specifications such that they could be reused as gearbox covers.[13] Ford's plant even had a vehicle disassembly operation! Henry Ford insisted that a business existed not to make profits but to provide a service to the public, and that waste reduction was the single most important way his company could cut costs and continue to sell its cars at a profit.[14] Although he did not speak in terms of "reducing the social costs of unmanaged waste" or "increasing resource efficiency," as a Corporation 2020 CEO might do today, Henry Ford ranks tall among the best of them. Ford Motor Company under his direction embodied an essential strand of the DNA of Corporation 2020: goal alignment with society.

Henry Ford also believed that the primary purpose of a corporation was not profit, but the betterment of society, including the community defined by the Ford Motor Company itself, its employees, and its current and future customers.[15] By 1916, Ford had reduced the price of the Model-T from its original $850 by almost half, mainly to make the car affordable to more Americans, and especially Ford's own employees. That led to his investment of company resources being challenged in court by the Dodge brothers (who owned a significant 10 percent of Ford Motor Company) and to the historic judgment in 1919 that overturned Ford's executive decision and firmly established the legal principle that "the purpose of a corporation is its own self-interest."[16] The law is blind, it is said, and it was certainly blind to Henry Ford's vision of a corporation whose goals were aligned to those of society at large. By a curious twist of destiny, this very court case (*Dodge v. Ford*, 1919) completes a transformative century at the end of which, by 1920, today's corporation had received its fully coded DNA.[17] How poignant it is that this crucible-like period which forged the corporation as we know it is lined with the legal ashes of Henry Ford's shattered vision of the corporation as a "force for good."[18]

The Four Strands of a New DNA

Goal alignment with society (and through that a reemergence of "social purpose") is an essential feature of Corporation 2020. However, if new DNA is indeed going to transform Corporation 1920, it will need to have not one but four major strands:

1. Goals that are closely aligned with those of society
2. A vision of the corporation as a capital factory
3. An understanding of the corporation's role as a community
4. A commitment to developing the corporation as an institute of learning

We'll now turn to each of these strands in more detail and explain how they are interwoven and interdependent.

Goal Alignment with Society

The goals of Corporation 2020 are the goals of human society: increased human well-being, increased social equity, improved social and communal harmony, reduced ecological scarcities, and reduced environmental risks. Goals clarify purpose, which answers the question Why are we here? Objectives define milestones toward our stated goals and answer the question What should we aim to do and by when?

Financial capital accretion (through profitability) is undoubtedly a key objective for Corporation 2020, which ensures its financial sustainability while pursuing these goals, but it is not the only objective. There are other important goals, not just those determined by the corporation's *share-holders*, but also those determined by the corporation's *stakeholders*, the public, those who are impacted by the corporation.

These beliefs are not new—they have been held in varying forms by business leaders for at least a century. We saw this in Henry Ford's belief that the primary purpose of a corporation was not profit,[19] but the uplifting of society, and in the irony of Corporation 1920 being built atop the legal ruins of Ford's desire for goal alignment with society.

Corporation 2020 is a type of evolved company, one which will survive and succeed because it is genuinely value-additive and because it secures corporations' social license to operate. Indeed, Corporation 2020 has a "constrained" social license to operate—because it is held accountable for its negative externalities and faces the risk of losing its freedom from taxes or penalties being imposed on these externalities if they grow larger and socially unacceptable. Corporation 2020 behaves in ways that are designed to deliver performance to shareholders and positive benefits to stakeholders. In that sense, and only in that sense, Corporation 2020 is a return to the "social corporation" concept of bygone years.

Corporation 2020 Is a Capital Factory

Tomorrow's corporation needs to be a capital factory, not just a goods-and-services factory. It creates financial capital through its operations, but without depleting (and ideally, while growing) natural capital, social capital, and human capital. Instead of a single-goal, cost-externalizing machine maximizing financial capital for its own shareholders, it maximizes financial capital, human capital, social capital, and natural capital for its shareholders and its stakeholders. It is rewarded for doing so by tax relief, policy incentives, staff commitment, and customer loyalty. All this sounds lovely, but can this vision square with traditional microeconomics?

In traditional microeconomics, firms are viewed simply as machines or factories, using labor and raw materials (sourced from "land") to produce goods and services. This "machine" view of firms is a useful starting point to understand modern production processes. In order to view the corporation through the lens of any sustainability metric, however, we need more. The traditional view can be polished to include subtleties such as life-cycle analyses and pollution impacts, but to really understand the corporation holistically, in terms of what it does or does not do for the economy and for society, one needs to think in terms of capital, and answer a key question: What is the impact of the corporation on the wealth of a nation or of the world?

Wealth comes in many forms, and its financial measure is called capital. Man-made assets and money are identified as physical and financial capital, and corporations use and generate both in good measure. There is, however, a larger world of capital that drives economies and human societies. The belief system that underlies free-market capitalism holds that marketization is nearly always desirable and that any inability to marketize public goods is a form of market failure. The reality is that public goods and services, by their very nature, are generally not delivered or priced by markets. And yet they do have value, including economic value, which is usually not visible to policy makers and businesses because no markets exist to price these values. This economic value can, however, be represented with shadow prices or accounting prices. Recognizing, demonstrating, and sometimes even capturing such value in economic terms—by the exchange of money—are ways of bringing such public goods and services into the fold where they matter.

The reinvestment of profits into new capital is the key to growth in any venture, whether it is on the scale of an individual or a corporation or a nation. A new definition of capital would state that anything that facilitates the production of income is capital. This is intuitive, but not often explicitly expressed in a business world where relationships, ideas, and natural resources are as important for producing income as physical and financial capital.

The more traditional view sees natural resources falling under the category of "inputs" to production, or simply "land." It fails to take into account the myriad services that nature provides that are undeniably beneficial and income-producing. Studies such as "The Economics of Ecosystems and Biodiversity" (TEEB) provide numerous examples of services that are provided by natural systems. They demonstrate not only that ecosystem services can become household income, but in expanding the scope of what is considered capital, they show that we must expand the notion that capital is always privately held. In reality, many types of capital are able to produce positive returns to a large group of people or to

society as a whole, but cannot provide income to individual private investors. An example of public capital would be public health. If overall health
in society were to improve, citizens' capacity to earn would increase by
losing fewer days to illness (which can be measured in socioeconomic research, in the form of disability-adjusted life years). Protected areas provide another example. They can increase the flow of essential goods and
services to poor rural communities by increasing nutrient and freshwater
flows from forests and wetlands to the farms and provide flood prevention and drought-control benefits, leaf litter for their cattle, and fuelwood
for cooking. In the absence of good stewardship of such capital, there can
arise a general neglect and a "tragedy of the commons" as resources get
exploited because they are owned neither privately nor communally. The
point is that responsibility for capital creation and maintenance across all
forms of capital, the resource optimization of public wealth and private
financial capital, is a shared responsibility of communities, governments,
and corporations, and that its "shared value" will not be optimized if
corporations do not see it as an important business objective.[20]

Profits are just one dimension of the economic value transformation
achieved by corporations as a result of their operations. The belief in
"shared value" requires that our conception of costs and benefits needs
to be expanded to be holistic.[21] As Michael Porter and Mark Kramer explain it, "shared value" is not about philanthropy; it is about developing
an economy that will continue to work for companies and society in the
long term.[22] Triple-bottom-line accounting is one way of assessing the
net value addition of corporations for society, but the complexities of
the estimations involved and limited exogenous pressure (which is not
very visible thus far from governments or accountancy bodies) has meant
that the incentive to produce such accounts has been minimal. Puma, the
branded sportswear maker, leads the field in this regard, having published
a set of triple-bottom-line accounts (valuing their social costs of carbon
emissions, freshwater usage, pollutants, land-use, and waste) in 2011. International initiatives such as the TEEB for Business Coalition and the
International Integrated Reporting Council seek to rectify this situation,
but they are still in their early stages.

There are certainly instances in which investing in public capital—either human, natural, or social—can provide positive private returns to

the organization making the investment. Infosys and Google are clear examples.

These positive private returns can come in new forms, such as savings on materials or energy use, better public relations, a larger applicant pool when hiring, less need for avoidance of taxes and regulations, less spending on lobbying, and the satisfaction of being responsible citizens. Some might question the last benefit, but a corporation is little more than a group of individuals and it stands to reason that sentiments such as the pride and responsibility of managers can be reflected in the actions of a corporation.

Corporation 1920, the old corporation, aims to maximize the physical and financial capital that it owns. Corporation 2020, on the other hand, recognizes that human capital, social capital, and natural capital are just as able to produce income as is financial capital. It is past the point of needing to view human and natural capital as ancillary to financial capital. It even recognizes that its true performance includes its creation or destruction of *public* wealth—be it natural or social capital—and not only its operating results in terms of owned financial capital. This is the central premise of "three-dimensional capitalism": that we must think beyond the traditional boundaries of what can be considered to create value.[23]

Corporation 2020 Is a Community

The loss of "community" around the world is a palpable result of our dominant economic model.[24] Tribes are rare nowadays, and the village community has been emaciated by labor mobility and long hours. Population migration from villages to towns is a global phenomenon, and we are increasingly entering an urban age. However, urban communities—the neighborhoods of old towns and cities—have also gradually lost their identity and pull. This is partly due to advances in communications and transportation, partly due to increased labor mobility, but also due to a marketplace that treats labor and skills as commodities and results in people either working the equivalent of two jobs or none at all. Corporation 2020 can be a modern-day community, tied by a shared culture created by its values, mission, goals, objectives, and governance. It can (and in the best of today's companies it already does) re-create the sense of belonging that has been lost due to the forces of modernization and globalization.

Recognizing the corporation's community moorings and doing what it can to build its business in the interest of this community is a key component of Corporation 2020. The role is not newly engineered—it has been present for at least two millennia. Throughout much of their history, governments have granted corporations, from the *sreni* of ancient India and the *societates publicanorum* of Rome,[25] to the joint stock corporations that built Britain's infrastructure for the Industrial Revolution, privileges that were held in check by a simple maxim: serve the public interest as a "social corporation" constituted for the benefit of society. In nineteenth-century India, J. N. Tata, founder of the Tata Group, believed that: *"In a free enterprise, the community is not just another stakeholder in business, but is in fact, the very purpose of its existence."*[26] This philosophy continues to be part of the corporate credo of the Tata Group even to this day. Ishaat Hussain, finance director of Tata Sons, the group holding company, clarifies: "This is not just altruistic; there is a lot of self interest as well. [The corporation] needs the goodwill of the people, its employees and customers."[27]

Peter Drucker wrote that "The organization is . . . more than a machine. . . . It is more than economic, defined by results in the marketplace. The organization is, above all, social. It is people. Its purpose must therefore be to make the strengths of people effective and their weaknesses irrelevant."[28]

Michael Hammer, cocreator of the "Six Sigma" business-process reengineering route for organizational value addition through a dual focus on clients and operational risks, wrote that "an organization is more than a set of products and services. It is also a human society, and like all societies, it nourishes particular forms of culture. . . . Every company has its own language, its own version of history (its myths), and its own heroes and villains (its legends), both historical and contemporary."[29]

Both Drucker and Hammer are describing what I term the community nature of tomorrow's corporation, built from a community of networks of relationships instead of a rigid, hierarchical, transfer-priced army of production units making goods to sell. This is, of course, related to the idea that the corporation's purpose is wider than just growing private financial capital creation for shareholders. In that sense, the community nature of Corporation 2020 relates to its nature as a capital factory whose goals are aligned with those of society—two other characteristics of Corporation 2020 that we have commented on above.

Corporation as Community: Natura

Founded in 1969, Natura today is Brazil's largest maker and seller of fragrances, cosmetics, and personal products. They are highly profitable: gross profit exceeds $400 million on a turnover of $2.7 billion. As a strategy, they source as much as possible naturally—around 80 percent of their formulae come from the rainforest, double what used to be the case 15 years ago, and this is quite unique. Its distribution strategy is also unique: *Natura uses no shops!* Their distribution model is relationship-based sales to friends, relatives, and neighbors by over a million housewives (Natura calls them "consultants"), who earn almost $900 million per year in consulting (sales) commissions (i.e., around one-third of Natura's turnover of $2.7 billion after sales commissions). These housewives in Brazil and neighboring countries are part of a silent cultural revolution, bringing employability and spending power into the hands of women in Latin America, which has historically been a male-dominated society.

Natura's CEO, Alessandro Carlucci, collectively refers to their million-plus consultant-housewives, the millions of customers of these housewives, thousands of Natura employees, and hundreds of Natura suppliers, as Natura's "community." In Brazil and Latin America, Natura is a powerful example what it means for a corporation to be an alternative form of community.

Corporation 2020 Is an Institute of Learning

Tomorrow's corporation must be an institute of learning and skills training, providing employees with an increasing base of knowledge and skills with which to add value to the corporation, and add to their earnings profile.

The annual positive human capital externality created by Infosys due to its formal training programme and its culture of people development, measured in terms of the value added to employees who leave the firm each year and apply learned skills elsewhere, is estimated at nearly $1.4 billion. That is equal to over half of the annual gross profits, or financial capital, created by Infosys for its shareholders. Infosys is truly a human-capital factory.

Today there are many corporations which, because of their size and significant annual trainee intake, do have large training programs. The notion of being an institute, however, takes it to another level. It requires an organizational culture of people development through a program that may have permanent or outsourced faculty or both, and a structure that is known and accepted by management and employees as meaningful, relevant, and of high quality. It is a senior-management commitment to use this program to build their employees into professional citizens of the future and develop their human capacities, not only in their narrow job skills but broadly, in their line of work and focused on their particular interests or talents. And of course, it also includes building their income-earning potential as skilled employees.

Pathways for Corporation 2020

Although more and more companies are willing to experiment with a broader set of goals than shareholder value, and more objectives than quarterly or annual profits, incentives are not aligned to make that thinking mainstream. This is because investments in public wealth rarely yield private returns, and private returns remain the only legal and widely accepted yardstick of company performance. In such cases, the need for new rules becomes apparent. These new rules could be in the form of regulations on disclosing externalities, new taxation structures, revised standards on advertising practices, laws to register new corporate forms such as B Corps, and checks on lobbying, to name a few.

These new rules, regulations, taxes, and incentives together comprise "enabling conditions" for Corporation 2020. They are related to and not dissimilar in concept to the enabling conditions of a green economy,[30] and they are focused largely around four major planks of change chosen to deliver the best return on mandate, effort, and investment.

Measuring and disclosing the externalities of corporations—resource use, pollution, and social impacts—is an essential step in encouraging the transformation of the corporation. As explained in Chapters 4 and 5 of this book, without measuring these external impacts and requiring corporations to provide information on them to the public, today's corporation is able to get away with converting public capital to private capital and calling it profit. The disclosure of externalities, however, will allow innovative firms to reap the benefits of innovation and genuine capital production.

Excessive or misused leverage has been at the heart of each of the last four major financial crises.[31] The practices of large financial institutions and other corporations (this list includes mortgage houses, insurance companies, car makers, and even airlines) which are now considered "too big to fail" need to be subjected to checks and balances that are appropriate in the context of the use of public funds (used for bailouts) as against private capital (used to invest in market equities). Chapter 7 discussed how moving toward a better set of standards and capital requirements for leverage will help to pave the way for the corporation of the future to become a safer producer of capital, and avoid yet more crises involving the excessive use, misuse, or abuse of leverage.

Shifting taxation away from taxing profits toward taxing resource extraction will do much to promote responsible use of nonrenewable natural capital. If such a change is tax-neutral, it will align incentives in such a way as to spur efficiency and innovation in resource and energy use.

Finally, advertising will be made more accountable—mainly because of an Internet- and social-media-induced change in the power balance between producer and consumer as to *who* has more say in product advertising. The consumer is indeed gaining ground, and leading corporations are spending more on smart listening and less on adding decibels and megabytes to be heard above the din of Corporation 1920 advertising. In addition, governments need to encourage evolving best practices in advertising, which will enable corporations that truly are Corporation 2020s to benefit from their early leadership.[32] The current lack of regulations for the advertising sector has lead to a situation in which mere "greenwashing" (i.e., exaggerated reporting or advertising of a token effort at sustainable business behavior as though it were a material achievement) often edges out truly ethical and responsible corporate leadership. Superficial packaging or bad practices should not be allowed to masquerade as virtue, and good companies should easily be able to inform consumers of their genuine and demonstrable merits.

The four planks of change advocated by this book—accounting for externalities, accountable advertising, limits to leverage, and resource taxation—are selected in terms of their potential impact. They are not the only solutions in the tool kit for change, but without them other changes might just not be sufficient. Among other solutions, a position paper presented by the Corporation 20/20 initiative[33] lays out a number of tools that can be used by various groups—investors, large business, small companies, civil society, government, labor, and media—to bring their principles to fruition, including the following:

- "Circuit breaker" opportunities, which arise whenever a company needs the permission of the government for licences or changes in regulations or fiscal incentives. These opportunities can be exploited to give more power to communities and labor as a means of refreshing (or withholding) the company's "social licence to operate"
- Changes in government procurement to reward responsible companies and shun irresponsible companies—in essence, a call for government policies to "walk the walk." This recommendation, in effect the greening of public procurement, is also advocated by the United Nations Environment Programme (UNEP)[34]
- Changes in government investment policies, again in a similar vein to the green-economy investments proposed by UNEP in 2011
- Introducing more effective laws to limit corporate lobbying and campaign contributions
- Addressing the "ownership" driver of corporate behavior with practical solutions, such as allowing only long-term investors to have voting rights; increasing short-term capital-gains taxes; and requiring some minimal target ownership of their companies by employees

The nature and powers of ownership, and how it can influence behavior to align a corporation's goals with those of society, is a vast subject, one that has been dealt with extensively by other authors, and one which remains extremely important. I do not believe there is enough time left for society to achieve material change in direction through propagating "B Corp"[35] status in other important jurisdictions around the world (it is progressing well in several states in the US), because the challenge

of achieving changes in charter and legal purpose for the typical large
MNC, operating across the dozens of jurisdictions and countries, is quite
forbidding.

Alternative Ownership Structures

Very few institutional owners have more than a token interest in the "long
term" or "public interest," as is evident in their constitutions, their investing behavior, and their performance metrics. As financial investors,
they exercise their shareholder votes either to reinforce short-term performance optimization, or they remain on the sidelines when the debate
turns to public interest.

Ownership models are critical determinants of corporate behavior,
and different forms of ownership and control can have very different outcomes in terms of positive and negative externalities—respectively, public
interest and public costs. Some of these alternative ownership models already exist.[36] For example, the *New York Times* is family controlled while
being publicly owned, and its mission is to create an informed electorate.
John Lewis Partnership, a major retail chain in the UK, is 100 percent
employee-owned, and its purpose is to optimize the wealth and well-
being of its employee-partners. Grupo Nueva, a conglomerate (forestry,
freshwater, cement) based in Chile, has a mission of sustainable development in Latin America and is controlled by a trust charged with blending
philanthropy and business operations.

Another model of business organization that succeeds time and again
in converting private enterprise into public interest is the cooperative.
Many success stories can be found. The Anand Milk Union Ltd. (Amul)
of India, launched in Gujarat in 1946, was used as a model for national
expansion by the National Dairy Development Board in 1965, turning
India's chronic milk shortages into a milk surplus while adding to the
incomes and livelihood security of millions of poor farmers across the
country. Organic Valley, a farmer-owned cooperative in the US, is jointly
owned by around 1,200 farmers and is operated in their wider interest.

Iconic of the cooperative and its potential for Corporation 2020 behavior is Spain's Mondragon Corporation.[37] This cooperative was started
1956 by a Jesuit priest, Don José Arizmendiarrieta, and based on the principle "Don't risk jobs to protect capital—risk capital to protect jobs."[38] It

began quite modestly as a company formed by five students from Don José's Business Ethics class in their employment-starved home state of Mondragón, in Basque Country. They raised $361,000 to buy Aladdin Kerosene Heaters, which they moved to Mondragón to provide their constituents a handful of new jobs. From those humble beginnings, Mondragon Corporation has grown to a complex of over 250 companies with revenues of over $24 billion.[39] Mondragon's corporate values are cooperation, participation, social responsibility, and innovation—nothing very different from those we see posted as the values at most large corporations. But unlike most such organizations, Mondragon was conceived from the outset as a community of enterprise bound by shared values that position social outcomes above profits. And as one examines their *operating principles* in key areas, however, it becomes obvious that they could not be more different than the typical Corporation 1920.

These principles are as follows:

- *Power Structure*. All employees are equal shareholders, each with one vote, and they elect a board of directors, which in turn hires their management team. Their community nature came through the 2008 financial crisis with flying colors, growing income 6 percent and recording a profit while absorbing the shocks throughout its diversified business.[40]
- *Financial Structure*. All workers invest savings in the cooperative, repayable on retirement. A bank (credit union) is part of the cooperative, and it finances new jobs in the Mondragón area. Creating jobs has priority over growing return on investment. Of the 103 cooperatives created over the thirty years from 1956 to 1986, only three were shut down—a survival rate of 97 percent, dispelling fears that there is more than an ordinary credit-risk downside to their business model.[41]
- *Education and Training*. Community-centered, focused on business skills and practical work programs for all, Mondragon is very much a Corporation 2020 *institute* in nature.
- *Pay Scales and Equity*. From 1955 until 1980, the top salary could not exceed six times the lowest salary. If management wanted a raise, everyone got a raise. In comparison, the US ratio of pay was 116 to 1 in 1955 and it has since increased to an estimated

600 to 1. Recently, Mondragon ratios were increased to 15 to 1 because the rest of Spain has realized how good Mondragon managers are and were hiring them away!

Examples such as Grupo Nueva, the *New York Times*, John Lewis, and Mondragon are powerful because they show that different organizational forms can and do take shape and conduct business in new, socially constructive ways. They create positive externalities and mitigate negative externalities by providing skills for their employees, build societal awareness, nurture the economies of local communities, and often place sustainability as a central plank of their strategy.

All of these examples are already very large corporations, so the key question is this: Are they merely icons of enthusiastic corporate evangelism or are they indeed replicable and scalable? In other words, will these models ever become mainstream and, indeed, the norm for sectors such as retailing, manufacturing, mining, or even oil and gas? On that vital issue, I believe the jury is out, but I do not hold high hopes.

Changes in ownership patterns may take ages, as they are evolutionary, often arising in a Schumpeterian transition from the commercial death of the current model to the commercial success of alternative models. To deliver results by 2020, however, we have to address two fundamental realities: the required change will have to be achieved by legislation and not by gradual evolution, and it will be resisted every inch of the way by powerful incumbents. Institutional shareholders are not likely to support such changes any more than turkeys vote for Thanksgiving or Christmas.

Nonetheless, behavioral change can be fostered, to at least some extent, by enforcing a new standard for performance metrics for the institutional investor community, metrics based on financial-accounting standards for the statutory annual reports of corporations.

Corporation 2020's "Theory of Change"

We live in a complex but increasingly democratic and free world and corporations are increasingly integral to most of it. Corporations have to change; however, changes do not happen simply because they seek visionary, virtuous, or profitable outcomes, or some combination thereof. If a particular change is profitable, and if it does not absorb corporate managerial bandwidth at the cost of other equally profitable changes, then chances are that particular change will indeed happen.

The rub is that it is *not always* the case that the four major planks of change described in this book, or any of the others that are laudable, are automatically and immediately profitable in the traditional "quarterly P&L" sense that does not account for externalities. Enabling conditions that help to internalize externalities—rules, regulations, taxes, subsidies, etc.—are within the power of governments to change, but they are too beholden to today's corporation to do so on their own. So it is back to the wide and complex world—informed and activist citizens and NGOs, visionary Corporation 2020 leaders and their inspired colleagues, electorally secure and visionary politicians, well-intentioned and powerful bureaucrats, and a host of human institutions—to collaborate in ingenious ways to create those enabling conditions such that Corporation 2020 grows increasingly successful, and Corporation 1920 becomes gradually unable to compete. And as most of these changes are positively reinforcing, the best outcomes may arise from such collaborations seeking to fire on all cylinders at once.

This may not sound simple, and indeed it is not. Complex problems require complex solutions.

It might result in an unsettling cacophony of changes over the next few decades at various levels and scales—and most probably, it will. There will be a period of turbulence when the economy contains both types of corporations, competing in a rapidly changing environment. This may be startling for human society, but it is a perfectly normal situation in the natural world. As environments change, dominant species decline, and emergent species become dominant. Pursuing changes in the business environment in four key arenas—externalities, leverage, advertising, and resource taxation—will create the business conditions that allow a new type of corporation to flourish. These are the enabling conditions needed for the DNA of Corporation 2020 to dominate our economy.

CHAPTER TEN

The World of Corporation 2020

We have always held to the hope, the belief, the conviction
that there is a better life, a better world, beyond the horizon.
— *Franklin D. Roosevelt*

The previous nine chapters have sought to explain the need for, the attributes of, and the pathways toward Corporation 2020. Yet, just as biological organisms both shape and are shaped by their environment, so do corporations respond to and influence the world in which they operate. It is time to expand our perspective in order to consider the broader changes necessary to bring about Corporation 2020 and the nature of the world that Corporation 2020 will in turn help to create.

The Decade of the Great Unraveling

We live in interesting times. The transition from the world of Corporation 1920 to that of Corporation 2020 is showing signs of significant turbulence, not smooth transition. There is increasing divergence between the fortunes of Corporation 1920 and the macroeconomy it produces: Corporation 1920 powers on while its world does not. The ever-ascending CEO pay packages of underperforming corporations came under pressure in spring 2012 from different quarters—that is, from the US Treasury Department, which announced a pay freeze for executives at AIG, Ally Financial, and General Motors in order to encourage repayment of debts to the government (between $10 billion and $50 billion each), and from the shareholders of financial giants Aviva, Barclays, Credit Suisse, and UBS, among others, who revolted at their AGMs.

We find ourselves in the midst of an uncertain recovery from the largest financial and economic crisis in history. This crisis triggered an unprecedented policy response from G-20 nations: Interest rates were dramatically reduced, in some cases close to zero, and trillions of dollars in liquidity support and fresh capital were provided to banking systems around the world. Beyond that, governments also deployed fiscal resources on an unprecedented scale, committing an estimated $3 trillion to reflate their economies.[1]

Such massive liquidity injections by central banks were certainly controversial, although they are not widely appreciated in a historical context. Most of the major central banks have injected liquidity and lowered interest rates at times of economic crisis. They did so at the onset of Long-Term Capital Management (LTCM)'s collapse and the Asian Debt crisis in 1998, again just after the 9/11 attack in 2001, and yet again in response to the Nasdaq and corporate governance meltdown in 2001 and 2002 that followed that tragedy. Importantly, the major central banks have almost never implemented liquidity *contraction* after any of these crises ended, thus leaving financial systems awash with more and more liquidity, opening up the risks of asset-price inflation and further financial meltdowns as this surplus liquidity in the banking system looked around for yields to earn. The 2008 liquidity injections were simply a continuation of a series of similar monetarist responses to previous crises, responses that had showed uncertain results in the past and promised no certainty of success in the future.

The financial system leading up to the mortgages (collateralized debt obligation, or CDO) crisis in 2008 has been aptly described as a patient with a drinking problem. These liquidity ministrations of central banks and fiscal stimulus by governments were therefore the equivalent of laying the patient down and prescribing intravenous alcohol in the hope of a cure. Liquidity injections and low interest rates had not succeeded in turning around the Japanese economy over almost two decades, so why was there such confidence that this strategy would succeed on a global scale?

The decade from 2000 to 2010 presented shocks and crises on many fronts—including food, fuel, and climate. In 2007, the upsurge in the prices of food cost developing countries $324 billion, the equivalent of

three years worth of global aid.[2] Although the recession has also brought
down food prices, food security remains a key problem. In 2008, oil prices
touched $147 per barrel. Although the recession brought a significant cor-
rection, to below $40 per barrel, the fuel crisis remains real. The Interna-
tional Energy Agency (IEA) forecasts oil prices to reach $200 per barrel
by 2030 due to increasing demand and increasingly constrained supply.[3]
At such prices, fossil-fuel-dependent developing nations may find their
projected development paths at risk. Freshwater availability has also continued to worsen, and the inability of poor nations to meet the Millennium Development Goals for freshwater and sanitation became evident.
Collectively, these crises exacerbate such persistent social problems as job
losses, socioeconomic insecurity, and poverty that threaten social stability
in developed as well as developing countries.[4] A 2009 report by the UNEP
aptly pointed out that

> although the causes of these crises vary, at a fundamental level,
> they shared a common feature: the gross misallocation of capital.
> In the last two decades, much capital has been poured into prop-
> erty, fossil fuels, and structured financial assets with embedded de-
> rivatives, but relatively little has been invested in renewable energy,
> energy efficiency, public transportation, sustainable agriculture,
> and land and water conservation.[5]

Nevertheless, while the economy struggles to rediscover a viable operating model and to lick its wounds from overuse of the brown-economy
model, Corporation 1920 powers ahead as if nothing has changed. The
number of large multinational corporations turning over more than $25
billion grew from around 210 in 2000 to over 330 in 2010. The number of
these megacorporations whose turnover exceeded 0.1 percent of *global*
GDP continued to rise, from about 100 to over 120.[6]

This divergence of fortunes between the macro and micro level cannot go on forever. Indeed, a decade of such disconnection is already quite
worrying. I see this divergence as symptomatic of the key problem of our
times: heightening systemic risks across several fronts due to our surprising willingness to live with the wrong economic model (brown economy)
and the wrong agency model (Corporation 1920).

Redefining Economic Success

Creating an environment that drives the evolution of a new kind of corporate DNA will require redefining success at the level of both corporations and nations, and implementing an array of policies that align the goals of corporations and society.

Thus far, I have argued that most of today's corporations "succeed" only insofar as they maintain a warped and limited definition of success. A utility company generating coal-fired electricity may report that it makes a huge profit, but who would not make huge profits in such circumstances when not counting their social costs? A too-big-to-fail financial institution counts itself a winner, but what gambler cannot build a lucky streak when someone else covers all their losing bets? In order to maximize the benefits of Corporation 2020's impact in the world, we need to redefine success at the level of national economies. What, we have to ask, is the economy for?

We currently know what the current economy is for as a function of the way in which we measure it. Gross domestic product (GDP)—its growth, its decline, its comparison among countries—is the *lingua franca* of the global economic system. And because GDP is what we measure, it is what countries seek to maximize. But all GDP tells us is the dollar value added by the activity of making and selling goods and services in a year. What our current economy is for, in other words, is making and selling as fast as possible, with little concern for whether all of our activity actually makes us better off.

The striking thing about GDP is that those who invented this metric never intended for it to define the goals of society. Nobel laureate Simon Kuznets helped to develop the system of national accounts that would eventually lead to GDP and the closely related measure Gross National Product (GNP). In 1934, as part of his first report to the US Congress, Kuznets wrote that "the welfare of a nation can . . . scarcely be inferred from a measure of national income." Likewise, the economist Richard Stone, who played a central role in refining GDP, noted in his Nobel Prize lecture that the measure only accounted for one part of national wealth. "The three pillars on which analysis of society ought to rest," Stone said, "are studies of economic, socio-demographic, and environmental phenomena."[7]

Like other, earlier national accounting measures, GNP and GDP came out of a particular historical milieu and were a response to a particular challenge. Developed during the Great Depression and brought to prominence during World War II, these measures were critical to the government's ability to manage the economy in times of crisis.[8] Yet the System of National Accounts (SNA) long outlasted the Third Reich, as well as the Marshall Plan and the Cold War. So, today, in a time characterized by a relative degree of peace, but also by ecological scarcity and inequity, economies around the world operate according to a measure meant to bend economies to a singular focus on industrial production. As Alan Krueger, now Chairman of the White House Council of Economic Advisers, put it at the 2007 Organization for Economic Cooperation and Development (OECD) World Forum, "GDP measures, in a certain sense, how much stuff we can produce that we can drop on an enemy. It's natural in the post–Cold War era that we would turn to other measures of how well our society is doing."[9]

The problems with GDP start with the fact that it counts all purchases of goods as actually *good*. If someone buys something, they have contributed to national progress, and never mind if what they bought was spaghetti or bricks to build a prison. Similarly, GDP ticks up even if what one buys destroys the value of previously invested capital. As Clifford Cobb, Ted Halstead, and Jonathan Rowe famously wrote in a 1995 *Atlantic Monthly* article, "By the curious standard of the GDP, the nation's economic hero is a terminal cancer patient who is going through a costly divorce. The happiest event is an earthquake or a hurricane. The most desirable habitat is a multibillion-dollar Superfund site. . . . It is as if a business kept a balance sheet by merely adding up all 'transactions,' without distinguishing between income and expenses, or between assets and liabilities."[10]

The fact that we don't value much of our social and natural capital makes GDP even more problematic. That a terminal cancer patient no longer buys as much food as a healthy person might partly balance the positive GDP impact of his payments for health care. But what of the clear-cutting of a piece of Amazon rainforest that precedes the creation of a factory? In that case, GDP not only counts the loss of the asset inherent in the forest as a gain, it also ignores the loss of income from the asset, in the form of a constantly replenished source of clean water, clean air, carbon sequestration, and many other unpriced services. Going down the list of all the things that aren't measured by GDP—from strong governing institutions to the preservation of wilderness, with much in between—it is not hard to find Robert F. Kennedy's assessment of it as accurate:

> Too much and for too long, we seemed to have surrendered personal excellence and community values in the mere accumulation of material things. Our Gross National Product, now, is over $800 billion dollars a year, but that Gross National Product—if we judge the United States of America by that—that Gross National Product counts air pollution and cigarette advertising, and ambulances to clear our highways of carnage. It counts special locks for our doors and the jails for the people who break them. It counts the destruction of the redwood and the loss of our natural wonder in chaotic sprawl. It counts napalm and counts nuclear warheads and armored cars for the police to fight the riots in our cities. It counts Whitman's rifle and Speck's knife, and the television programs which glorify violence in order to sell toys to our children.
>
> Yet the gross national product does not allow for the health of our children, the quality of their education or the joy of their play. It does not include the beauty of our poetry or the strength of our marriages, the intelligence of our public debate or the integrity of our public officials. It measures neither our wit nor our courage, neither our wisdom nor our learning, neither our compassion nor our devotion to our country, it measures everything in short, except that which makes life worthwhile. And it can tell us everything about America except why we are proud that we are Americans.[11]

Knowing these problems with GDP as a measure of success, modern society has still continued to use it—almost to the exclusion of other metrics. The reasons for that, I believe, are incumbency and inertia: GDP is relatively easy to measure, and simple in concept to explain to the electorate, albeit by omitting to mention its most glaring defects. Fortunately, we seem to have reached a point where it is possible to move beyond GDP and, in so doing, redefine the purpose of national economies.

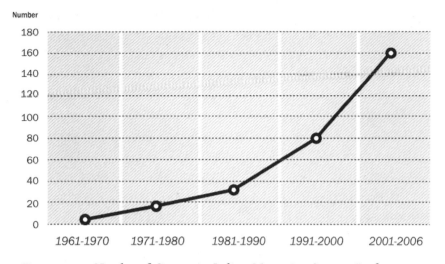

Figure 10-1   Number of Composite Indices Measuring Country Performance
Source: Romina Bandura, "A Survey of Composite Indices Measuring Country
Performance: 2006 Update," UNDP/ODS Working Paper (2006).

Recent years have seen an explosion of new indicators aimed at providing a more holistic view of the wealth of nations. Some of these new indicators describe aspects of societal health, such as development, welfare, or environmental health, in primarily qualitative terms. Others represent attempts to replace or fundamentally redesign the existing accounting.

At the heart of new approaches to green national accounting is the need to move beyond metrics that account only for financial and manufactured wealth—physical capital. An inclusive wealth approach, for example, would tally the value of not only a nation's physical capital, but also, via nonmarket-valuation techniques, its natural capital or ecological infrastructure (its forests, wetlands, rivers, coral reefs, etc.), and its social/human capital (institutional infrastructure, communal harmony, knowledge and skills, and human health). In the inclusive-wealth version of holistic national accounting, a successful nation would be one that increases the per capita "total wealth" of its citizens over time. Another related approach is "green accounting," in which economists use nonmarket-valuation techniques to give prices specifically to reflect externalities such as the significant invisible ecosystem services from natural capital. Green accounting takes into account the present value of activities that cause future costs (such as the health costs of pollution) or future incomes (such as higher incomes thanks to education), which are not reflected in the current mainstream model, the UN's System of National Accounts (SNA). National accounts can then show an adjusted or "Green GDP" that reflects both gains in physical capital and any resultant drawdown or increase in natural capital. Tallied year-on-year, Green GDP provides a picture of whether a nation's "genuine savings" are increasing or decreasing over time.[12]

Little more than two decades ago, many of the national accounting ideas now emerging would not have been conceivable, much less implementable. New computing and remote sensing technology have been crucial to modeling ecological dynamics in a way that allows economists to estimate stocks and value natural capital. So too has the emergence and rapid evolution of the field of ecological economics itself. In 1997, a team of ecological economists and scientists writing in *Nature* shocked the world by stating that the global value of natural production was $33 trillion,[13] larger than the standard global GDP measure of $30 trillion.[14] Their exercise was criticized on methodological grounds, but it served as a wake-up call for a world which for too long had ignored the implications of the economic invisibility of nature. Since then, natural-capital-valuation techniques have become increasingly sophisticated as well as more practicable, as documented in the 2010 international study "The Economics of Ecosystems and Biodiversity" (TEEB).

Green accounting and inclusive-wealth approaches to national accounting are now making their way into the realm of real-world decision making. In India, a project known as the Green Accounting for Indian States Project (GAISP), implemented by GIST,[15] a research NGO, has been measuring the external costs to natural capital of rapid economic growth. The results so far have been striking. In the state of Uttar Pradesh, for instance, the condition of the state's surface- and groundwater is so poor that the cost of restoring their water quality would amount to 17.5 percent of the state's net domestic product.[16] Some Indian states have likewise seen massive losses of capital in the forest sector, while in others with extensive protected areas, natural capital has been a boon for the overall "genuine savings" picture.

With the success of research projects such as GIST (in India) and

TEEB (a global report), the World Bank has called for a more advanced treatment of natural capital to be an addendum to national accounts, and a group of experts is moving forward with the goal of making this a reality for a pilot group of some ten developing and developed nations. The only argument left in favor of GDP may be that it benefits vested interests—that changing the global system will be hard. Undoubtedly, this is true—no one wants to look at the bill after an extravagant dinner—but it actually argues for immediate change. For Corporation 1920, a new, more honest system of national accounting is a threat. But for Corporation 2020, a system that values all forms of capital, by further contributing to the "Great Realignment" of societal and business goals, will be an immense boon.

A story helps to illustrate the point. In the United States, a modest effort at implementing green accounting was attempted in the 1990s. A proposed bill to do so did reach Congress, but it was ultimately stymied in the House Appropriations Committee by two representatives from coal states. One of them, Alan Mollohan (a Democrat from West Virginia), quickly cut to the chase. "Somebody is going to say," he declared, "that the coal industry isn't contributing anything to the country."[17]

Indeed. As we have seen, the externalized and unpriced economic impacts of air pollution on the US GDP show that once health costs of air pollution are added, the damages inflicted by coal on the national economy are far more than the value added by the industry.[18] Looking at that number, somebody—indeed anybody—is going to say that it is time to measure the coal industry's contribution differently.

Enabling the World of Corporation 2020

Simply redefining success is far from sufficient. We have touched on some of the policy options for creating the enabling conditions we need, but a key question remains: How can national governments and other policy-making bodies best combine different tools in the real world? Answering this question is critical, because, while we do have the tools we need to enable the creation of Corporation 2020, no *single* tool will suffice. Moreover, combining different kinds of policy options in a way that achieves desired results is nearly always a difficult and messy task.

To paraphrase a saying sometimes used for describing the tools available for addressing climate change: "There is no silver bullet, but we do have a whole lot of bronze buckshot."

Transparency, Measurement, and Disclosure

Policies that create incentives for transparency, measurement, and disclosure (TMD) form a foundation upon which it is possible to erect other policies that drive change. If it is true that "you cannot manage what you do not measure," it is also true that you can neither manage nor measure what you cannot see. Because policies that improve the quantity and quality of available information tend to generate relatively minor complications and impose few burdens (aside, perhaps, from an occasional bout of healthy embarrassment), TMD initiatives are often among the easiest and least risky kinds of policy tools to wield.

We have already detailed some varieties of TMD policy. Policies that bring externalized costs into either corporate or national accounting are a critical prerequisite for many other public policies or corporate practices aimed at managing externalities. Likewise, policies that incentivize the disclosure of environmental or social impacts in advertising can play a valuable role in empowering consumers as agents of change.

It is also important to bring transparency to tax and subsidy regimes. Subsidies in particular have a tendency to produce perverse results at odds with the public interest. Because of the difficulty of taking subsidies away from special interests, they often turn into zombies: Long after they should have died, they keep on receiving funding! Transparency, measurement, and disclosure of taxes and subsidies can help policymakers to manage their adverse or unintended effects.

The importance of an improved System of National Accounts (SNA) which includes changes in natural and human capital (which are treated as externalities) cannot be overemphasized, as it is the catchall metric that will require new thinking among policy makers. However, at the micro level, there is also no denying the need for a better *corporate* accounting framework, one that reflects both positive and negative externalities in a corporation's statutory annual reports, and thus makes transparent not only its holistic impact on the economy, society, and the environment, but also its exposure to risks of resource constraints and regulation. After an externalities estimation has been mandated and standardized, next comes assurance and disclosure—the need to *audit and report* what has been calculated as the externality.

Transparency is only finally achieved through standardization and disclosure, which in turn needs to be driven by regulators. There is some initial progress on that count. In response to the publication of "TEEB for Business," the Institute of Chartered Accountants of England and Wales (ICAEW) has hosted a program whose main task is to arrange for the study and calculation of major corporate externalities, and to provide valuation and accounting standards. An ambitious program of first prioritizing and then computing the top 100 global externalities is being launched even as this book is being written. Standardization and disclosure of externalities will ensure that investors are adequately aware of the broad set of relevant risks faced by any corporation with large externalities, as opposed to the narrower risks that are currently being recognized, reported, and managed.

Taxation

Taxation will play a central role in enabling the world of Corporation 2020. We have singled out resource taxes as particularly important, both because they incentivize extractive industry corporations to pay the costs they currently externalize, and because the resulting increases in resource prices drive innovation in less resource-intensive technologies. The strategy for limiting leverage discussed in Chapter 7 would involve reducing or selectively eliminating the tax deduction for debt-based leverage in financial institutions. Still, there are a wide variety of tax options we have not already discussed that could help create the world of Corporation 2020.

Of course, like any major policy prescription, taxes often produce unintended consequences. Indeed, it is telling that even in a publication such as the OECD's "Taxation, Innovation, and Environment," which argues for the value of taxes in driving innovation, none of the taxes cited in a number of case studies produced exactly the expected or desired results. Instead, we find policymakers constantly have to adapt to changing circumstances, and constantly to be (at least a little) surprised by outcomes.[19]

For a specific and instructive example of how policymakers can respond with ingenuity to unintended consequences in even the most dynamic taxation situations, we can look to Singapore's long-running experiment with road congestion. Over the past four decades, Singapore has experienced a trend common to many large Asian cities, in which a booming middle class leads to rapid increases in car ownership, resulting in traffic jams and excessive vehicular pollution. Given Singapore's status as an island city-state, it has not surprisingly faced a particularly severe variation on the problem.[20] As such, beginning in the early 1970s, the Singaporean government began setting about attempting to limit traffic congestion.

Singapore's first effort involved making vehicles more expensive by raising import taxes and adding a registration tax of 25 percent to the price of new vehicle purchases. This approach failed to have a substantial impact on congestion, however, and in 1975 Singapore pioneered the world's first zoned urban-road pricing system, known as the Area Licensing Scheme. Under it, drivers had to purchase daily or monthly licenses to enter into a Restricted Zone. The scheme did reduce traffic to the Restricted Zone by up to 45 percent, but it also ushered in a series of other, unpredictable effects. Over the next fifteen years, Singapore struggled to constrain car ownership levels and deal with traffic jams occurring just outside the Restricted Zone and on expressways.

At various points, the government implemented a 100 percent increase in parking fees at public housing facilities and larger fuel taxes, to little effect. Next came a Certificate of Entitlement (COE) Scheme, in which people wanting to purchase new cars had to bid on expensive licenses costing as much as $58,000. Finally, in 1998, Singapore instituted a dynamic Electronic Road Pricing scheme, which charges drivers tolls based on the time of a particular trip, the type of vehicle, and the zone of travel. This system has been hailed as a success, but it's nonetheless clear that the situation on Singapore's roads, while under control, remains under pressure.[21]

One of the most intriguing points to emerge from the Singapore experience is the fact that behavioral economic mechanisms may be at work. The relatively new field of behavioral economics differs from classical economics in that it does not treat people as entirely rational. Instead, it holds that humans regularly act on the basis of cognitive biases—predictable errors of thinking. In the Singapore case, a cognitive bias related to sunk costs may explain why simply increasing the price of vehicles did not reduce congestion. Since people had paid more for their vehicles, they felt compelled to drive them more. Similarly, a "salience bias" may explain why Electronic Road Pricing rates reduced congestion but gasoline taxes did not, even where the actual costs were equal. The Electronic Road Pricing costs were more visible to drivers and thus had a greater effect.[22]

Taken as a whole, Singapore's experience suggests the near impossibility of getting taxes exactly right on the first try, and the importance of not letting the perfect be the enemy of the good when designing new policies.

Looking at Germany's Ecological Tax Reform (ETR) bill, which was passed in 1999, leads us to a similar conclusion. The idea behind the bill was to raise energy taxes, thereby internalizing previously externalized costs and using the resulting revenues to increase employment by lowering payroll taxes.[23] Proponents hailed the bill as a "central project of the modern age" and expected it to "simultaneously address many environmental, economic, and social problems." Almost immediately after the bill's passage, however, both traditional opponents of ecological taxes *and* traditional supporters of ecological taxes began to criticize the measure. What could be done in reality, it seems, fell far short of what could be done in theory.

A scholarly report released after the ETR passed delineated several of the controversies that grew out of the "second-best" nature of many of the components of the ETR. One controversy related to the fact that political horse trading led to energy-intensive industries receiving a break in the bill. Another controversy related to worries about the impossibility of ensuring steady revenues from environmental taxes. A representative of a business association put it this way: "Either the tax is ecologically useless [doesn't reduce energy use] or it will not provide any revenue [reduces energy use and in so doing fails to provide revenue]." Still another controversy stemmed from the fact that Germany was not able to directly tax actual sources (primary energy) but, because of trade restrictions in the European Union, had to settle on the less efficient tax point of energy consumption (final energy).

The list of gaps between theoretical possibilities and real-world results goes on. And yet, the report on Germany's ETR bill comes to a general conclusion that it was still important that the bill was passed, even in imperfect form. To paraphrase the title of the concluding section of the report, outside the ivory tower policymaking often looks more like "muddling through."[24]

Government Investment and Public Procurement

The idea that private finance and private companies can and should drive the shift to a green economy, supported in this transition by a fair business environment that enables Corporation 2020 behavior, is a core tenet of this book. In this context, government investment and spending also has an important role to play. Working in tandem with TMD and taxation policies aimed at setting the stage for the world of Corporation 2020, government investment in green-economy ventures and green public procurement can be effective short-term catalysts that bring about long-term results.

There are a number of areas where such government investment and spending can make a big difference. The first is in the arena of innovation. Economists have long recognized that free markets provide less than the optimal amount of innovation.[25] In part, this is because an individual company investing heavily in innovation does not reap all the benefits of its effort; many of the gains flow to society as a whole, in the form of "spillovers" reducing the company's incentive to focus on R&D.[26] At the same time, innovation often requires large amounts of up-front capital and entails large risks, which dissuades private innovation. In the case of energy, for example, a 2011 report produced by a consortium of business leaders, including Bill Gates, Jeff Immelt, and John Doerr, noted that "Slow turnover of capital assets combined with the need for large up-front investments mean that the sector as a whole is subject to a high degree of inertia, a tendency to avoid risk, and domination by incumbent firms."[27] The report's central conclusion was that government must play a key role in creating the conditions that allow the energy industry to push forward into new areas.

Another area where government investment is essential is in the creation of appropriate infrastructure. In the world of Corporation 2020, this infrastructure is "green infrastructure," which includes everything that allows for more efficient and equitable use of natural resources, from a mass transit system in China to a system to deliver the latest crop prices to farmers via cell phone in Kenya. What is important about this infrastructure is that it drives the creation of entirely new markets, laying the groundwork for the powerful machinery of corporations to act in alignment with the goals of society.

Yet all government investment faces a fundamental difficulty: constrained budgetary resources. Particularly in difficult economic times, it is worthwhile to consider not only new initiatives, but also how to reallocate existing spending. Governments at all levels spend roughly 15 to 20 percent of their countries' GDP on procurement of goods and services (or 7 to 9 percent when compensation is excluded).[28] Given the enormous role governments play in driving national economies, simply shifting procurement to certain kinds of goods and services—such as those that are environmentally friendly and also enhance welfare and equity—can create and help to develop new markets.[29]

Ultimately, the success of government investment and procurement initiatives will hinge, like the success of other policies aimed at bringing about the world of Corporation 2020, on how well they are combined with other policies. In the arena of financing, for example, studies have shown that a dollar of public lending can leverage between three and fifteen private financing dollars.[30] Yet making this happen requires much more than a well-designed public-private finance mechanism. Indeed, it requires a whole constellation of policies and institutions that help to provide the private sector with the incentives and assurance of stability necessary to invest.

For another example, we might turn back to the energy industry. In a 2011 report, a team from the Harvard Kennedy School of Government presented models aimed at determining how the United States could dramatically accelerate energy innovation to meet climate-mitigation goals by the year 2050. Though the report recommends a large investment in public energy R&D investments, it also characterizes as "deeply wrong" the idea that public R&D investments alone will ever be sufficient. According to the authors, success will depend on the United States' ability to also put a price on carbon, ideally through economy-wide policies such as a cap or tax, or through clean energy, vehicle efficiency, and building standards.[31] The problem of energy, like many problems we face, is simply too

large and multifaceted for any government to buy its way out of. Though
public investment is important, it works best in tandem with policies that
also incentivize private innovation.

Finally, it is critical to recognize the reality and problems of existing
government spending. One of the simplest ways to characterize some of
the environmental and social failures of the past century is to say that we
have misallocated an enormous amount of capital. And nowhere is our
misallocation of capital on more vivid display than in perverse subsidies
that actively work against progress. We have already seen the numbers
describing the existing subsidy for fossil fuels, but they are so large as to
merit repeating. Some $650 billion, or *about 1 percent of global GDP*, goes
to fossil fuels each year in the form of either consumption or production
subsidies. This figure excludes any so-called implicit subsidies such as a
government-funded highway system that supports private car traffic and
thus constitutes a large subsidy for car transport and thus fossil fuels.[32]

The problem of perverse subsidies is, of course, not limited to fossil
fuels. In many areas where we are most in need of government support
to align business and societal interests, we find the opposite. Agricultural subsidies in wealthy countries (totalling $273 billion annually in
OECD nations[33]) have long been implicated in distorting markets in a
way that perpetuates scarcity, ecological degradation, and poverty in
the developing world.[34]

In terms of designing policy aimed at change, the problems with existing subsidies suggest a few conclusions. One is that the argument that
the free market can simply provide improvements like renewable energy
holds little water. In reality, thanks in large part to lobbying, the "free
market" in many sectors already tilts substantially in the direction of Corporation 1920. Given this reality, we have two options. The easier of the
two is to create new subsidies that help to counteract the barriers created
by existing subsidies. This, of course, is far from ideal. Do we really want
to use more taxpayer money to battle misused taxpayer money? A better
solution, though often less politically feasible, would be to target reductions in perverse subsidies and finally to eliminate them altogether. Any
consideration of government spending should also be a consideration of
how to reduce maladaptive government spending.

In instances where government investment is desirable, past experience with spending leads us to a set of principles that can help to design programs that are beneficial rather than perverse. Like any single investor, the government is ill-suited to pick technological "winners and losers." To the extent possible, investment should be neutral about particular solutions. Additionally, far from replacing private enterprise, investment should be aimed at developing market forces that can take over after public spending fades. Finally, and perhaps most importantly, new investment initiatives should be accompanied by transparent, measurable, and enforceable time-limitation and cost-control mechanisms.

Regulation

The final tool available to policymakers seeking to lay the groundwork for the world of Corporation 2020 is regulation. Though one of the more straightforward kinds of policy options available, regulations actually serve a wide variety of purposes. For the purposes of this book, three kinds of regulations—command and control policies, standards, and laws that create property rights—are particularly worth considering.

Command and control policies encompass what the average person likely thinks of when they hear the word *regulation*. Rather than using TMD policies, taxes, or investment to nudge corporate action in a certain direction, command and control policies make it illegal for corporations to take certain actions. In general, command and control policies are most useful for completely eliminating certain kinds of activities. Because it is not feasible to ban smoking outright, governments typically use taxes rather than regulation to reduce tobacco consumption. Yet it is both feasible and desirable to eliminate all tobacco related advertising, and in this area many governments use command and control regulation. The inflexibility of command and control regulation makes it critical for policymakers to be aware of and responsive to changes in industries, and to also have an in-depth understanding of how particular industries function.

Standards are another useful type of regulatory policy. Though many standards are mandatory, some are simply designed to create demand for certain goods and services. A good example of a demand-oriented policy can be found in EnergyStar ratings, which serve to make consumers aware of energy-efficient appliances. Like taxes on negative externalities, standards have often been shown to drive innovation. That being said, however, standards also run the risk of creating a "ceiling of mediocrity" in which companies innovate to a certain point, and then have no incentive to innovate further. Moreover, complex standards may be easier for large corporations to interpret and meet than smaller corporations or private businesses. As with command and control policies, a general rule for standards is that policymakers should strive to balance their inherent inflexibility with a commensurate level of care, attention, and adaptability over time.

A final category of regulatory policy that is often overlooked, but will be crucial, consists of policies that assign and enforce property rights. One of the best-supported axioms of the social sciences is that people are more likely to abuse and overuse resources for which no one has clear rights. This refers not only to individual rights, but also community rights, and they need not be just ownership rights—they could be rights of access, sustainable harvest, and management, or the right of exclusion of access and use by others. Only by creating a regulatory framework that clearly allocates rights to resources can governments avoid the "tragedy of the commons." Furthermore, to implement effective economic mechanisms that reward responsible stewardship of natural commons (e.g., mechanisms such as "REDD+" and other forms of payments for ecosystem services), property rights will have to be recognized. Property-rights regulation also includes restrictions on the use of property, and in cases where social or environmental problems have a strong spatial component, strong zoning regulations can be effective solutions. For example, zoning regulations can ensure that polluting industries are located in land distant from human populations or in areas with the least impact on wildlife and natural resources.

The Macroeconomic Implications

Like many of the realities associated with the modern corporation, the state of the global economy seems to present a riddle. Why does it persist? Like a business that doesn't implement efficiency measures that would produce financial gains (to say nothing of welfare improvements), it seems that we are collectively walking by piles of cash, choosing not to pick them up.

One critical reason is that no single, rational being runs the global economy; many different actors have a role. Corporations, with their interest in generating financial returns for a small group of shareholders while offloading costs onto society, are among the most powerful, and that has dramatically shifted the playing field for the whole of the human enterprise.

So it should come as little surprise that we have a global economy that systematically excludes large swaths of society and borrows from the future. It is as if there is indeed a new world on the way but many of our most powerful institutions are busy blocking her progress. Corporation 2020 provides for a new economic actor with incentives for a more holistic form of capitalism and a new kind of economy.

Internalizing negative externalities can kick off a virtuous cycle. Even as corporations gain an incentive to reduce their own externalities, they also affect other actors. Who would doubt that an executive at Adidas was one of the first to read Puma's groundbreaking evaluation of its impacts on natural resources? It is similarly easy to envision how Puma's actions to reduce its externalities will bring about change in its suppliers and, via transparent advertising, its consumers.

The power that a corporation can have on its sector of the economy is so profound that it bears delving deeper into a particular instance—the case of Victoria's Secret.

In late 2004, the company was mailing roughly a million lingerie catalogs a day, many of which were printed on paper sourced from old-growth boreal forests. Around that time, a small environmental campaign group called ForestEthics was looking for a way to draw attention to the problem of destructive logging practices in the boreal forest. Victoria's Secret was not the only company using boreal products, and ForestEthics was not the first group to try to slow boreal logging. Yet ForestEthics took a different approach from campaign groups of the 1990s. Rather than having people chain themselves to trees *in the boreal*, they followed paper that came out of the boreal *down the supply chain* to the point at which it entered consumer consciousness. One place boreal-forest-produced paper entered the consumer consciousness in a big way was via Victoria's Secret's direct-mail marketing.[35]

ForestEthics began targeting Victoria's Secret. First, it launched a campaign designed to engage the company directly. When that didn't change practices, ForestEthics kicked off a public campaign. The campaign consisted of hundreds of protests around the country, but most importantly an advertisement published in the West Coast edition of the *New York Times*. It featured a lingerie model holding a chainsaw with a headline reading "Victoria's Dirty Secret."

Within days of the advertisement's publication, ForestEthics had received press from a number of prominent national news outlets, and it wasn't long before Victoria's Secret was prepared to meet with the group. About two years after ForestEthics began its campaign, Victoria's Secret announced a major deal to begin switching to sustainably sourced paper and reducing its overall catalog mailings.

What happened next is what is most instructive. Not only did Victoria's Secret begin exerting pressure on its suppliers, it began to call on more corporations to change their practices. Moreover, it took a role in lobbying the Canadian government for new standards and studies of forest ecology.[36] Recently, 21 forest product companies and nine environmental groups signed the Boreal Forest Agreement—touted as the largest conservation deal in history—which has the potential to reshape logging practices in the far north. Although the agreement was not entirely the result of ForestEthics or Victoria's Secret's efforts, their actions stand out as one of the primary catalysts that led to the deal.[37]

In short, a small group was able to use a very small amount of money to achieve change on an issue in a distant land involving many companies that most consumers had never heard about. And they did it all by leveraging the immense marketplace and societal power of the corporation. If we simply imagine this phenomenon writ large we begin to see the power of Corporation 2020. Each new Corporation 2020 exerts its influence up and downstream on its suppliers and on its consumers. It also touts its performance over its competitors, forcing horizontal market change. Finally, the new Corporation 2020 puts pressure on the government to continue to establish conditions that benefit it.

It is not enough for a corporation to simply "do no harm." Corporation 2020's goals are the same as society's goals: to increase human well-being, to increase social equity, to improve communal harmony, to reduce ecological scarcities and environmental risks. Proper valuation of social,

financial, and natural capital will allow corporations to go beyond minimizing costs to actually gaining from social- and environmental-positive
business propositions. For Natura or Tata, which already conceive of their
mission more broadly, the competitive advantage of a world in which the
rules favor Corporation 2020 will be immense.

Before going any further, we should ask: Where—that is, to what parts
of global society—will the benefits of Economy 2020 flow? For answers,
it is necessary only to examine who would benefit from investment in currently invisible social and natural capital.

One obvious answer is the young. Their education and training are investments in human capital that will provide future returns, so the youth
throughout the world possess immense potential. Young people will also
inherit many of the uncounted costs of today's corporate activities. Another answer is the poor, who rely disproportionately on the world's natural and social capital, and so would benefit disproportionately from its
valuation and increase.[38]

If these answers seem too pat, too facile to solve a number of the
world's most pressing problems, it is no coincidence. We are living in the
world of Corporation 1920, and Corporation 1920 plays by rules that
render the needs and potential of a large swath of the present population, and even more of the world's future population, invisible. Corporation 2020, in contrast, recognizes the value of social and natural capital,
measures and manages its impact on these categories of public assets as
part of its measure of true performance, and recognizes the reality that
business as usual will depend on using resources in a sustainable way.

The Nine-Billion-Ton Hamster and the Butterfly

In an animated video produced by the New Economics Foundation, the
narrator tells the story of an unusual hamster. Like all hamsters, it dou-
bles in size every week between its birth and puberty. Unlike all hamsters,
it continues to grow at the same rate after puberty, soon reaching 100,
then 200, then 400 pounds. By its first birthday, the hamster has hit 9 billion tons, and is capable of consuming all the world's corn in a day. With a
roar, it sets off on a Hamsterzilla rampage, destroying buildings, eventually consuming the planet and floating off, fat and happy, into space. "There
is a reason why in nature things grow in size only to a certain point," says

the narrator. "So why do most economists and politicians think that the economy can grow forever, and ever, and ever?"[39]

Though funny, the video drives home the frightening reality of our economic system. We know of no example of a biological organism or natural system that grows indefinitely—and yet we expect the natural world to sustain indefinite economic growth.

If nature suggests we have a Hamsterzilla problem, we might look to nature for solutions. How do natural organisms, and natural systems, grow? The answer is often via complexity. We recognize this on a human level; long after we have reached physical maturity we continue to become wiser, more capable, and more productive. In the natural world, the term to describe growth via complexity is *intussusception*, and its best-known example may be the metamorphosis of a caterpillar into a butterfly. The biologist and conservationist Tom Lovejoy, interviewed for this book, told me that "what we need is growth by intussusception—the *economic* equivalent of a caterpillar becoming a butterfly."

Obviously, hamsters and butterflies do not explain the global economy, but they can serve as a metaphor for the power of a new corporate form and a new economy. Aligning the goals of the corporation with the interests of society will set the stage for a much-needed shift away from growth via *size* and toward growth via *complexity*. We must go from an economy based on cutting, burning, and digging to one based on conservation, resource efficiency, and most important, innovation.

The necessity of decoupling economic growth from resource use, and particularly the most damaging kinds of resource use, is clear. A 2011 report from the United Nations Environment Program (UNEP) estimated that, on our present course, the human impact on the planet will grow dramatically between now and 2050. We will consume 57 percent more energy, resulting in a 71 percent increase in CO_2 emissions, use 70 percent more water, and produce 19 percent more waste.[40] Our farm and pasturelands will continue to grow to cover a total area over five times as large as the entire United States' land area; we will cut down a total of nearly seven Germanys of forests; and global fish catch will halve as overfishing leads stocks to decline. The "business as usual" scenario might, in short, be better known as the "best way to end business for a very long time."[41]

Delving into a particular sector, energy, clarifies the role that innovation can play in shifting away from business as usual. Because of its many dimensions, meeting energy demand without drawing down natural capital is perhaps both the most well-studied and most vexing challenge we face. In a number of papers, researchers have developed scenarios examining how we might meet future demand. Absent innovation, the task presents stark choices among accommodating the welfare of much of the world's population, pursuing energy resources in ever-more extreme and fragile environments, and mitigating the impacts of climate change.[42] It is only via substantial and sustained innovation that we will be able to meet the energy demands of a growing and rapidly developing world without pushing our natural resources to the brink.[43] As the IEA put it in 2008: "Current global trends in energy supply and use are patently unsustainable—environmentally, economically, socially. . . . What is needed is nothing short of an energy technology revolution."[44]

That thought, along with the statistics presented throughout this chapter, run the risk of inducing paralysis. The challenges ahead are large, and innovation can sound like a *deus ex machina*, magically available to extract us from a crisis in our collective history. Yet innovation does not happen by magic. Now, more than at any time in history, we know how to incentivize innovation on a societal scale. The key, as we have already argued, will be to align the goals of corporations, government, and civil society.

It is, finally, important to note that innovation means more than developing new gizmos and gadgets. New means of financing energy efficiency, such as Property-Assessed Clean Energy loans that help municipalities pay for renewable energy and efficiency projects through the issuance of property-secured bonds, also count as innovation—as do economic mechanisms for rewarding ecosystem services that are now being created and that will become more prevalent by the better valuation of natural capital. The essential message is that while we cannot predict the shape of the future, we need as much creativity in meeting it as possible. While we don't know how we will meet our collective resource challenges, what we do know is that we urgently need to align our most powerful institutions—corporations in particular—to the task of innovation.

The Costs and Benefits of the Green Economy

Often, the task of "greening" the global economy is cast in terms of fundamental tradeoffs—between environmental sustainability and economic progress, development, and the preservation of nature. I argue that, on the contrary, transitioning from a brown economy to a green economy holds great economic opportunity, whether we measure it in GDP, or by newer, more inclusive standards for evaluating human progress.

We can determine the tradeoffs associated with switching from a brown to a green economy via scenarios that map the choices ahead with hard numbers. As part of its 2011 report on the prospects for a global Green Economy, the United Nations Environment Program (UNEP) developed a comprehensive model exploring the dynamic relationship between the global economy and the environment. This model considers, *inter alia*, what the economy and its footprint would look like over time if, each year, 2 percent of global GDP were invested in greening the economy *instead of* investing in business-as-usual. At current levels, the amount 2 percent of global GDP is around $1.3 trillion. Global gross capital formation (GCF) is around $13 trillion, so this would not be additional investment, but rather a redirection of one-tenth of what the word invests anyway from public and private sources each year. Seen in that light, and for what the model predicts a green-economy transition would deliver, the investment required is by no means unreasonable. It would stabilize atmospheric CO_2 at 450 parts per million. Forest lands and fisheries stocks would begin to recover from decades of degradation. Average soil quality would improve, and by 2050, water use and energy use per capita would go down 40 percent and 22 percent respectively. Growth in output and jobs would be lower for 5–15 years but would then recover to higher trajectories than with a business-as-usual scenario.

But where is the *money* to finance a green economy? the cynics will ask. My answer is that it is there, and always was. Taxpayers' money is at present being wasted on almost a trillion dollars per year of perverse subsidies—for fossil fuels, intensive agriculture, unsustainable ocean fisheries, and the like. Trillions of dollars of public and private financial capital has been misallocated for decades on brown-economy growth plans which have helped Corporation 1920 privatize its profits and socialize its losses, delivered us a string of global recessions, and hit the poorest and most vulnerable people the hardest. Natural capital has been misallocated as well, and when it comes to nature, there are no central banks or fiscal largesse to help, no bailouts from ecological disaster.

The time has come to end all this waste and capital misallocation, and invest in a real future. We have to rebuild today's economy and transform it into a green economy, a sustaining economy which takes the poor out of poverty and delivers well-being to all, an economy of permanence. To do so, we urgently need to transform today's dominant Corporation 1920 model of business into Corporation 2020.

Notes

Introduction

1. "BP CEO Tony Hayward (VIDEO): 'I'd Like My Life Back,'" Huff Post Green, www.huffingtonpost.com/2010/06/01/bp-ceo-tony-hayward-video_n_595906.html.

2. Tony Hayward, "Entrepreneurial Spirit Needed: Tony Hayward, British Petroleum," YouTube, www.youtube.com/watch?v=FwQM00clxgM&noredirect=1.

3.

Accidental Oil Spills	Year	Estimated amount of oil spilled (in gallons)
BP—Gulf of Mexico	2010	206 million
Ixtoc I—Gulf of Mexico	1979	140 million
Atlantic Empress—Trinidad & Tobago	1979	90 million
Kolva River—Russia	1983	84 million
Exxon Valdez—Alaska	1989	11–32 million

Source: Laura Moss, "The 13 largest oil spills in history," Mother Nature Network, www.mnn.com/earth-matters/wilderness-resources/stories/the-13-largest-oil-spills-in-history.

4. Steve Hargreaves, "BP's $70 billion whipping," CNN Money, money.cnn.com/2010/06/01/news/companies/BP_analysts/index.htm.

5. "'No Underwater Oil Plumes': BP CEO Tony Hayward Denies Scientists' Research," Energy Boom Policy, www.energyboom.com/policy/no-underwater-oil-plumes-bp-ceo-tony-hayward-denies-scientists-research.

6. Ian Urbina, "BP Used Riskier Method to Seal Oil Well Before Blast," *New York Times*, www.cnbc.com/id/37370432/BP_Used_Riskier_Method_to_Seal_Oil_Well_Before_Blast.

7. US companies led the way in asking for a weakening of safety equipment that added to drilling risks in the gulf of Mexico, arguing for the removal of sound-triggered sealing switches costing over $500,000 per bore at the head of every well in the Gulf of Mexico, which, incidentally, BP did have in place in its own drilling platforms in the North Sea. (See: Robert F. Kennedy Jr., HuffPost Green, December 1, 2010, www.huffingtonpost.com/robert-f-kennedy-jr/sex-lies-and-oil-spills_b_564163.html.) This "cost saving" proved costly. Environmental attorney Mike Papantonio told Ed Schultz on MSNBC's Ed Show that it was Dick Cheney's Energy Task Force that rejected the proposal on grounds that "the switches, which cost $500,000, were too much a burden on the industry." (See: Michael Tomasky, The Guardian: Michael Tomasky's Blog, May 3, 2010, www.guardian.co.uk/commentisfree/michaeltomasky/2010/may/03/usa-dickcheney.) Halliburton is directly implicated in the disaster, since the Houston-based oilfield services corporation was under contract to pump cement around the wellhead to seal any leaks. Workers had just completed the cementing process when the well exploded. (See: Tim Wheeler, "Cheney blasted for blocking oil well safety valve," People's World, peoplesworld.org/cheney-blasted-for-blocking-oil-well-safety-valve/.)

8. Robert Costanza, David Batker, John Day, Rusty A. Feagin, M. Luisa Martinez, Joe Roman, "The Perfect Spill: Solutions for Averting the Next *Deepwater Horizon*," *Solutions Journal*, no. 12/1 (June 2010), www.thesolutionsjournal.com/node/629.

9. BP, "BP Establishes $20 Billion Claims Fund for *Deepwater Horizon* Spill and Outlines Dividend Decisions." www.bp.com/genericarticle.do?categoryId=2012968&content Id=7062966.

10. Anne Landman, "BP's 'Beyond Petroleum' Campaign Losing Its Sheen," Center for Media and Democracy, PR Watch, www.prwatch.org/node/9038.

11. Third Nobel Laureate Symposium on Global Sustainability, Stockholm, Sweden, May 16–19, 2011.

12. Adam Smith, author of several important works including *An Inquiry into the Nature and Causes of the Wealth of Nations* (1776), was a Professor in Moral Philosophy at Glasgow University in Scotland. Although one of the founding fathers of economics, he was not labeled an "economist" until much later. His much-quoted phrase "invisible hand" appears in *The Theory of Moral Sentiments* (London: A. Millar, 1759).

13. See, for example, Joseph E. Stiglitz, *The Roaring Nineties: A New History of the World's Most Prosperous Decade* (New York: W. W. Norton, 2003).

14. The total cost in the United States of caring for people with health problems caused by cigarette smoking has been estimated at $72.7 billion annually, according to health economists at the University of California in 1998. Smoking accounted for almost 12 percent of all medical expenditures in the United States according to this study. See Chapter 6, "Accountable Advertising," for a more detailed treatment of cigarette smoking and breast milk substitutes, two heavily advertised products.

15. "Universal Ownership: Why Environmental Externalities Matter to Institutional Investors" (report prepared by Trucost, 2010).

16. I discuss Infosys, Natura, and other examples of positive externalities in greater detail in Chapter 3, "Corporation 1920."

17. Foreign direct investment is discussed in Chapter 2, "The Great Alignment: 1945–2000."

18. See Chapter 6, "Accountable Advertising."

19. Joel Bakan, *The Corporation: The Pathological Pursuit of Profit and Power* (New York: Free Press, 2004).

20. For an overview of some of the issues of the shareholder-stakeholder dialogue, see: Renee Adams, Amir N. Licht, and Lilach Sagiv, "Shareholders and Stakeholders: How Do Directors Decide?" *Strategic Management Journal* 32 (2011); H. Jeff Smith, "The Shareholders vs. Stakeholders Debate," *MIT Sloan Management Review*, Summer (2003); Bidhan L. Parmar, R. Edward Freeman, Jeffrey S. Harrison, Andrew C. Wicks, Lauren Purnell, and Simone De Colle, "Stakeholder Theory: The State of the Art," *Academy of Management Annals* 4, no. 1 (2010).

21. In 2010 TruCost, estimated these externalities—the environmental and social costs of corporate activity—at US$2.15 trillion for the top 3,000 listed corporations. (See: Trucost, *Universal Ownership*.)

22. Officially, she is the winner of the Sveriges Riksbank Prize in Economic Sciences in Memory of Alfred Nobel, 2009.

23. Personal communication, Hyderabad, 2011.

24. United Nations Environment Programme, "Enabling Conditions: Supporting the Transition to a Global Green Economy," in *Towards a Green Economy: Pathways to Sustainable Development and Poverty Eradication: A Synthesis for Policy Makers* (2011).

25. Subsidies for fossil-fuel use include $550 billion in price subsidies and $100 billion in production subsidies, as reported in *Towards a Green Economy*.

26. The World Bank estimated subsidies for agriculture at around US$273 billion; global agricultural output is approximately US$2.3 trillion. See: *World Development Report 2008: Agriculture for Development* (The World Bank, 2007).

27. "Global 500," *Forbes*, July 26, 2010.

28. Based on 2010 global data; see: IHS, "IHS Global Insight: Country & Industry Forecasting," www.ihs.com/products/global-insight/index.aspx.

29. Data is from 1998 for the 64 countries for which the ILO collected data. See: Messaoud Hammouya, *Statistics on Public Sector Employment: Methodology, Structures, and Trends* (Geneva: International Labour Office Bureau of Statistics, 1999).

30. Data is for OECD countries over the period 1965–2009. See: Organization for Economic Co-operation and Development, *Revenue Statistics—Comparative Tables* (2011).

31. Amol Agrawal, "The Ubiquitous Crony Capitalist," livemint.com, January 16, 2011, www.livemint.com/2011/01/16211456/The-ubiquitous-crony-capitalis.html?h=B#.

32. Simon Johnson, "The Quiet Coup," *Atlantic Monthly*, May 2009.

33. The "revolving door" refers to the easy flow of very senior people between Wall Street and the US Treasury. Donald Regan, CEO and Chairman of Merrill Lynch, became US Treasury Secretary in the Reagan Administration in 1981—one of the first high-profile turns of the revolving door. This practise allowed Henry Paulson, former chief of Goldman Sachs, to become US Treasury Secretary in 2006 while an unfolding CDO credit crisis (in which his firm was already involved) had not yet grown into the full-blown banking crisis of 2008. It also allowed the selection of former Goldman Sachs lobbyist Mark Patterson as chief of staff to Treasury Secretary Timothy Geithner. Earlier, in 1996, it had enabled departing US Deputy Secretary of the Treasury Frank Newman to move to the ailing US financial giant Bankers Trust; just two years later, as its chairman and CEO, he negotiated the firm's sale to Deutsche Bank as well as his reported exit package of US$55 million.

34. Corporation 20/20 is a group convened by Allen White and Marjorie Kelley of Tellus Institute. The "20/20" in their name represents perfect vision, as against a deadline for significant change (the year 2020) argued in this book; however, there is considerable congruence of goals, so the two groups have now formed a close collaboration. See: www.corporation2020.org.

35. Marjorie Kelly and Allen White, "Corporate Design: The Missing Business and Public Policy Issue of Our Time" (Tellus Institute, 2007).

36. See www.corp2020.com for an explanation of the "2020" timeline of "Corporation 2020."

37. Title of economist J. C. Kumarappa's iconic work *Economy of Permanence*, 1945. Kumarappa was popularly known as M. K. Gandhi's favorite economist.

38. In *Towards a Green Economy*, (2011) UNEP defines a green economy as one which increases human well-being and increases social equity, while decreasing environmental risks and ecological scarcities.

39. James Gustave (Gus) Speth, personal communication, 2008; also the title of his speech "New Economy, Sustaining Economy" at the E. F. Schumacher Society, May 28, 2009.

40. Beyond GDP was an international conference of policy makers and thinkers held in the EU Parliament, November 2007, to debate and evolve alternative and more holistic metrics for measuring national performance than the UN's prevailing standard "System of National Accounts." Beyond GDP is also the name of a project launched by the EU Commission to further this aim.

41. WAVES (Wealth Accounting and Valuation of Ecosystem Services) is the name of a project for improving national-performance measurement that includes the economic impacts of ecosystem services and the costs of their ongoing loss. It was announced by World Bank president Robert Zoellick at the UN CBD COP-10 meeting in Nagoya, Japan, in October 2010. Its members are a balanced mix of early adopters, from both the developed and developing world, who seek to evolve a common approach toward integrating natural capital into national accounts.

42. See: United Nations Environment Programme, *Towards a Green Economy*.

Chapter 1 Notes

1. Vikramaditya Khanna, *The Economic History of the Corporate Form in Ancient India*, (University of Michigan Law School, 2005). Some uncertainty about limited liability in the *sreni* persists, due to a deficiency of evidence regarding how liabilities in excess of pooled capital would be resolved.

2. See: Ramesh Chandra Majmudar, *Corporate Life in Ancient India* (Calcutta: Surendra Nath Sen, 1922), 71–77. See also: P. N. Agrawala, *A Comprehensive Business History of India* (2004), 259.

3. Khanna, *The Economic History of the Corporate Form in Ancient India*, 39–40.

4. William Blackstone, quoted in Oscar and Mary Handlin, "Origins of the American Business Corporation," in *Enterprise and Secular Change*, ed. Frederic Lane (Homewood, IL: Richard Irwin, 1953).

5. John Micklethwait and Adrian Wooldridge, *The Company: A Short History of a Revolutionary Idea*, Modern Library Chronicles (New York: Modern Library, 2003), 4.

6. See: E. Badian, *Publicans and Sinners: Private Enterprise in the Service of the Roman Republic* (Dunedin, NZ: University of Otago Press, 1983), 68–69. There is evidence that these *societates publicanorum* were numerous, but in fact only one actual contract of association has been discovered. See also: Karl and David Lewis Moore, *Foundations of Corporate Empire* (London: Financial Times/Prentice Hall, 2001), 97.

7. Ulrike Malmendier, *Societas Publicanorum* (Cologne/Vienna: Böhlau Verlag, 2002), 249–51.

8. Henry Hansmann, Reinier Kraakman, and Richard Squire, "Law and the Rise of the Firm," Yale Law & Economics Research Paper 326 (2006), 1361. The authors go on to present further evidence that the *societates publicanorum* had a significant amount of entity shielding (i.e., in which the company's assets are legally partitioned from the owners' other assets). See also: Badian, *Publicans and Sinners*, 69.

9. The Roman state also outsourced the duty to collect taxes to the *publicani*. But when this approach proved unprofitable, the *publicani* joined together in a cartel during the first century to demand that the fees they paid the state for this business be returned to them. Julius Caesar promised to do so if he won the Roman Civil War, and he thus gained their support. See: Tenney Frank, *An Economic History of Rome*, 2nd Edition (Baltimore: The Johns Hopkins Press, 1927), 182.

10. It is interesting to note that the idea of some individuals acting as a representative for others, as is common in modern business, was present in the *societates publicanorum*, but seems to have been limited to the largest banking partnerships for much of Roman history. It was not until the emperor Justinian's rule in the sixth century that this began to be utilized by regular *societates*. See: W. W. Buckland, *A Text-Book of Roman Law from Augustus to Justinian* (Cambridge, UK: Cambridge University Press, 1921), 507, 510; John Crook, *Law and Life of Rome* (Ithaca, NY: Cornell University Press, 1967), 234.

11. Remarkably, to this day the Corporation of London, originating in the twelfth century, owns a fourth of all the land in the City of London (as well as three private schools, four markets, and the 790-acre park Hampstead Heath). See: Micklethwait and Wooldridge, *The Company*, 12.

12. William Blackstone, *Commentaries on the Laws of England*, vol. 1 (Oxford: Clarendon Press, 1765–69), 467–69; Ron Harris, *Industrializing English Law: Entrepreneurship and Business Organization, 1720–1844 (Political Economy of Institutions and Decisions)* (Cambridge, UK, and New York: Cambridge University Press, 2000).

13. The oldest public-sector corporation is likely the Aberdeen Harbour Board, which was established in 1136. See: Micklethwait and Wooldridge, *The Company*, 12.

14. See: Sir George C. M. Birdwood, *Report on the Old Records of the India Office, with Supplementary Note and Appendices* (London: W. H. Allen & Co., 1891); and William Foster, *The Register of Letters &c. of the Governour and Company of Merchants of London Trading into the East Indies, 1600–1619* (London: B. Quaritch, 1893).

15. Glenn Joseph Ames, *The Globe Encompassed: The Age of European Discovery, 1500–1700 (Connections)* (Upper Saddle River, NJ: Pearson Prentice Hall, 2008), 102–3.

16. Nicholas B. Dirks, *The Scandal of Empire: India and the Creation of Imperial Britain* (Cambridge, MA: Belknap Press of Harvard University Press, 2006), 82–90.

17. Ron Harris, "The Bubble Act: Its Passage and Its Effects on Business Organization," *Journal of Economic History* 54, no. 3 (1994); see also: "Bubble Act," in 6 Geo. 1, c. 18 (Great Britain, 1719).

18. See: J. W. Hurst, *The Legitimacy of the Business Corporation in the Law of the United States* (Charlottesville, VA: University of Virginia Press, 1970).

19. However, some companies attempted to circumvent the Bubble Act, which sometimes led to prosecutions. See: *The King v. Webb*, (1811) 104 Eng. Rep. 658; *The King v. Dodd*, (1808) 103 Eng. Rep. 670 (K.B.); see Ron Harris, "The Bubble Act," 78–79.

20. Joseph Kinnicut and Samuel Ames Angell, *A Treatise on the Law of Private Corporations Aggregate* (Boston: Hilliard, Gray, Little & Wilkins, 1832), 35. For general discussions of state corporate charters, see: Lawrence Meir Friedman, *A History of American Law*, 2nd ed. (New York: Simon & Schuster, 1985), 177–202; Kermit Hall, William M. Wiecek, and Paul Finkelman, *American Legal History: Cases and Materials* (New York: Oxford University Press, 1991), 115–17; Morton J. Horwitz, *The Transformation of American Law, 1780–1860: Studies in Legal History* (Cambridge, MA: Harvard University Press, 1977), 63–139.

21. *McCulloch v. Maryland*, 17 U.S. 316, (U.S. Supreme Court, 1819), 518–25, 626.

22. Ibid. 635, 636.

23. Ibid.

24. Cited in Margaret M. Blair, "Locking in Capital: What Corporate Law Achieved for Business Organizers in the Nineteenth Century," *UCLA Law Review* 51 (2003), 387, 389n. 3. There are now closer to 6 million corporations in the United States (5,857,000 in 2008). See: U.S. Census Bureau, *Business Enterprise: Sole Proprietorships, Partnerships, Corporations* (2008).

25. See, for example: Act Relating to Joint Stock Corporations, 1837 Conn. Pub. Acts 49, 49 (permitting incorporation of any "lawful" business); *Nesmith v. Sheldon* (1849), 48 U.S. (7 How.), 812, 817–18; see also President Jackson's veto of the Second Bank of the United States: "If [the government] would confine itself to equal protection, and, as Heaven does its rains, shower its favors alike on the high and the low, the rich and the poor, it would be an unqualified blessing." (Andrew Jackson, Veto Message [2], in *Messages and Papers of the Presidents*, 576, 590 [1896].)

26. *Louisville, Cincinnati, and Charleston Railroad Co. v. Letson*, 43 U.S. (2 How.) 555 (1844). See also *Marshall v. Balt. & Ohio R.R. Co.*, 57 U.S. (16 How.) 314, 328 (1853) (holding that for diversity purposes a corporation should be deemed a resident of its place of incorporation). This led to the current rule, adopted in 1958, under which a corporation is for diversity purposes a citizen of both the state in which it is incorporated and the state in which it has its principal place of business. [28 U.S.C. § 1332(c)(1) (2006)]

27. Frank H. Easterbrook and Daniel R. Fischel, "Limited Liability and the Corporation," *Univ. of Chicago Law Review* 52 (1985), 89.

28. See: Ronald M. Green, "Shareholders as Stakeholders: Changing Metaphors of Corporate Governance," *Washington & Lee Law Review*, no. 50 (1993), 1409, 1414–20 (which utilizes various corporate "disasters" to make a case for why limited liability may not always be helpful for a society); see also: H. Hansmann and R. Kraakman, "Toward Unlimited Shareholder Liability for Corporate Torts," *Yale Law Journal* 100, no. 7 (1991), 1879, 1880–81 (which explains that limited liability eliminates some of the incentive for corporations to avoid environmental damages, workplace accidents, etc.).

29. See: "Should Shareholders Be Personally Liable for the Torts of Their Corporations?" *Yale Law Journal* 76, no. 6 (1967), 1190, 1191 (in which the authors criticize limited liability on the basis of its application to corporate torts). For a more modern critique, see, for example: David Millon, "Piercing the Corporate Veil, Financial Responsibility, and the Limits of Limited Liability," *Emory Law Journal* 56, no. 5 (2007), 1305, 1307.

    There is strong historical evidence that limited liability was never meant to extend to involuntary creditors and tort liability, a benefit that had not been readily available to individuals until the twentieth century. However, the dilemma at present is not simply that the shareholders are excessively protected by limited liability in tort, but that much of the externalized social and environmental harm caused by corporations is not considered tortious at all. Thus, in the multinational context, the problem is not limited liability protecting shareholders, but the immunity of liability that the corporation enjoys more broadly. The concern is no longer that the corporation is undercapitalized in resolving its debts—rather, it's that the corporation is not being asked to pay for those environmental and social debts in the first place.

30. The *Times* of London published this relevant editorial in 1824:
    Nothing can be so unjust as for a few persons abounding in wealth to offer a portion of their excess for the information of a company, to play with that excess—to lend the importance of their whole name and credit to the society, and then should the funds prove insufficient to answer all demands, to retire into the security of their unhazarded fortune, and leave the bait to be devoured by the poor deceived fish. (*Times* [London], May 25, 1824. as reprinted in Paul Halpern, Michael Trebilcock, and Stuart Turnbull, "An Economic Analysis of Limited Liability in Corporation Law," *Univ. of Toronto Law Journal* 30, no. 2 (1980), 117)

31. "Limited Liability," *Law Magazine* 23 (1855), 215, 215–17. Quoted in Kahan, "Shareholder Liability for Corporate Torts," 1085, 1095.

32. See "Limited Liability Act," in 18 & 19 Vict., c. 133 (Parliament of the United Kingdom, 1855). See also J. Saville, "Sleeping Partnership and Limited-Liability, 1850–1856," *Economic History Review* 8, no. 3 (1956), 428–31 (describing in detail the process leading up to the adoption of the 1855 Act).

33. Andrew Haldane, "The Doom Loop," *London Review of Books* 34, February 4, 2012.

34. Ibid.

35. "Limited Liability Partnerships Act" (Parliament of the United Kingdom, 2000) and

"Limited Liability Partnerships Act (Northern Ireland)" (Northern Ireland Assembly, 2002).

36. Craig Holman, "Origins, Evolution and Structure of the Lobbying Disclosure Act" (Public Citizen, 2006).

37. *Siegman v. Electric Vehicle Co.*, 140 F. 117, 118 (D.N.J. 1905); see also: *Munson v. Curtis*, 223 N.Y. 313, 323 (1918) ("Directors are the exclusive, executive representatives of the corporation and are charged with the administration of its internal affairs and the management and use of its assets. Clearly the law does not permit the stockholders to create a sterilized board of directors." [citation omitted]).

38. See, e.g.: *Abbott v. Am. Hard Rubber Co.*, 33 Barb. 578 (N.Y. Gen. Term 1861).

39. General Corporation Act of New Jersey, N.J. Comp. Stat. § 51 (1896); see also: id. § 104 (authorizing mergers).

40. Michael A. Schaeftler, "Ultra Vires—Ultra Useless: The Myth of State Interest in Ultra Vires Acts of Business Corporations," *Journal of Corporate Law*, no. 9 (1983), 81, 89.

41. R. S. Avi-Yonah, "Corporations, Society, and the State: A Defense of the Corporate Tax," *Virginia Law Review* 90, no. 5 (2004), 1193, 1227, 1232.

42. Sherman Anti-Trust Act (1890), Ourdocuments.gov, www.ourdocuments.gov/doc .php?flash=true&doc=51.

43. See: Merchant Marine Act, in Vol. XLIX (United States, 1936).

44. *Dodge v. Ford Motor Co.*, 170 N.W. 671 (Mich. 1919).

45. Henry Ford, in *My Life and Work* (Garden City, NY: Doubleday, 1922), 162; see also: "Ford Makes Reply to Suit Brought by Dodge Brothers," *Detroit Evening News*, Nov. 4, 1916.

46. *Dodge v. Ford Motor Co.*, in 204 Mich. 459, 170 N.W. 668. (Michigan Supreme Court, 1919), 684.

47. *Santa Clara County v. Southern Pacific Railroad Company*, in 118 U.S. 394 (United States Supreme Court, 1886).

48. The critical statement, often attributed to Chief Justice Waite, reads: "The court does not wish to hear argument on the question whether the [Equal Protection Clause] . . . applies to these corporations. We are all of the opinion that it does." Interestingly, this statement was found in a summary to the case written by the court reporter. In other words, the finding that corporations enjoyed the same rights under the Fourteenth Amendment as natural persons was not decided by the Court. The court reporter, a former president of the Newburgh and New York Railway, in a case that specifically avoided the constitutional application of the Equal Protection Clause of the Fourteenth Amendment, may well have shifted the tide of history.

49. The full list of supportive cases includes *Minneapolis and St. L. R. Co. v. Beckwith* (1889) (Corporation's right for judicial review on state legislation); *Noble v. Union River Logging R. Col.* (1893) (Corporation's right for judicial review for rights infringement by federal legislation); *Hale v. Henkel* (1906) (Corporation's right to protection "against unreasonable searches and seizures" as per the Fourth Amendment); *Armour Packing C. v. United States* (1908) (Corporation's right to trial by jury as per the Sixth Amendment); *Pennsylvania Coal Co. v. Mahon* (1922) (Corporation's right to compensation for government takings); *Fong Foo v. United States* (1962) (Corporation's right to freedom from double jeopardy as per the Fifth Amendment); *Ross v. Bernhard* (1970) (Corporation's right to trial by jury in civil case as per the Seventh Amendment); *Virginia Pharmacy Board v. Virginia Consumer Council* (1976) (Corporation's right to free speech for purely commercial speech as per the First Amendment); *First National Bank of Boston v. Bellotti* (1978) (Corporation's right to corporate political speech as per the First Amendment); *Pacific*

Gas and Electric Company v. Public Utility Comm. of California (1986) (Corporation's right against coerced speech as per the First Amendment); *Citizens United v. Federal Election Commission* (2010) (Corporation's right for unlimited spending on elections as per the First Amendment).

50. W. O. Douglas, "Stare Decisis," *Columbia Law Review* 49, no. 6 (1949), 735–58.
51. Ample evidence of this can be found in banking. Note, for example, the fines imposed on investment banks after the 2008 recession, as discussed in Congressional testimony on banking practices in 2008–9.

Chapter 2 Notes

1. Hong Kong is a real success story for the "Chicago school" (a neo-classical school of economic thought built on underlying beliefs in human rationality, economic liberalism, and self-regulating free markets, notwithstanding extensive evidence of irrational human behavior and recent outcomes such as the 2008 financial crisis that would appear to challenge their faith in free markets to self-regulate), although its protagonists have changed since 1997, and that may spell a very different future. Chile is a contrived success story because much of its successes – achieved through sustained investments in education, healthcare and institutions – were actually state-driven, and not due to the "invisible hand" of markets in Chile's post-Pinochet decades.
2. Quoted by Frances Hesselbein, Marshall Goldsmith, and Richard Beckhard, The Organization of the Future, Drucker Foundation Future Series (San Francisco: Jossey-Bass Publishers, 1997).
3. Daniel C. K. Chow and Thomas J. Schoenbaum, *International Trade Law: Problems, Cases, and Materials* (New York: Aspen Publishers, 2008).
4. For example, Google, Microsoft, and Facebook are leading members of the Computer and Communications Industry Association (CCIA), which has a permanent office in Geneva.
5. "Beyond Doha," *The Economist*, October 9, 2008.
6. Alan Beattie, "Business Loses Heart in Doha Drudgery," *Financial Times*, July 24, 2008.
7. The OECD's estimate of the world "total GDP including proxy component" is 2,733.5 billion international dollars in 1913, and 5,329.7 billion in 1950. Source: Angus Maddison, "Table 7-1: Coverage of World GDP Sample and Proportionate Role of Proxy Measures, 1820–2001," in *The World Economy: Historical Statistics* (OECD, 2003). World export data is in current values. Source: "International Trade Statistics, 1900–1960" (UN Statistics Division, 1962). See also: World Bank, "World Development Indicators."
8. William J. Bernstein, *A Splendid Exchange: How Trade Shaped the World* (New York: Atlantic Monthly Press, 2008).
9. Instituted by the Act to Regulate Commerce of 1887, the ICC was initially charged with preventing and correcting rate discriminations by railroads. With the Transportation Act of 1920, however, the US Congress expanded the ICC's policy scope to include the promotion, encouragement, and development of water transportation, service, and facilities in connection with US commerce, and the fostering and preservation of both rail and water transportation.
10. For example, leading up to the passage of the Merchant Marine Act of 1936, the cargo industry in America was rife with corporate efforts to influence policy, ultimately leading to scandal in early 1935 due to illicit corporate payments to Congressional officials in an effort to secure maritime mail-hauling contracts. Political response to the scandal was relatively soft and similar to that of 50 years earlier, when burgeoning railroad

corporations openly paid congressional officials in the halls of the Capitol building in return for favorable legislation. (See: Michael T. Hayes, *Lobbyists and Legislators: A Theory of Political Markets* [New Brunswick, NJ: Rutgers University Press, 1981].) While such forms of unbridled and unethical corporate influence have been significantly curtailed through modern legislation in the developed world, these examples nonetheless provide insight into the way today's corporations behave in a deregulated trade environment: when market innovations create opportunity, corporations seek to gain as much political influence as possible in order to seize that opportunity.

11. Stewart Taggart, "The 20-Ton Packet," *Wired*, October 1999.
12. Ibid. See also: Marc Levinson, "Container Shipping and the Economy: Stimulating Trade and Transformations Worldwide," *TR News*, no. 246 (2006).
13. Andrea Goldsmith, *Wireless Communications* (Cambridge, UK, and New York: Cambridge University Press, 2005).
14. John H. Dunning, *International Production and the Multinational Enterprise* (London, Boston: Allen & Unwin, 1981).
15. Maurice Obstfeld and Alan M. Taylor, "Globalization and Capital Markets," in *Globalization in Historical Perspective*, ed. Michael D. Bordo, Alan M. Taylor, and Jeffrey G. Williamson (Chicago: University of Chicago Press, 2003).
16. Zbigniew Zimny, "Foreign Direct Investment in the World and in Africa: Long-Term Trends and Current Patterns," in *UNCTAD Virtual Institute Training Package on Economic and Legal Aspects of International Investment Agreements (IIAs), Module 1, Concepts, Trends and Economic Aspects of Foreign Direct Investment* (2008).
17. Nicholas Hildyard and Sara Sexton, "Cartels, 'Low Balls,' Backhanders and Hand-Outs: Privatization in the UK," *The Ecologist* 26, no. 4 (1996).
18. Yves Albouy and Reda Bousba, "The Impact of IPPs in Developing Countries—Out of the Crisis and into the Future" (The World Bank Group, 1998).
19. See also Chapter 7, "Limiting Financial Leverage," which describes the role of M&A in driving up the use of financial leverage.
20. Imed Chkir and Jean-Claude Cosset, "The Effect of International Acquisitions on Firm Leverage," *Journal of Financial Research* XXVI, no. 4 (2003).
21. Richard M. Levich, "The Euromarkets after 1992," NBER Working Paper No. 3003 (1991).
22. Ibid.
23. In a swap, as well as other derivative instruments, the notional amount does not represent the amount of money exchanged but is rather a reference number to which rates, percentages, or other calculations are applied in order to derive the respective payment obligations of the parties to the transaction. The change in total notional amount provides a sense of the growth in that market, but does not represent the actual amount at risk. The figures shown here come from Investopedia, "An Introduction to Swaps," www.investopedia.com/articles/optioninvestor/07/swaps.asp#axzz1bNEnGsgK.
24. Ronen Palan, "The history of tax havens," History & Policy, www.historyandpolicy.org/papers/policy-paper-92.html.
25. Ibid.
26. International Monetary Fund Monetary and Exchange Affairs Department, "Offshore Financial Centers: IMF Background Paper" (2000).
27. Organisation for Economic Co-operation and Development, "Towards Global Tax Co-operation: Report to the 2000 Ministerial Council Meeting and Recommendations by the Committee on Fiscal Affairs" (2000).
28. Ibid.

29. As a simple example of a derivative instrument, let's consider a "plain vanilla" interest-rate swap. In that transaction, two institutions would agree to exchange cash flows, but one set of cash flows would be fixed and the other would be variable, essentially allowing each party to bet against the other on the direction of interest rate changes. Let's assume the notional of the transaction is $1,000,000 and that the twelve-month LIBOR rate stands at 3 percent at the transaction date. The contract could be structured so that party A pays party B an annual fixed amount of 5 percent of the notional (or $50,000) and party B pays party A the twelve-month LIBOR rate plus 2 percent on the notional, which initially would total 5 percent for the same $50,000 annually. On the contract date, the derivative's value is zero because both sets of cash flows offset perfectly, and no payments are needed. However, if the LIBOR rate rises, party B's payments will exceed its receipts from party A, producing a net loss for party B. If the LIBOR rate falls, party A will pay party B an amount over its own receipts. In this way, contracted cash flows can be exchanged with no net initial investment. This type of instrument can be used to hedge against interest-rate risk or to speculate.

30. "Metallgesellschaft," Turtle Trader, www.turtletrader.com/adtrade.html.

31. "Long-Term Capital Management," MoneyScience, v2.moneyscience.com /Information_Base/Long_Term_Capital_Management_%28LTCM%29.html.

32. Gene D. Guill, "Bankers Trust and the Birth of Modern Risk Management" (The Wharton School of the University of Pennsylvania, 2009).

33. CNN Money, "CSFB loss hits Credit Suisse," money.cnn.com/1999/03/16/worldbiz /merchant/.

34. Manuel Castells, *The Rise of the Network Society, The Information Age: Economy, Society and Culture*, Vol. I (Malden, MA: Blackwell Publishers, 1996).

Chapter 3 Notes

1. Example courtesy Prof. Rajiv Sinha, W. P. Carey School of Business, Arizona State University. See also: "Who is in charge of bread supply in London?" *Skeptic Lawyer* 26, September 2010 skepticlawyer.com.au/2010/09/26/who-is-in-charge-of-bread-supply -in-london/.

2. Marjorie Kelly and Allen White, "Corporate Design: The Missing Business and Public Policy Issue of Our Time" (Tellus Institute, 2007).

3. Joel Bakan, *The Corporation: The Pathological Pursuit of Profit and Power* (New York: Free Press, 2004).

4. See: R. H. Coase, "The Nature of the Firm," *Economica—New Series 4*, no. 16 (1937). The size of a firm (as framed by Coase) is measured by how many contractual relations are "internal" to the firm and how many "external." It is a result of finding an optimal balance between the costs of competing paths for the firm. In general, making the firm larger will initially be advantageous, but decreasing returns indicated above will eventually kick in, preventing the firm from growing indefinitely.

5. There is a natural limit to what can be produced internally, however. Coase notices "decreasing returns to the entrepreneur function," including increasing overhead costs and increasing propensity for an overwhelmed manager to make mistakes in resource allocation. This is a countervailing cost to the use of the firm.

6. Coase, "The Nature of the Firm."

7. Tom McCarthy, *Auto Mania: Cars, Consumers, and the Environment* (New Haven: Yale University Press, 2007), 61–63.

8. Ibid.

9. Fred Thompson, "Fordism, Post-Fordism, and the Flexible System of Production," www.willamette.edu/~fthompso/MgmtCon/Fordism_&_Postfordism.html.

10. See Chapter 2, "The Great Alignment."

11. U.S. Financial Crisis Inquiry Commission. "The Financial Crisis Inquiry Report: Final Report of the National Commission on the Causes of the Financial and Economic Crisis in the United States" (2011).

12. C. William Thomas, "The Rise and Fall of Enron," *Journal of Accountancy* (2002).

13. "The Rise and Fall of Enron: A Brief History," CBC News, May 25, 2006.

14. Obtained from Enron Corporation's form 10-K annual report, filed with the Securities and Exchange Commission (SEC) for the fiscal year that ended December 31, 2000. Online access to such financial reports is available at www.sec.gov/edgar/searchedgar /companysearch.html.

15. Thomas, "The Rise and Fall of Enron."

16. Estimates differ among company reports. See: Center for Media Research, "2012 Ad Spending Outlook" (2011).

17. A couple of definitions are in order. *Need*—something that is essential. It is often argued that there are only four basic needs, viz., food, clothing, shelter, and healthcare; however, advertising has the power to make people believe they "need" much more than these four essentials. *Want*—something you would like to have . . . and note that there are no limits to human wants, but only if they are perceived as "needs" will they command priority and purse.

18. Teresa Moran Schwartz and Alice Saker Hrdy, "FTC Rulemaking: Three Bold Initiatives and Their Legal Impact, in 90th Anniversary Symposium of the Federal Trade Commission Consumer Protection Panel (2004).

19. Schwartz, "FTC Rulemaking."

20. Federal Trade Commission, "Do Not Call Registrations Exceed 10 Million," www.ftc .gov/opa/2003/06/dncregistration.shtm.

21. Schwartz, "FTC Rulemaking."

22. Ibid.

23. "Global 500 Annual Ranking of the World's Largest Corporations," *Forbes*, July 26, 2010.

24. Richard Munson, *From Edison to Enron: The Business of Power and What It Means for the Future of Electricity* (Westport, CT: Praeger Publishers, 2005).

25. The American Clean Energy and Security Act of 2009 was a bill put before the US Congress (which was approved by the House of Representatives, but was never passed in the Senate) that proposed a cap-and-trade system for greenhouse-gas emissions in the United States. It also included renewable energy requirements for electric utilities, subsidies for clean energy and other technologies, and consumer protection for energy price rises. See: Marianne Lavelle, "The Climate Change Lobby Explosion," The Center for Public Integrity, www.publicintegrity.org/investigations/climate_change /articles/entry/1171/.

26. Marianne Lavelle to iwatch news, April 21, 2009, www.iwatchnews.org/2009/04/21/2 885/%E2%80%98clean-coal%E2%80%99-lobbying-blitz.

27. Anne C. Mulkern, "IRS Disclosures Show Extent of Oil and Coal Groups' Outreach," *New York Times*, 2009.

28. Alex Kaplun, "Lobbyist Apologizes to House Climate Panel for Forged-Letter 'Scheme,'" *New York Times*, October 29, 2009.

29. Australia's "Resource Super Profits Tax"—RSPT. See Chapter 8, "Resource Taxation."

30. Tony Abbott, "K-Rudd's killing the goose that laid Australia's golden egg," *Daily Telegraph* (Sydney), May 7, 2010.

31. Global data from 2010. See: IHS, "IHS Global Insight: Country & Industry Forecasting," www.ihs.com/products/global-insight/index.aspx.

32. Data from 1998 for the 64 countries for which the ILO collected data. See: Messaoud Hammouya, "Statistics on Public Sector Employment: Methodology, Structures, and Trends" (Geneva: International Labour Office Bureau of Statistics, 1999).

33. See: Organisation for Economic Co-operation and Development, www.oecd.org/home/0,2987,en_2649_201185_1_1_1_1_1,00.html.

34. Jules Pretty, "Agroecological Approaches to Agricultural Development" (RIMISP—Latin American Center for Rural Development, 2006).

35. Note that the term "lobbying" in this book refers to the use of persuasion with government or industry regulators or lawmakers to create advantage through laws, regulations, taxes, and public investment to promote private profit. Lobbying is as ubiquitous in business as the pursuit of profit, and it presents an outstanding return on the investment of management time.

36. This following discussion of lead in gasoline is based largely on the research work of William Kovarik. See: William Kovarik, "Ethyl: The 1920s Environmental Conflict over Leaded Gasoline and Alternative Fuels," American Society for Environmental History (2003).

37. United States Environmental Protection Agency Region 10, "Leaded Gas Phaseout," yosemite.epa.gov/R10/airpage.nsf/webpage/Leaded+Gas+Phaseout.

38. Kovarik, "Ethyl."

39. Ibid.

Chapter 4 Notes

1. Paul Krugman, "Willie Sutton Wept," *New York Times*, February 17, 2011.

2. "Willie Sutton Rule," *Farlex Financial Dictionary*, financial-dictionary.thefreedictionary.com/Willie+Sutton+Rule.

3. "BrainyQuote," www.brainyquote.com/quotes/keywords/profit.html.

4. "Profit Quotes," Thinkexist.com, thinkexist.com/quotes/with/keyword/profit/3.html. Also see: Chapter 1, "The Legal History of the Corporation."

5. Gethin Chamberlain, "Vedanta and the holy mountain," www.newsandpics.com/Photojournalism/Vedanta-and-the-holy-mountain/13030929_tfneQ/1/943677730_Tbfgg#943672782_LD8ps.

6. "Vedanta would invest $2 billion less in India in next 2 years," *Economic Times*, October 7, 2010.

7. Sung-Bae Mun and Ishaq Nadiri, "Information Technology Externalities: Empirical Evidence from 42 U.S. Industries," NBER Working Paper Series, no. 9272 (NBER, 2002), www.nber.org/papers/w9272.pdf?new_window=1.

8. Zhiqiang Liu, "Foreign Direct Investment and Technology Spillover: Evidence from China," http://58.194.176.234/gjtzx/uploadfile/200904/20090401143359232.pdf.

9. (Bloom et al 2012) http://www.stanford.edu/~nbloom/bsv_2010.pdf.

10. American Society for Training and Development, "Training Industry FAQ," www.astd.org/ASTD/aboutus/trainingIndustryFAQ.htm.

11. Matt Barney and Infosys Technologies Ltd., *Leadership @ Infosys* (New Delhi: Portfolio, 2010), 1.

12. Andrew Tanzer, "Passage to India," Forbes.com, www.forbes.com/forbes/2000/1030/6612080a.html.

13. "Form 20-F: Infosys Technologies Limited," United States Securities and Exchange Commission, www.sec.gov/Archives/edgar/data/1067491/000106749107000015/form20f.htm#item6. (See "Recruiting" section.)
14. Barney, *Leadership @ Infosys*, viii.
15. "Form 20-F" (See "Training and Development" section.)
16. Infosys, "Smt. Sonia Gandhi Inaugurates Infosys' Global Education Center - II in Mysore," www.infosys.com/newsroom/press-releases/Pages/global-education-center-II.aspx.
17. "Goodbye, folks. March on with values . . . ," Infosys, www.infosys.com/investors/reports-filings/annual-report/annual/Documents/AR-2011/Theme-Pages/goodbye_folks.html.
18. International Labour Organization, "Working Time Around the World—One in five workers worldwide are putting in 'Excessive' hours: New ILO study spotlights working time in over 50 countries," www.ilo.org/global/about-the-ilo/press-and-media-centre/news/lang--en/WCMS_082827.
19. Gustavo J. Bobonis, "Is the Allocation of Resources within the Household Efficient? New Evidence from a Randomized Experiment," *Journal of Political Economy* 117, no. 3 (2009).
20. D. Thomas, "Intrahousehold Resource Allocation: An Inferential Approach," *Journal of Human Resources* 25, no. 4 (1990).
21. Michael Schuman, "At Toyota's Home Base, Townspeople Are Worried," *Time World*, February 10, 2010. It has been reported that in 2009, after the Toyota company laid off more than 9,000 contract workers, the city responded by changing its name back to Koromo. See: Malcolm Moore and Julian Ryall, "Rebuilding Japan: Hitachi's residents put faith in 'family' company," *Telegraph* (London), April 18, 2011.
22. P. Kuhn and F. Lozano, "The expanding workweek? Understanding trends in long work hours among US men, 1979–2006," *Journal of Labor Economics* 26, no. 2 (2008).
23. The study by Kuhn and Lozano is quoted and summarized in: David R. Francis, "Why High Earners Work Longer Hours," The National Bureau of Economic Research, www.nber.org/digest/jul06/w11895.html.
24. International Labour Organization, "Working Time Around The World."
25. I say "most likely" because so little work that values externalities comprehensively has been done on other major negative externalities of the corporation, such as its impacts on human health.
26. Nicholas Z. Muller and Robert Mendelsohn, "Measuring the damages of air pollution in the United States," *Journal of Environmental Economics and Management* 54 (2007).
27. N. Z. Muller, R. Mendelsohn, and W. Nordhaus, "Environmental Accounting for Pollution in the United States Economy," *American Economic Review* 101, no. 5 (2011).
28. Developed in 2006 by Dr. Robert Repetto, who was at the Yale School of Forestry and Environmental Studies at the time, and Professor Daniel Dias at the University of Illinois.
29. Robert Repetto and Daniel Dias, "TRUEVA: A New Integrated Financial Measure of Environmental Exposure," in Yale Center for Environmental Law & Policy Working Paper Series, ed. Anastasia O'Rourke (2006).
30. K. G. Berger and S. M. Martin, "II.E.3.—Palm Oil," www.cambridge.org/us/books/kiple/palmoil.htm.
31. Food and Agriculture Organization, "FAOSTAT" (2010).
32. US Department of Agriculture Foreign Agricultural Service, "Indonesia: Palm Oil Production Growth to Continue" (2009).

33. W. F. Kee, "Market and Technical Foresights for Oleochemical Industry, and Market Outlook for SouthEast Asia Region" (2010).

34. "The other oil spill," *The Economist*, June 24, 2010.

35. "Fact Sheet Norway-Indonesia Partnership REDD+," www.norway.or.id/PageFiles /404362/FactSheetIndonesiaGHGEmissionMay252010.pdf.

36. Ellie Brown and Michael F. Jacobson, "Cruel Oil: How Palm Oil Harms Health, Rainforest, & Wildlife" (Washington, DC: Center for Science in the Public Interest, 2005).

37. "The Other Oil Spill."

38. Greenpeace, "How Sinar Mas is pulping the planet" (2010), www.greenpeace.org /international/en/publications/reports/SinarMas-APP.

39. David Gilbert, "Cargill customers cancel with Sinar Mas while Cargill continues to support rainforest destruction," Rainforest Action Network: The Understory, understory.ran.org/2010/03/17/cargill-still-committed-to-rainforest-destruction -despite-global-exodus/.; Greenpeace, "Burger King cancels palm oil contract with rainforest destroyer Sinar Mas," www.greenpeace.org/usa/en/media-center/news -releases/Burger-King-cancels-palm-oil-contract-with-rainforest-destroyer-Sinar-Mas-/; Mongabay, "Forest destruction by Sinar Mas undermines efforts to develop and promote greener palm oil," news.mongabay.com/2009/1214-sinar_mas.html; Cargill, "Cargill's Position on Sinar Mas (PT SMART)," www.cargill.com/corporate -responsibility/pov/palm-oil/response-to-pt-smart/index.jsp.

40. John Roach, "Alaska Oil Spill Fuels Concerns over Arctic Wildlife, Future Drilling," *National Geographic* News, 2006.

41. Francis G. Beinecke, "No to Arctic Drilling," *New York Times*, August 17, 2011.

42. "Total Oil Consumption by Country," Globalfirepower.com, www.globalfirepower. com/oil-consumption-by-country.asp.; see also: Spencer Swartz and Shai Oster, "China Tops U.S. in Energy Use," *Wall Street Journal*, July 18, 2010.

43. Beinecke, "No to Arctic Drilling."

44. Michael Whitney, "BP and MMS Agree: 'Seals, Sea Otters, and Walruses' Live in Gulf of Mexico," MyFDL, my.firedoglake.com/michaelwhitney/2010/05/19/bp-and -mms-agree-seals-sea-otters-and-walruses-live-in-gulf-of-mexico/.

45. Kate Sheppard, "BP's Gulf Oil Spill 'Plan,'" *Mother Jones*, May 26, 2010; Holbrook Mohr, Justin Pritchard, and Tamara Lush, "BP's gulf oil spill response plan lists the walrus as a local species. Louisiana Gov. Bobby Jindal is furious.," *Christian Science Monitor*, June 9, 2010.

46. This refers to the following lines in the article by Mohr et al., "BP's gulf oils spill response plan": "In the spill scenarios detailed in the documents, fish, marine mammals and birds escape serious harm; beaches remain pristine; water quality is only a temporary problem. And those are the projections for a leak about 10 times worse than what has been calculated for the ongoing disaster." And: "BP's site plan regarding birds, sea turtles or endangered marine mammals ('no adverse impacts') also have proved far too optimistic."

47. Whitney, "BP and MMS Agree."

48. Office of the Inspector General of the US Department of the Interior, "Investigative Report: Island Operating Company et al." (2010).

49. Ibid.

50. Center for Biological Diversity, "Catastrophe in the Gulf of Mexico: Devastation Persists," www.biologicaldiversity.org/programs/public_lands/energy/dirty_energy _development/oil_and_gas/gulf_oil_spill/index.html.

51. "BP oil spill: 9 strange facts," *The Week*, May 27, 2010.

52. TEEB 2010, a UN-hosted global study of the value of biodiversity and ecosystems and of the economic and social consequences of their ongoing loss, refers to the underlying cause of the problem as "the economic invisibility of nature."

53. Paul Wiseman and Tim Watson, "Future losses from BP oil spill worry Gulf Coast businesses," *USA Today*, June 9, 2010.

54. Jaquetta White, "Economic impact of Gulf of Mexico oil spill varies by industry," www.nola.com/news/gulf_oil-spill/index.ssf/2010/05/economic_impact_of_gulf_of _mex.html.

55. Marcus Baram and Gideon Pine, "How the Economic Impact of the Oil Spill Is Spreading Beyond the Gulf," www.huffingtonpost.com/2010/07/15/oil-spill -economic-impact_n_646016.html.

56. Lisa Flam, "Spill Study Envisions Huge Losses for Florida Tourism," AOL News (2010), www.aolnews.com/2010/06/08/spill-study-envisions-huge-losses-for -florida-tourism/.

57. "Jindal calls stimulus 'irresponsible' in GOP response," CNNPolitics.com (2009), www.cnn.com/2009/POLITICS/02/24/sotn.jindal.speech/index.html.

58. Jake Tapper and Bradley Blackburn, "BP Oil Spill: Gov. Jindal Asks for Permission to Build Barrier Islands," *ABC World News*, May 24, 2010.

59. Josh Harkinson, "Bobby Jindal: Oil Spill Hero or BP's BFF?" *Mother Jones*, June 2, 2010.

60. Stephen Power, John Kell, and Siobhan Hughes, "BP, Oil Industry Take Fire at Hearing," *Wall Street Journal*, June 16, 2010; Gideon Pine, "Exxon, BP CEOs: It Was 'Embarrassment' to Include Walruses in Gulf Response Plan," Huff Post Green, www.huffingtonpost.com/2010/06/15/exxon-bp-ceos-it-was-emba_n_612837.html.

61. Associated Press, "Punitive Damages Ruled Possible in Gulf Oil Spill," *New York Times*, August 26, 2011.

62. Brad Johnson, "BP funds push for more offshore drilling in oil-soaked Louisiana," Grist, www.grist.org/oil/2011-08-05-bp-funds-push-offshore-drilling-louisiana -gulf-of-mexico.

63. "Chemical firm to pay Rs200cr for defying SC orders," *Times of India*, July 25, 2011.

64. "Corporate responsibility," Information for Action, www.informaction.org/cgi-bin /gPage.pl?menu=menua.txt&main=corpres_causes.txt&s=Corporate+Responsibility.

65. Marianne Lavelle to iwatch news, April 21, 2009, www.iwatchnews.org/2009/04/21/2 885/%E2%80%98clean-coal%E2%80%99-lobbying-blitz.

66. See Chapter 6, "Accountable Advertising."

67. Tim Wheeler, "Cheney blasted for blocking oil well safety valve," People's World (2010), peoplesworld.org/cheney-blasted-for-blocking-oil-well-safety-valve/.

68. John W. Schoen, "BP $20 billion fund may not cover spill costs," MSNBC.com (2010), www.msnbc.msn.com/id/37736098/ns/business-us_business/t/bp-billion-fund-may -not-cover-spill-costs/.

69. Colman McCarthy, "A CEO who cares: Whole Foods founder John Mackey thinks profits and ethics can mix," Business Library (2005), findarticles.com/p/articles/mi _m1141/is_6_42/ai_n15956843/.

70. Whole Foods Market, "About Whole Foods Market" (2012) www.wholefoodsmarket .com/company/index.php.

71. Mike Musgrove, "Sweatshop Conditions at iPod Factory Reported," *Washington Post*, June 16, 2006.

72. Danny Bradbury, "Apple risks green makeover with CSR snub," BusinessGreen, www.businessgreen.com/bg/news/1800821/apple-risks-green-makeover-csr-snub.

Chapter 5 Notes

1. Center for Climate and Energy Solutions, "Global Anthropogenic GHG Emissions By Sector," www.pewclimate.org/facts-figures/international-emissions/sector.

2. *Stern Review* estimates damages in terms of a social cost of carbon of $85 per tonne of CO2. Nicholas Stern, "The Economics of Climate Change: Executive Summary," *Stern Review* (2006).

3. For example, Daniel Esty and Andrew Winston's *Green to Gold* (2006) included BP as a leading "Wave Rider"; however, based on this company's alarming oil spills, it seems reasonable to question whether voluntary measures by corporations will ever lead to a truly green economy.

4. L'Oreal, "The Body Shop," www.loreal-finance.com/site/us/marques/marque5.asp.

5. The Body Shop, "Our History," www.thebodyshop-usa.com/about-us/aboutus _history.aspx.

6. Patagonia, "Our Reason for Being," www.patagonia.com/us/patagonia. go?assetid=2047. See also: Rocky Mountain Institute, "Doing Well by Doing Good: Why Patagonia Makes a Profit, Naturally," Treehugger, www.treehugger.com /corporate-responsibility/doing-well-by-doing-good-why-patagonia-makes-a-profit -naturally.html.

7. Fair Trade Federation, "Interim Report on Fair Trade Trends" (2008).

8. Fairtrade Foundation, "Global Fairtrade sales increase by 22%," www.fairtrade.org .uk/press_office/press_releases_and_statements/jun_2009/global_fairtrade_sales _increase_by_22.aspx.

9. Geoffrey M. Heal, "Corporate Environmentalism: Doing Well by Being Green," Working Paper Series (2007).

10. Geoffrey Heal, "Environmental disaster—not all bad news," *Financial Times*, October 30, 2000.

11. General Electric, "Fact Sheet," www.ge.com/company/factsheets/corporate.html.

12. General Electric, "Awards & Recognition," www.gecapital.com/en/our-company /careers/awards-recognition.html.

13. Kirsten Korosec, "Why General Electric Is Pouring $10B into Its Ecomagination Brand," CBS News, June 25, 2010.

14. TEEB for Business showcases analyses as complex as the economic impact of deforestation in China due to its construction industry, or the economic impact of freshwater losses in the Aral Sea due to the cotton industry in Central Asia. See: "The Economics of Ecosystems and Biodiversity for Business and Enterprise" (2011).

15. The International Integrated Reporting Committee (IIRC) was formed in 2010 by the Prince's Accounting for Sustainability Project (A4S) and the Global Reporting Initiative (GRI). See: Wisegeek, "What Is Integrated Reporting?" www.wisegeek.com/what-is -integrated-reporting.htm.

16. Puma, "PUMA Completes First Environmental Profit and Loss Account Which Values Impacts at €145 million," about.puma.com/puma-completes-first-environmental -profit-and-loss-account-which-values-impacts-at-e-145-million/.

17. Ibid.

18. Puma, "PUMA's Environmental Profit and Loss Account Three-Stage Development Process," about.puma.com/wp-content/themes/aboutPUMA_theme/media/pdf /2011/en/epl1116.pdf.

19. Carbon Disclosure Project, "View responses and CDP findings," www.cdproject.net /en-US/Results/Pages/overview.aspx.

20. Carbon Disclosure Project, www.cdproject.net/en-US/WhatWeDo/CDPNews
    ArticlePages/commercial-interests-driving-ghg-emissions-reduction-at-worlds-largest
    -companies.aspx.

21. Robert G. Eccles, Michael P. Krzus, and George Serafeim, "Market Interest in Non
    financial Information," Harvard Business School Working Paper (2011).

22. Marcus Norton, "The Water-Energy-Food Security Nexus: Understanding the Risks &
    Opportunities for Private Finance" (German Federal Government publication, 2011).

23. See, for example: The Coca-Cola Company, "Securities Exchange Act Reports," www
    .thecoca-colacompany.com/investors/pdfs/10-K_2010/04_Coca-Cola_Item1A-1B.pdf.

24. The Rainforest Alliance, "Quality Sustainable Coffee for a Growing Global Market,"
    www.rainforest-alliance.org/sites/default/files/publication/pdf/coffee_servicesheet
    .pdf.

25. Thehistoryof.net, "The History of Insurance—Risk Through the Ages," www.the
    historyof.net/the-history-of-insurance.html.

26. AboutBritain.com, "The Great Fire of London, 1666," www.aboutbritain.com/articles
    /great-fire-of-london.asp. See also: Gresham College, "Protecting London—The Phoe-
    nix: Rebuilding London after the Great Fire and the Origins of the London Fire Bri-
    gade," www.gresham.ac.uk/lectures-and-events/protecting-london-the-phoenix
    -rebuilding-london-after-the-great-fire-and-the.

27. Jennifer Ann Carlson, "The Economics of Fire Protection: From the Great Fire of Lon-
    don to Rural/Metro," in IEA Discussion Paper (2005). See also: P. G. M. Dickson, *The
    Sun Insurance Office* (Oxford: Oxford University Press, 1960), 11.

28. Carlson, "The Economics of Fire Protection."

29. Maldives Monetary Authority, "Insurance Industry Regulations," www.mma.gov.mv
    /laws/insurance%20regulations.pdf.

30. Heal, "Environmental disaster—not all bad news."

31. National Conference of State Legislatures, "State Cigarette Excise Taxes: 2010" (2010).

32. Brian Tumulty, "Tobacco tax increase expected to reduce smoking," *USA Today*, March
    27, 2009.

33. "Denmark introduces world's first food fat tax," BBC News, October 1, 2011.

34. Ryan Jaslow, "Denmark's 'fat tax' targets butter, burgers," CBS News, October 3, 2011.
    See also: Dan Evon, "Fat Tax Spreading: France Follows in Denmark's Footsteps," The
    Inquisitr, October 6, 2011.

35. Justin G. Trogdon, Eric A. Finkelstein, Charles W. Feagan, and Joel W. Cohen, "State-
    and Payer-Specific Estimates of Annual Medical Expenditures Attributable to Obesity,"
    Obesity (2011).

36. W. Reed Walker, "The Transitional Costs of Sectoral Reallocation: Evidence From the
    Clean Air Act and the Workforce" (2011).

37. "New Mexico Approves Mandatory Greenhouse Gas Reporting Regulations," *Environ-
    mental Leader*, October 12, 2007.

38. Esther Duflo, Michael Greenstone, Rohini Pande, and Nicholas Ryan, "Towards an
    Emissions Trading Scheme for Air Pollutants in India" (Center for Energy and Envi-
    ronmental Policy Research, 2010).

39. Jesse Shoemaker-Hopkins and Meggin Thwing Eastman, "Dodd-Frank Not Just about
    Banks: Conflict Mineral Reporting Requirements Will Affect Chipmakers, Other
    Electronics Firms," RiskMetrics, www.msci.com/insights/responsible_investing
    /riskmetrics/.

40. "The other oil spill," *The Economist*, June 24, 2010.

41. Trucost, "EU Accounts Modernisation Directive," www.businessandbiodiversity.org
    /pdf/EU%20accounts%20and%20modernization%20Directive.pdf. See also: Gordon
    L. Clark and Eric R. W. Knight, "Institutional Investors, the Political Economy of
    Corporate Disclosure, and the Market for Corporate Environmental and Social Re-
    sponsibility: Implications from the UK Companies Act (2006)," 2008 Industry Studies
    Conference Paper (2008).
42. Ibid.
43. Clark and Knight, "Institutional Investors."

Chapter 6 Notes

1. Estimates of global advertising turnover differ among company reports. This estimate
   comes from the Center for Media Research, "2012 Ad Spending Outlook" (2011).
2. Niall Dunne (formerly of Saatchi & Saatchi S. and head of EMEA, now chief sustainability officer of British Telecom) explaining that the right kind of advertising is about
   "selling good, not just good selling" through the power and penetration of brands.
   Personal communication with author, 2011.
3. Tobaccodocuments.org, "Review of Female Targeted Brands" (1988), tobaccodocu
   ments.org/product_design/507124752-4797.html.
4. Amanda Amos and Margaretha Haglund, "From social taboo to 'torch of freedom':
   the marketing of cigarettes to women," *Tobacco Control 9*, no. 1 (2000).
5. Allan M. Brandt, *The Cigarette Century: The Rise, Fall, and Deadly Persistence of the Product That Defined America* (New York: Basic Books, 2007).
6. Centers for Disease Control and Prevention, "Highlights: Marketing Cigarettes to
   Women," www.cdc.gov/tobacco/data_statistics/sgr/2001/highlights/marketing/.
7. Philip Morris Incorporated, "Virginia Slims Performance in San Francisco," legacy.
   library.ucsf.edu/tid/jzq18e00.
8. "Virginia Slims ads (1968)," archive.org/details/tobacco_ndo23e00.
9. Marc C. Willemsen and Boudewijn de Blij, "Tobacco advertising," *Tobacco Control
   Resource Centre*.
10. US National Library of Medicine, "The Reports of the Surgeon General: The 1964
    Report on Smoking and Health," profiles.nlm.nih.gov/ps/retrieve/Narrative/NN
    /p-nid/60.
11. "Tobacco Advertising in the United States," *Mediascope Press* (1997).
12. Martin Lindstrom, *Buy-ology: Truth and Lies about Why We Buy*, 1st pbk. ed. (New York:
    Broadway Books, 2010).
13. Centers for Disease Control and Prevention, "Economic Facts about U.S. Tobacco Pro-
    duction and Use," www.cdc.gov/tobacco/data_statistics/fact_sheets/economics
    /econ_facts/.
14. Patricia McBroom, "$72.7 Billion: Smoking's Annual Health Care Cost," *Public Affairs*
    (1998), berkeley.edu/news/berkeleyan/1998/0916/smoking.html.
15. The Tobacco Atlas, "Tobacco Company Profits," www.tobaccoatlas.org/industry
    /tobacco_companies/profits/.
16. State of California Department of Justice, "Tobacco Master Settlement Agreement
    Summary," /caag.state.ca.us/tobacco/resources/msasumm.php. See also: Joy Johnson
    Wilson, "Summary of the Attorneys General Master Tobacco Settlement Agreement,"
    academic.udayton.edu/health/syllabi/tobacco/summary.htm. For more information,
    see: "Master Settlement Agreement," web.archive.org/web/20080625084126/http://
    www.naag.org/backpages/naag/tobacco/msa/msa-pdf/1109185724_1032468605
    _cigmsa.pdf.

17. This calculation uses an inflation rate of 2 percent and a discount rate of 3 percent for the costs of smoking, and a 5 percent rate for the payments by the companies, which incorporates the 2 percent inflation rate.

18. E. Sokol, V. Aguayo, and D. Clark, "Protecting Breastfeeding in West and Central Africa: 25 Years Implementing the International Code of Marketing of Breastmilk Substitutes" (UNICEF Regional Office for West and Central Africa, 2007).

19. M. F. Picciano, "Nutrient composition of human milk," *Pediatric Clinics of North America* 48, no. 1 (2001).

20. Sokol et al., "Protecting Breastfeeding in West and Central Africa."

21. Ibid.

22. Ibid.

23. See: World Health Organization, "International Code of Marketing of Breast-Milk Substitutes" (Geneva, 1981).

24. UNICEF, "Infant and Young Child Feeding," www.unicef.org/nutrition/index _breastfeeding.html.

25. Brainyquote, "David Ogilvy Quotes," www.brainyquote.com/quotes/quotes/d /davidogilv103337.html.

26. KPMG and FICCI, "Hitting the High Notes: FICCI-KPMG Indian Media and Enter-tainment Industry Report 2011" (2011).

27. Adam Werbach, interview with author conducted in San Francisco, CA, March 8, 2012—see www.corp2020.com.

28. ODDEE, "15 Most Offensive, Banned and Rejected Ads," www.oddee.com/item _ 96502.aspx.

29. Maura Judkis, "Vatican takes legal action over pope-imam, Obama-Chavez kissing Benetton ad," *Washington Post*, November 16, 2011.

30. "China: Don't Spit at the Olympics," *RedOrbit*, February 8, 2007.

31. Jack Neff, "Agencies Also on the Hook for P&G's Green Scorecard," *Advertising Age*, May 12, 2010.

32. Yahoo! Finance, "Publicis Groupe (PUB.PA)," finance.yahoo.com/q/ks?s=PUB.PA +Key+Statistics.

33. The term "Polman Effect" is known throughout the industry and refers to the work of Paul Polman, who took over as chairman of Unilever in January 2009; earlier, Polman was CFO at Nestlé, and before that he spent 27 years at Procter & Gamble in finance roles and later as group president for Europe.

34. Andrew McMains, "Unilever Set to Join Cost-Cutting Push," *Adweek*, June 7, 2009.

35. "Clock-watchers no more," *The Economist*, May 14, 2009.

36. The Bubble Project, "Manifesto," thebubbleproject.com/.

37. "Bubble Project," www.flickr.com/groups/bubble_project/.

38. Adbusters, "São Paulo: A City without Ads," www.adbusters.org/magazine/73/Sao _Paulo_A_City_Without_Ads.html.

39. Vincent Bevins, "São Paulo advertising goes underground," *Financial Times*, September 6, 2010.

40. CUTS International, "Consumer Rights and Its Expansion," www.cuts-international .org/consumer-rights.htm.

41. Consumers International, "History of the Consumer Movement," www.consumersin ternational.org/who-we-are/we-are-50/history-of-the-consumer-movement.

42. Ted Thornhill, "Gone in 60 seconds: 168 million emails, 700,000 Google searches . . . a mind-boggling snapshot of what happens on the Internet in just ONE MINUTE," *Mail Online*, June 21, 2011.

43. Saqlain Abbas, "Verizon Withdraws Its Plan to Charge $2 as Fee for Online Payments," *Tribune News*, January 1, 2012.
44. Mark Sweney, "Unilever goes crowdsourcing to spice up Peperami's TV ads," *The Guardian*, August 25, 2009.
45. David Tiltman, "Unilever to crowdsource content for 13 global brands," *Brand Republic*, April 20, 2010.
46. Bob Garfield, *The Chaos Scenario* (Stielstra Publishing, 2009).
47. Aayush Arya, "Internet users exceed 100 million in India; mobile net usage still in infancy," *Next Web*, November 8, 2011.
48. Goos Poos, "Mobile Internet Usage in India: Statistics, Facts & Opportunities," www.goospoos.com/2011/05/mobile-internet-usage-in-india/.
49. "Missed call campaign on Lokpal bill a hit," *Deccan Herald*, June 15, 2011.
50. Gallup, "Business and Industry Sector Ratings," www.gallup.com/poll/12748/Business-Industry-Sector-Ratings.aspx.
51. Gallup, "Honesty/Ethics in Professions," www.gallup.com/poll/1654/honesty-ethics-professions.aspx.
52. Brainy Quote, "David Ogilvy Quotes," www.brainyquote.com/quotes/authors/d/david_ogilvy.html#ixzz1i5vhN6Yk.
53. Ibid.
54. Truthmove, "Advertising & Public Relations Propaganda," www.truthmove.org/content/advertising-public-relations/.
55. Dean Rieck, "The Brilliant Words of Leo Burnett," Direct Creative, www.directcreative.com/the-brilliant-words-of-leo-burnett.html.

Chapter 7 Notes

1. See our arguments in Chapter 1, "The Legal History of the Corporation," and Chapter 2 "The Great Alignment."
2. See: Chapter 2, "The Great Alignment."
3. Richard P. Nielsen, "High-Leverage Finance Capitalism, the Economic Crisis, Structurally Related Ethics Issues, and Potential Reforms," *Business Ethics Quarterly* 20, no. 2 (2010).
4. Ben Bernanke, John Campbell, and Toni Whited, "U.S. Corporate Leverage: Developments in 1987 and 1988," Brookings Papers on Economic Activity 1990, no. 1 (1990).
5. C. William Thomas, "The Rise and Fall of Enron," *Journal of Accountancy* (2002).
6. Ibid.
7. "The rise and fall of Enron: A brief history," CBC News, May 25, 2006.
8. Obtained from Enron Corporation's form 10-K annual report filed with the Securities and Exchange Commission (SEC) for the fiscal year ended December 31, 2000. Online access to such financial reports is available at: www.sec.gov/edgar/searchedgar/companysearch.html.
9. Thomas, "The Rise and Fall of Enron."
10. Simi Kedia and Thomas Philippon, "Enron's Final Accounting," Sternbusiness (2006), w4.stern.nyu.edu/sternbusiness/spring_2006/enron.html.
11. Thomas, "The Rise and Fall of Enron."
12. James Flanigan, "Enron Is Proving Costly to Economy," *Los Angeles Times*, January 20, 2002.
13. US Financial Crisis Inquiry Commission, "The Financial Crisis—Inquiry Report," (2010).

14. McKinsey Global Institute, "Debt and deleveraging: The global credit bubble and its economic consequences" (2010).

15. McKinsey Global Institute, "An economy that works: Job creation and America's Future" (2011).

16. See our website, www.corp2020.com, for a more-detailed explanation of the links between leverage and these four financial crises.

17. National banks were, by law, barred from making loans to any single borrower in excess of 10 percent of the bank's capital and surplus. In 1979, the US Office of the Comptroller of the Currency (OCC), likely under the pressure of lobbying and against better judgment, issued an interpretation of the law that enabled banks to treat individual agencies of sovereign governments as separate entities for the 10 percent rule instead of aggregating them and treating them as one entity. Had it ruled the opposite way, many banks would probably have been out of compliance with the law and would have had to reduce their exposure to these loans. Source: US Federal Deposit Insurance Corporation, "Chapter 5: The LDC Debt Crisis," *Volume I: An Examination of the Banking Crises of the 1980s and Early 1990s* (Library of Congress, 1997), http://www.fdic.gov/bank/historical/history/vol1.html.

18. US Federal Deposit Insurance Corporation, "The Savings and Loan Crisis and Its Relationship to Banking," in *An Examination of the Banking Crises of the 1980s and Early 1990s*, Vol. I (Library of Congress, 1997), www.fdic.gov/bank/historical/history/vol1.html.

19. Timothy Curry and Lynn Shibut, "The Cost of the Savings and Loan Crisis: Truth and Consequences," FDIC Banking Review (2000).

20. Paul Krugman, "What Happened to Asia?" web.mit.edu/krugman/www/DISINTER.html.

21. US Financial Crisis Inquiry Commission, "The Financial Crisis Inquiry Report: Final Report of the National Commission on the Causes of the Financial and Economic Crisis in the United States" (2011).

22. See: Chapter 2, "The Great Alignment," and Chapter 3, "Corporation 1920."

23. See: Chapter 2.

24. Board of Governors of the Federal Reserve System, "Reserve Requirements," www.federalreserve.gov/monetarypolicy/reservereq.htm.

25. European Central Bank, "How to calculate the minimum reserve requirements," www.ecb.int/mopo/implement/mr/html/calc.en.html.

26. Stephane Rottier and Veron Nicolas, "Not All Financial Regulation Is Global" (Peterson Institute for International Economics, 2010).

27. Adrian Blundell-Wignall and Paul Atkinson, "Thinking Beyond Basel III: Necessary Solutions for Capital and Liquidity," *OECD Journal: Financial Market Trends 2010*, no. 1 (2010).

28. Ibid.

29. The Banking Act of 1933, or the Glass-Steagall Act, was enacted in June 1933. Among other items, this act established the Federal Deposit Insurance Corporation (FDIC) and introduced reforms in the banking sector such as required separation between commercial and investment banking. This last item was repealed through the Gramm-Leach-Bliley Act of 1999.

30. Stephen Labaton, "U.S. regulator's 2004 rule let banks pile up new debt," *New York Times*, October 3, 2008.

31. Romesh Sobti, interviewed by Pavan Sukhdev and Rafael Torres, 2011.

32. Revenue Watch Institute, "Revenue Watch Index" (2010).

33. Anne P. Villamil, "The Modigliani-Miller Theorem," *New Palgrave Dictionary of Economics*, www.econ.uiuc.edu/~avillami/course-files/PalgraveRev_ModiglianiMiller _Villamil.pdf.

34. Obtained from Thomson Financial via Ernst & Young, "2011 ripe for uptick in deal making if confidence and clarity return" (2010).

35. "Thomson Reuters Says Global M&A Activity Value Rose 22.9% In 2010—Update," *RTT News* (2011), www.rttnews.com/Story.aspx?type=bn&Id=1523040.

36. Donald M. DePamphilis, "Financing Transactions," Chapter 13 in *Mergers, Acquisitions, and Other Restructuring Activities: An Integrated Approach to Process, Tools, Cases, and Solutions*, 5th ed. (Waltham, MA: Academic Press, 2009).

37. Steven Kaplan, "Campeau's acquisition of Federated: Post-bankruptcy results," *Journal of Financial Economics* 35 (1994).

38. DePamphilis, "Financing Transactions."

39. Ibid.

40. Aloke Ghosh and Prem C. Jain, "Financial leverage changes associated with corporate mergers," *Journal of Corporate Finance* 6 (2000).

41. Craig H. Furfine and Richard J. Rosen, "Mergers increase default risk," *Journal of Corporate Finance* 17 (2011).

42. In some cases, such as distressed-asset books and structured-credit-derivatives books, the opposite may hold true: too much provision is taken for future risks and costs, but conversely, this may result, in future years, in teams earning bonuses for performance which includes a large component of reserve releases alone, rather than genuine performance.

43. Company remuneration reports have been challenged at a number of corporations in spring 2012—questioning the pay packages of chief executives at AstraZeneca, Aviva, Barclays, Citibank, Inmarsat, Trinity Mirror, and UBS, inter alia (*Financial Times*, May 4, 2012).

Chapter 8 Notes

1. International Energy Agency, "2011 Key World Energy Statistics."

2. Ibid.

3. "Mankind using Earth's resources faster than replenished," *The Independent* (2009), www.independent.co.uk/environment/mankind-using-earths-resources-faster-than -replenished-1827047.html. Note that American Public Media features an online game based on a report from the Global Footprint Network, an international think tank. The game is available online at sustainability.publicradio.org/consumerconsequences/.

4. Mineral data were obtained from the US Geological Survey's online resources. For more information see: minerals.usgs.gov/minerals/pubs/mcs/.

5. This is a conclusion shared by two major global studies, the MEA and TEEB. See: "The Economics of Ecosystems and Biodiversity," www.teebweb.org/; see also "Millenium Ecosystem Assessment," www.maweb.org/en/index.aspx.

6. See Chapter 6, "Limiting Leverage."

7. OPEC, IEA, OECD, WORLD BANK, "Analysis of the Scope of Energy Subsidies and Suggestions for the G-20 Initiative" (2010).

8. European Commission, "Eurostat: Environment" (2011).

9. IEA, "Analysis of the Scope of Energy Subsidies and Suggestions for the G-20 Initiative," June 16, 2010.

10. Toby Price, "Fossil fuels received more than €320 billion in aid in 2010," *Renewable Energy Magazine*, January 17, 2012. See also: Roger Harrabin, "Harrabin's Notes: Mission impossible?" BBC, January 19, 2011.

11. Global Subsidies Initiative, "Mexico's 2008 fuel subsidies higher than previously predicted," www.iisd.org/gsi/news/mexicos-2008-fuel-subsidies-higher-previously-predicted.

12. Paul Segal, "'El petroleo es nuestro': The Distribution of Oil Revenues in Mexico," in *The Future of Oil in Mexico* (James A. Baker III Institute for Public Policy at Rice University, 2011), 20.

13. This chapter recognizes the complexities of resource subsidization in developing countries, and the equity issues involved with removing subsidies for resources such as petroleum. Notably, developing countries themselves are revising subsidization policies given the financial burden these regulations have created. Jordan is an example of a developing country with high fuel subsidies which has, over the last three years, gradually eliminated these subsidies and compensated low-earning employees (who would feel the pinch) with a series of transfer payments. Iran and Saudi Arabia are other examples.

14. The World Bank, "World Development Indicators" (2011).

15. "The global debt clock," *The Economist*, www.economist.com/content/global_debt_clock.

16. Adriene Hill, "Companies sit on huge reserves of cash," American Public Media, *Marketplace*, August 17, 2011.

17. Note that the Global Resource Tax Assessment does not include materials sourced from biological sources, such as timber and fish stocks, as it does similar resources in global depletion.

18. David G. Victor and Richard K. Morse, "Living with Coal: Climate Policy's Most Inconvenient Truth," *Boston Review* (2009), www.bostonreview.net/BR34.5/victor_morse.php.

19. IEA, "Coal Information" (2010).

20. These numbers may not reflect the actual total tax bill to the IRS (which is confidential), but are rather based on GAAP figures available in the companies' 10-K filings.

21. Specifically, the taxation ranges from –2.1 percent for Westmoreland Coal to 11.53 percent for CONSOL Energy. These numbers are estimates, as the taxes paid by some of the companies are for activities other than coal extraction.

22. Using 2009 values.

23. Negotiations are under way to compensate Ecuador for lost petroleum sales if the country forgoes oil extraction in the Yasuni National Park. A coalition of governments, corporate interests, and activists have raised over $100 million to reimburse the Ecuadorian government for disallowing drilling in Yasuni. Scientists believe the park to contain more mammal, bird, amphibian, and plant species than any location in the world. Similar revenue models are in development for extractive industries in ecologically rich areas. See: John Vidal, "World pays Ecuador not to extract oil from rainforest," *The Guardian*, December 30 2011.

24. Interestingly enough, Bill Gates recognizes the failures in current energy markets to spur innovation. Today, with several prominent former and current US CEOs, such as Jeff Immelt of General Electric and Norman Augustine of Lockheed Martin, Gates contributed to the founding of the American Energy Innovation Council (AEIC). The AEIC published a market report detailing the innovation barriers in the current energy economy, which is available online at www.americanenergyinnovation.org/.

25. Note that Joseph Schumpeter was an Austrian-American economist and political scientist prominently known for his popularization of the phrase "creative destruction," which referred in part to the integration of new technologies and services into business cycles.

26. Note that these country descriptions are implied generally to illustrate principles described in this book. The author recognizes that all countries hold some consumer, producer, and managerial characteristics.

27. NationMaster.com, "Energy Statistics," www.nationmaster.com/index.php.

28. Jerome Cukier, "Revenues from green taxes have dropped despite increased use (data update—01/07/2011)," blog.oecdfactblog.org/?p=13.

29. Center for Sustainable Systems at University of Michigan, "U.S. Material Use" (2010).

30. University of Michigan Center for Sustainable Systems, "Residential Buildings" (2011).

31. US Energy Information Administration, "Annual Energy Outlook 2011 with Projections to 2035" (2011).

32. Institute for Energy Research, "Coal," www.instituteforenergyresearch.org/energy-overview/coal/. See also: Energy Information Administration, *Coal Data: A Reference* (Washington, DC: US Department of Energy, 1995), 31.

33. See: Erik Shuster, "Tracking New Coal-Fired Power Plants" (National Energy Technology Laboratory, Office of Strategic Energy Analysis & Planning, 2011). See also: "The writing on the wall," *The Economist*, May 7, 2009.

34. N. Z. Muller, R. Mendelsohn, and W. Nordhaus, "Environmental Accounting for Pollution in the United States Economy," *American Economic Review* 101, no. 5 (2011).

35. Paul R. Epstein, Jonathan J. Buonocore, Kevin Eckerle, Michael Hendryx, Benjamin M. Stout, R. Heinberg, Richard W. Clapp, et al., "Full Cost Accounting for the Life Cycle of Coal," *Annals of the New York Academy of Science* (2011): 73–98.

36. Ibid.

37. Ibid.

38. Clean Air Task Force, "The Toll from Coal: An Updated Assessment of Death and Disease from America's Dirtiest Energy Source" (2010). In the Climate Progress blog, Joe Romm writes: "Note that several organizations have released studies on integrated costs and benefits of coal-fired power. The National Research Council found that in 2009, coal-fired power produced damages upwards of $120 billion per year, counting emissions of mercury and greenhouse-gas emissions" ("Life-cycle study: Accounting for total harm from coal would add 'close to 17¢/kWh of electricity generated," Climate Progress, February 16, 2011, http://thinkprogress.org/romm/2011/02/16/207534/life-cycle-study-coal-harvard-epstein-health/). The American Lung Association estimates that coal electricity is directly responsible for over 13,000 premature deaths in 2010, along with 10,000 hospitalizations and 20,000 heart attacks each year. Source: American Lung Association, "American Lung Association Energy Policy Development: Electricity Generation Background Document" (2011). Source for drunk driving statistics: Centers for Disease Control and Prevention, "Drinking and Driving: A Threat to Everyone," www.cdc.gov/vitalsigns/drinkinganddriving/?s_cid=vitalsigns-092-bb.

39. Pamela L. Spath, Margaret K. Mann, and Dawn R. Kerr, "Life Cycle Assessment of Coal-Fired Power Production" (National Renewable Energy Laboratory, 1999).

40. See: Keith Bradsher, "China Outpaces U.S. in Cleaner Coal-Fired Plants," *New York Times*, May 10, 2009. See also: World Coal Association, "Improving Efficiencies," www.worldcoal.org/coal-the-environment/coal-use-the-environment/improving

-efficiencies/. And: EurActiv.com, "Analysis: Efficiency of coal-fired power stations—evolution and prospects," www.euractiv.com/energy/analysis-efficiency-coal-fired-power-stations-evolution-prospects/article-154672.

41. Richard Munson, *From Edison to Enron: The Business of Power and What It Means for the Future of Electricity* (Westport, CT: Praeger Publishers, 2005).

42. The Waxman-Markey Bill is the colloquial name for HR 2454: the American Clean Energy and Security Act of 2009. The legislation's colloquial name stems from the names of its Congressional lead authors, Henry Waxman and Edward Markey. For further information on the bill, see www.govtrack.us/congress/bill.xpd?bill=h111-2454. See also: Marianne Lavelle, "The Climate Change Lobby Explosion," The Center for Public Integrity, www.publicintegrity.org/investigations/climate_change/articles/entry/1171/.

43. Lavelle, "The Climate Change Lobby Explosion."

44. George Monbiot, "The need to protect the internet from 'astroturfing' grows ever more urgent," *The Guardian*, February 23, 2011, www.guardian.co.uk/environment/georgemonbiot/2011/feb/23/need-to-protect-internet-from-astroturfing.

45. Antonio Regalado and Dionne Searcey, "Where Did That Video Spoofing Gore's Film Come From?" *Wall Street Journal*. August 3, 2006.

46. Center for Responsive Politics, www.opensecrets.org/lobby/top.php?showYear=a&indexType=i.

47. National Science Foundation/Division of Science Resources Statistics, "Survey of Industrial Research and Development," 2007.

48. Marianne Lavelle to iWatch News, April 21, 2009, www.iwatchnews.org/2009/04/21/2885/%E2%80%98clean-coal%E2%80%99-lobbying-blitz.

49. Eric Pooley, *The Climate War: True Believers, Power Brokers, and the Fight to Save the Earth* (New York: Hyperion, 2010), 172–86.

50. Ki Mae Heussner, "Coal Campaign Pulled after Heavy Criticism," *ABC News*, December 12, 2008.

51. Central Intelligence Agency, "Electricity-Consumption," www.cia.gov/library/publications/the-world-factbook/rankorder/2042rank.html.

52. This calculation is meant to demonstrate the potential size of tax revenues. It does not take into account any decrease in demand that might occur.

53. Internal Revenue Service, "SOI Tax Stats—Individual Statistical Tables by Tax Rate and Income Percentile," www.irs.gov/taxstats/indtaxstats/article/0,,id=133521,00.html.

54. Ibid.

55. Again, these calculations are not based on a full model and so do not take into account changes in demand, but are rather meant to provide some sense of the scale of the numbers.

56. US Energy Information Administration, "Annual Energy Outlook 2011 with Projections to 2035."

57. This chapter recognizes the complexities of environmental taxation on the supply-and-demand elasticity of electricity and related supply chain in the electric-power industry. Manufacturing relies on razor-thin margins for profitability, and the author recognizes that policy precautions for US energy-intensive industries would be required to balance any transition from incumbent power sources to cleaner, more efficient power sources.

58. Matt Siegel, "Australia's Lower House Narrowly Passes Carbon Tax," *New York Times*, October 12, 2011.

59. Australian Bureau of Statistics, "Australia's Production and Trade of Minerals" (2010).
60. Australian Department of Foreign Affairs and Trade, "Australia in brief: Trading with the world," www.dfat.gov.au/aib/trade_investment.html.
61. Simon R. James, *Taxation: Critical Perspectives on the World Economy*, vol. 1 (London, New York: Routledge, 2002).
62. "Timorous tax on gold," *The Age*, May 18, 1982.
63. Bloomberg, "Income Statement for BHP Billiton PLC (BLT)," www.bloomberg.com/quote/BLT:LN/income-statement.
64. "How will Rio Tinto and its fellow miners spend their fortunes?" *The Economist*, February 16, 2011.
65. Richard Wachman, "BHP and Rio Tinto hit by Australian supertax," *The Guardian*, May 4, 2010.
66. European Commission, "Germany—Energy Mix Fact Sheet" (2007).
67. McKinsey and Company, "Energy efficiency: A compelling global resource" (2010).
68. International Energy Agency, "Selected 2008 Indicators for United States," www.iea.org/stats/indicators.asp?COUNTRY_CODE=US. See also: International Energy Agency, "Relation with Member Countries—Germany," www.iea.org/country/m_country.asp?COUNTRY_CODE=DE.
69. "Germany to Phase Out Nuclear Power by 2022," *Spiegel* Online International (2011), www.spiegel.de/international/germany/0,1518,765594,00.html.
70. For clarity, in his interview with German newspaper *Der Spiegel*, Heinrich Hiesinger's reference to "reunification" refers to the political merging of the former West and East Germany.
71. "An Effort Comparable to Reunification" *Spiegel* Online International (2011), www.spiegel.de/international/spiegel/0,1518,777944,00.html.
72. Michael Kohlhaas, "Ecological Tax Reform in Germany: From Theory to Policy," in *Economic Studies Program Series* (American Institute for Contemporary German Studies, 2000).
73. Susanna Kim, "5 Shocking Gas Prices Around the Globe," *ABC News*, April 12, 2011.
74. Romain Davoust, "Gasoline and Diesel Prices and Taxes in Industrialized Countries" (Institut Français des Relations Internationales, 2008).
75. Ibid.
76. Federal Ministry for the Environment, Nature Conservation, and Nuclear Safety, "Electricity from Renewable Energy Sources: What Does It Cost?" (2009).
77. Markus and Benjamin Görlach Knigge, "Die Ökologische Steuerreform—Auswirkungen auf Umwelt, Beschäftigung und Innovation" (Berlin: Ecologic Institut für Internationale und Europäische Umweltpolitik gGmbH, 2005).
78. Kohlhaas, "Ecological Tax Reform in Germany."
79. Anne and Monika Zulauf Power, "Cutting Carbon Costs: Learning from Germany's Energy Saving Program" (What Works Collaborative, 2011).
80. Ibid.
81. Ibid.
82. Ibid.
83. Data from 2002–4. Source: Federal Ministry of Economics and Technology (BMWi), "Energy Efficiency—Made in Germany: Energy Efficiency in Industry and Building Services Technology."

Chapter 9 Notes

1. See, for example: Ram Nidumolu, C. K. Prahalad, and M. R. Rangaswami, "Why Sustainability Is Now the Key Driver of Innovation," *Harvard Business Review* (September 2009).
2. Daniel C. Esty and Andrew S. Winston, *Green to Gold: How Smart Companies Use Environmental Strategy to Innovate, Create Value, and Build Competitive Advantage*, rev. and updated ed. (Hoboken, NJ: Wiley, 2009).
3. This data is based upon the largest companies in the US and UK. See: Ben W. Heineman Jr. and Stephen Davis, "Are Institutional Investors Part of the Problem or Part of the Solution?" (Committee for Economic Development and Millstein Center for Corporate Governance and Performance, 2011).
4. Don Tapscott and David Ticoll, *The Naked Corporation: How the Age of Transparency Will Revolutionize Business* (New York: Free Press, 2003).
5. Dov Seidman, *How: Why How We Do Anything Means Everything . . . in Business (and in Life)* (Hoboken, NJ: John Wiley & Sons, Inc., 2007).
6. R. K. Pachauri, "Obama Administration Should Lead Energy Transition," *Science News*, January 3, 2009, 32.
7. Ann Graham, "Too good to fail," Tata, www.tata.com/company/Articles/inside.aspx?artid=HCy+RNqd0vk.
8. Ishaat Hussain, interview conducted by Pavan Sukhdev and Meenakshi Menon for Corporation 2020, August 2011.
9. Marjorie Kelly and Allen White, "Corporate Design: The Missing Business and Public Policy Issue of Our Time" (Tellus Institute, 2007).
10. Santander Bank, São Paolo, interviewed by Linda Murasawa, November 21, 2011.
11. Opportunitynow, "Santander," www.bitcdiversity.org.uk/about_us/members/on_champions/santander.html.
12. "Ford Predicts Fuel from Vegetation," *New York Times*, September 20, 1925.
13. See: Tom McCarthy, *Auto Mania: Cars, Consumers, and the Environment* (New Haven: Yale University Press, 2007).
14. Ibid.
15. William T. Allen, "Our Schizophrenic Conception of the Business Corporation," *Cardozo Law Review* 14:261 (1992–93), 267–68.
16. *Dodge v. Ford*, 1919—see: Chapter 1, "The Legal History of the Corporation."
17. See: Chapter 1, "The Legal History of the Corporation."
18. Tomorrow's Company, "About Us," www.tomorrowscompany.com/aboutus.aspx.
19. One of the quotes attributed to Ford that expresses this sentiment is: "A business that makes nothing but money is a poor business." See: Wikiquote, en.wikiquote.org/wiki/Henry_Ford.
20. M. E. Porter and M. R. Kramer, "Creating Shared Value," *Harvard Business Review* 89, nos. 1–2 (2011).
21. Ibid.
22. Ibid.
23. See author's website, www.pavansukhdev.com, for an exposition of "3-D Capitalism."
24. The main thesis of Stephen A. Marglin's book *The Dismal Science: How Thinking Like an Economist Undermines Community* (Cambridge, MA: Harvard University Press, 2008).
25. Groups of investors (the *publicani*) would bid on state contracts for activities deemed vital for the advancement of the republic. Limitations on liability, tied to risk tolerance as the primary investor would pledge land and estates as security for contract performance by a multi-owner firm, demonstrated one of history's first advanced systems of

limiting the liability of commercial entities, and represents an early appearance of the corporation.

26. Ann Graham, "Too good to fail," www.tata.com/company/Articles/inside.aspx?artid =HCy+RNqd0vk.

27. Ishaat Hussain, interviewed by Pavan Sukhdev and Meenakshi Menon for Corporation 2020, August 2011.

28. Peter F. Drucker, Introduction to *The Organization of the Future*, ed. Frances Hesselbein, Marshall Goldsmith, and Richard Beckhard (San Francisco: Jossey-Bass Publishers, 1997).

29. Michael Hammer, "The Soul of the New Organization," in *The Organization of the Future*. Adapted from: Michael Hammer, *Beyond Reengineering: How the Process-Centered Organization Is Changing Our Work and Our Lives* (New York: HarperBusiness, 1996).

30. United Nations Environment Programme, "Towards a Green Economy: Pathways to Sustainable Development and Poverty Eradication" (2011).

31. See: Chapter 7, "Limiting Financial Leverage."

32. See: Chapter 6, "Accountable Advertising."

33. Kelly, "Corporate Design."

34. "Towards a Green Economy," United Nations Environment Programme, 2011.

35. "B Corps" (benefit corporations) or "Flexible Purpose Corporations" are companies whose Memorandum and Articles of Association expressly permit social purpose, in addition to profitability, as the purpose of the corporation. Several states in the US, including California, have already enacted legislation that enables such "B Corps."

36. Case studies on the *New York Times*, the John Lewis Partnership, and Grupo Nueva are drawn from Kelly, "Corporate Design."

37. Joel A. Barker, "The Mondragon Model—A New Pathway for the Twenty-First Century," in *The Organization of the Future*.

38. Ibid.

39. Rina Kuusipalo, "Mondragón Co-operative Corporation," Participedia, participedia.net/cases/mondrag-n-co-operative-corporation.

40. Ibid.

41. William Foote Whyte and Kathleen King Whyte, *Making Mondragón: The Growth and Dynamics of the Worker Cooperative Complex*, Cornell International Industrial and Labor Relations Report (Ithaca, NY: ILR Press, 1988).

Chapter 10 Notes

1. "Global Green New Deal—A Policy Brief," UNEP, 2009.

2. Oxfam International, "G20 must put fight against poverty at the center of global economic reforms," www.oxfam.org/en/pressroom/pressrelease/2008-11-13/g20-global -economic-reforms.

3. Businessgreen.com, "IEA warns oil will hit $200 a barrel by 2030," November 7, 2008, www.businessgreen.com/business-green/news/2230069/soaring-oil-price-encourage.

4. For a more detailed discussion, see: ILO, "The financial and economic crisis: A Decent Work response," ILO Governing Body 304th Session, Geneva, March 2009.

5. UNEP, "Global Green New Deal—A Policy Brief," 2009.

6. See Figures 2.1 and 2.2 in Chapter 2, "The Great Alignment: 1945–2000."

7. See: P. Sukhdev and C. Feger, "Green Accounting for Everyone," in *The Economics of Nature* (Delhi: Business Standard Books, 2012). See also: Clifford Cobb, Ted Halstead, and Jonathan Rowe, "If the GDP Is Up, Why Is America Down?" *The Atlantic* Online (1995), www.theatlantic.com/past/politics/ecbig/gdp.htm.

8. Ibid. In a 1995 *Atlantic* article, Clifford Cobb, Ted Halstead, and Jonathan Rowe wrote that "In the United States the Manhattan Project got much more glory. But as a technical achievement the development of the GNP accounts was no less important. The accounts enabled the nation to locate unused capacity, and to exceed by far the production levels that conventional opinion thought possible. To their great surprise, American investigators learned after the war that Hitler had set much lower production targets, partly for lack of sophisticated national accounts."

9. Stephan Faris, "A Better Measure than GDP," *Time*, November 2, 2009.

10. Cobb et al., "If the GDP Is Up, Why Is America Down?"

11. Robert F. Kennedy, "Remarks of Robert F. Kennedy at the University of Kansas, March 18, 1968," www.jfklibrary.org/Research/Ready-Reference/RFK-Speeches/Remarks-of-Robert-F-Kennedy-at-the-University-of-Kansas-March-18-1968.aspx.

12. Sukhdev and Feger, "Green Accounting for Everyone."

13. R. Costanza et al., "The value of the world's ecosystem services and natural capital," *Nature* 387, no. 6630 (1997).

14. World Bank, World Development Indicators.

15. Green Indian States Trust, a public charity in India since 2004.

16. Pushpam Kumar, Sanjeev Sanyal, Rajiv Sinha, and Pavan Sukhdev, "Accounting for freshwater quality in India," Green Accounting for Indian States Project (2007).

17. Cobb et al., "If the GDP Is Up, Why Is America Down?"

18. Nicholas Z. Muller, Robert Mendelsohn, and William Nordhaus, "Environmental Accounting for Pollution in the United States Economy," *American Economic Review* 101, no. 5 (2011).

19. Organization for Economic Co-operation and Development, "Taxation, Innovation and the Environment" (2010).

20. . . . Though not the most severe. That honor goes to Bangkok, where the average car spends the equivalent of 45 days a year stuck in traffic. See: Hannah Beach, "The Capital of Gridlock," *Time*, February 8, 2008.

21. Mark Goh, "Congestion management and electronic road pricing in Singapore," *Journal of Transport Geography* 10, no. 1 (2002).

22. Yii Der Lew and Wai Yan Leong, "Managing Congestion in Singapore—A Behavioural Economics Perspective," *Journeys* (2009).

23. The 1999 ETR Bill only included a hike in energy taxes. The social-policy part of the concept—reducing payroll taxes—was addressed separately, via a 1998 bill, but both laws went into effect at the same time.

24. Michael Kohlhaas, "Ecological Tax Reform in Germany: From Theory to Policy," in Economic Studies Program Series (American Institute for Contemporary German Studies, 2000).

25. United Nations Environment Programme, "Towards a Green Economy: Pathways to Sustainable Development and Poverty Eradication" (2011).

26. The concept of "spillovers" was introduced and described in Chapter 4 as a form of "positive externality" of the corporation.

27. American Energy Innovation Council, "A Business Plan for America's Energy Future."

28. The exact figures for procurement are as follows: weighted average of OECD countries is 19.96 percent of GDP (9.17 percent excluding compensation), and of non-OECD countries 14.48 percent (6.89 percent excluding compensation). Data is from 1997–98. See: Denis Audet, "Government Procurement: A Synthesis Report" *OECD Journal on Budgeting* (OECD, 2002).

29. International Institute for Sustainable Development, "Building accountability and transparency in public procurement" (2008).

30. United Nations Environment Programme and Partners, "Catalysing low-carbon growth in developing economies: Public Finance Mechanisms to scale up private sector investment in climate solutions" (2009).

31. Laura Diaz Anadon, Matthew Bunn, Gabriel Chan, Melissa Chan, Charles Jones, Ruud Kempener, Audrey Lee, Nathaniel Logar, and Venkatesh Narayanamurti, *Transforming U.S. Energy Innovation* (Cambridge, MA: The Harvard Kennedy School Belfer Center for Science and International Affairs, 2011).

32. International Energy Agency, "World Energy Outlook" (2008).

33. The World Bank, *World Development Report 2008: Agriculture for Development* (2008).

34. Organization for Economic Co-operation and Development, "Taxation, Innovation and the Environment."

35. ForestEthics, "Victoria's Dirty Secret Exposed—ForestEthics Launches New Environmental Campaign Targeting Victoria's Secret," forestethics.org/victoria146s-dirty -secret-exposed---forestethics-launches-new-environmental-campaign-targeting -victoria146s-secret-1. See also: Native Forest Network, "What's Victoria's Dirty Secret?" www.nativeforest.org/events/victorias_secret.htm.

36. "Strange bedfellows," *The Economist*, May 22, 2008. See also: Seasons Fund For Social Transformation, "Getting Results: ForestEthics," seasonsfund.org/case-studies /forest-ethics/.

37. "The Canadian Boreal Forest Agreement," canadianborealforestagreement.com/index .php/en/. See also: Canopy, "The Canadian Boreal Forest Agreement," canopyplanet .org/index.php?page=the-canadian-boreal-forest-agreement. And: ForestEthics, "ForestEthics and the Canadian Boreal Forest Agreement: A Historic Opportunity," forestethics.org/boreal-forest-agreement-media-kit.

38. United Nations Environment Programme, "Towards a Green Economy."

39. Andrew Simms to NEF, February 8, 2010, www.neweconomics.org/blog/2010/02/08 /growth-is-good-isnt-it1.

40. Different scenarios produce different figures. The cited UNEP report numbers are relatively conservative. For instance, the IEA predicts an increase in energy consumption of 1.5–3 times by 2050. See: United Nations Environment Programme, "Towards a Green Economy."

41. Ibid.

42. Anadon, "Transforming U.S. Energy Innovation."

43. Reyer Gerlagh, and Lise Wietze, "Carbon taxes: A drop in the ocean, or a drop that erodes the stone? The effect of carbon taxes on technological change," *Ecological Economics* 54, nos. 2–3 (2005).

44. International Energy Agency, "World Energy Outlook 2008."

Index

About Island Press

Since 1984, the nonprofit Island Press has been stimulating, shaping, and communicating the ideas that are essential for solving environmental problems worldwide. With more than 800 titles in print and some 40 new releases each year, we are the nation's leading publisher on environmental issues. We identify innovative thinkers and emerging trends in the environmental field. We work with world-renowned experts and authors to develop cross-disciplinary solutions to environmental challenges.

Island Press designs and implements coordinated book publication campaigns in order to communicate our critical messages in print, in person, and online using the latest technologies, programs, and the media. Our goal: to reach targeted audiences—scientists, policymakers, environmental advocates, the media, and concerned citizens—who can and will take action to protect the plants and animals that enrich our world, the ecosystems we need to survive, the water we drink, and the air we breathe.

Island Press gratefully acknowledges the support of its work by the Agua Fund, Inc., The Margaret A. Cargill Foundation, Betsy and Jesse Fink Foundation, The William and Flora Hewlett Foundation, The Kresge Foundation, The Forrest and Frances Lattner Foundation, The Andrew W. Mellon Foundation, The Curtis and Edith Munson Foundation, The Overbrook Foundation, The David and Lucile Packard Foundation, The Summit Foundation, Trust for Architectural Easements, The Winslow Foundation, and other generous donors.

The opinions expressed in this book are those of the author(s) and do not necessarily reflect the views of our donors.